Russian Literature

an introduction

For Alan.

Robert Lord

Russian
Literature

an introduction

TAPLINGER PUBLISHING COMPANY, NEW YORK

First published in the United States in 1980 by
TAPLINGER PUBLISHING CO., INC.
New York, New York

Library of Congress Catalog Card Number: 79-63625.
ISBN 0-8008-6940-0

Contents

Preface

This book is not so much an encyclopaedic survey as a general guide. My models have been those guides to noble ruins that, whilst seeking not to mislead, are yet not squeamish about indulging their pet fancies. If the reader is looking for an impartially balanced introduction, this is not it; there are rather too many personal views, and a few too many hares started. My aim is to provoke readings or re-readings of the works of Russian writers: no more.

I wish to acknowledge my debt to those authors who have trodden this path before, with contributions more weighty than my own. They have been a source of encouragement. Their names are already well-known and to list them here would be little better than name-dropping. The reader will find reference to them in my appendix.

Robert Lord, 1979.

A note on Russian pronunciation

The reader is most likely aware that the English language transliteration of Russian renders only approximately the pronunciation of the original. It is not my intention here to go into the niceties of Russian pronunciation. I wish only to draw the reader's attention to the more general features of Russian vowel sounds.

In the transliteration used here, the equivalent English pronunciations of Russian vowels are as follows:

Transliteration	English equivalent sound
a	approximately the vowel sound in 'cut or 'nut'
e	ye as in 'yet' (except when otherwise indicated)
i	ee as in 'cheese'
o	aw as in 'thaw', or ou in 'thought'
u	oo as in 'tool'

y
(i) when between two consonants (e.g. Russ. byt), approximately the sound of the second vowel in 'label' or 'level';
(ii) when immediately before or after another vowel, approximately as in 'yacht' or 'boy' (e.g. Russ. Yásha, Tolstóy);
(iii) in the endings of personal names it has become conventional to use 'y' to represent different varieties of ending in Russian. Pronunciation as in English 'whisky' e.g. Russ. Tómsky, Górky).

Stress

In Russian the pronunciation of a word depends very much on the location of the stress, each word having a single stress. In the transliteration used here stress is indicated by an accent placed over the vowel thus: á, é, ý, etc. In a Russian word only the vowel with the stress is given prominence, the prominence being achieved by force, loudness and timbre. The remaining vowels are given less prominence (i.e. they are less loud, less forcefully pronounced, and less distinct), and in some cases alter their quality. (This is particularly the case with 'o', which is only pronounced as in English 'thought' or 'thaw' when stressed. For example, in *Dostoévsky*, the first 'o' is pronounced roughly as the 'e' in English 'the lot'; and the second 'o' roughly as the vowel sound in 'nut'. Here, the modifications depend on the position of the stress, which in this word comes later than either of the 'o' sounds.)

I have not attempted to be entirely consistent, but have chosen a middle path between established conventions and the demands of accuracy. Thus, I have been consistent in marking stresses on the names of writers, their characters, and their works (when these are given as transliterations), but have not extended this practice to better-known place-names (e.g. Kiev) and well-known modern political figures (e.g. Stalin). When it has become conventional to refer to a Russian person by his European name equivalent (e.g. Nicholas, Alexander etc.) I have usually followed this convention.

Foreword

Nowadays Russian literature in translation is so much a part of the English reader's diet that he has sometimes read whole sections of Russian classics like Chékhov or Dostoévsky before even getting round to, say, Hardy or Melville. The phenomenon is not that easy to account for. Many readers find the Russian novel difficult enough. Yet they keep on going to the bitter end, long after they have lost their way in a forest of unfamiliar names; and for the newcomers it is only dogged persistence or blind fascination which brings them through. Mystique is no doubt at least part of the explanation; for, legendarily, Russian literature is something sensational, tormented, monstrous even. D. H. Lawrence described it as 'a surgical outcry, horrifying or marvellous'.

Even the violence incurred in the process of translation does not seem to make much difference. Despite the undeniably high quality of many recent translations, readers go on putting up with the stock renderings of some of the older translations in prose which would make them put down an English or American novel after a couple of pages. But even the best translation leaves the original stripped of most of its colour and flavour, its weight, irony, humour and poetry. To Virginia Woolf the Russian writers seemed 'like men deprived by our earthquake or a railway accident, not only of all their clothes, but also of something subtler and more important – their manners, the idiosyncrasies of their characters'.

Russian literature, even so, means something vastly different to us from what it did to Lawrence or Virginia Woolf. The thoughts of the modern reader turn not only to the classic novelists of the last century, but also to those writers who have survived and somehow manage to go on surviving in the Russia of Stalin and his heirs; figures who sometimes seem more like heroes of some great human resistance movement than mere writers. These include Borís Pasternák, Ánna Akhmátova, and Nadézhda Mandelstám, who defied the most devilish terror apparatus of all time and lived to attain world acclaim; writers like Sinyávsky, Daniél, and Bródski, who were subjected to show trials, arctic imprisonment, and in due time granted the favour of being able to choose exile; and especially Alexander Solzhenítsyn who survived all the worst horrors of 'Campland' to pass beyond all fear. It is the experience of the past half century of Stalinism, in its successive forms, that has raised not only literature in Russia, but literature in general, on to a different plane. Literature has gone beyond enriching our lives and cultural existence. It is salvaging what is left of humanity among us, and the only hope of restoring us to ourselves. The word itself has been drying up, and without the living word mankind is finished. As Nadézhda Mandelstám wrote in *Hope Abandoned*: 'A word is too easily transformed from a meaningful sign into a mere signal, and a group of words into an empty formula, bereft even of the sense such things have in magic. We begin to exchange set phrases, not noticing that all living meaning has gone from them. Poor, trembling creatures – we don't know what meaning is; it has vanished from a world in which there is no room any more for the Logos. It will return only if and when people come to their senses and recall that man must answer for everything, particularly for his own soul.'*

Literature, oral and written, has a very long history in Russia. Some of the epic ballads, surviving as a great oral tradition, not quite extinct even in Soviet Russia, undoubtedly go back to pagan antiquity and perhaps even to classical times. When writing came with Christianity at the bidding of Prince Vladímir of Kiev in A.D. 988 it seems as if literature was only waiting for its new garb. Within a very short period of time, not only a liturgical style, but other written traditions

* loc. cit., trans. Max Hayward, London, 1974.

became established throughout Kievan Russia as far as the north-western cities of Nóvgorod and Pskov. The domestic use of writing is usually taken as an index of literacy and the existence of a literary standard; and if this is so, then the citizens of Nóvgorod who recorded details of ordinary everyday matters indicates the widespread use of writing only a relatively short time after the introduction of writing itself.

Púshkin and Gógol are not the beginning but the first representatives of the culmination of a long tradition. Russia's peculiar geographical situation has meant that its poets, writers and artists have commonly not only been exposed to Western influences, but at the same time have sometimes been great exponents themselves of the various European genres, whilst having their roots firmly planted in another lore, a borderland lore taking its ingredients not only from its own ill-defined regions and its own pagan past, but also from its neighbours. For 'border' in Russia's case implies plurality: Byzantium, Persia, India, and more distantly, Egypt and China. The Russian writer seems to have little to learn from his European counterparts, having mastered their crafts seemingly with effortless ease; but he compounds this mastery into his own totally different dimension, derived from his own indigenous Russian nature. This is as true of the anonymous author of the twelfth century epic poem *The Lay of Igor's Campaign* as it is of Púshkin's *Evgény Onégin* or Dostoévsky's *The Brothers Karamázov*.

A proof of how indispensable a writer has become to a particular public does not depend upon how many people find his work pleasing, but upon the extent to which, if his writings were by some magic suddenly abolished, the works of that writer would be felt as a lack or absence. Despite those English readers who find some, if not necessarily all, Russian writers uncongenial, 'unhealthy', or even, as D. H. Lawrence eventually did, 'crude' and 'insensitive', the retrospective abolition of a Tolstóy or Dostoévsky would be as painful a loss as if the same thing had happened to any of our own writers. It is for this reason that the classic Russian prose writers have in a very real sense been adopted by the English reading public. Even if the latter view is open to question, the matter is entirely beyond dispute in the case of the theatre. Very few would deny that Chékhov is more at home among our theatregoing public than any other foreign dramatist.

My purpose in writing this book is neither to provide background information nor a comprehensive survey. There are many excellent books that do this already, including the splendid critical surveys compiled by Marc Slonim, Janko Lavrin, and others. I shall be writing in the main about the writers who interest me and about whom I know a little. In consequence, a number of writers will seem to have been passed over in indecent haste, and perhaps ignored altogether, when they deserved better. It seemed to me best, owing to restrictions of space, to adopt a longitudinal approach. This is not entirely satisfactory as many of the writers I deal with find themselves chopped clumsily down the middle; for many major Russian writers are important in all three spheres: prose, poetry, and the theatre. Also, there is a fairly intimate relationship between all three modes. Some of the finest Russian poetry is to be found in a 'novel in verse', and one of the greatest novels was conceived by its author as a poem. I make no excuses for devoting so much space to the poets. Russian literature, especially in more modern times, is not fully comprehensible without a fairly extensive treatment of them. Also, there are grounds for supposing that in the future the number of bilingual translations of the Russian poets will grow considerably. Bilingual translations are most useful texts for those with even less than a modicum of Russian, and an even more powerful incentive to learn more of the language. It will be obvious that my study shares with many others the disadvantage of concentrating on the modern period only, beginning as it does with Púshkin. It is to be hoped that, as more and more translations of earlier writers become available, the next generation of surveys will devote more attention to what in earlier surveys has hardly been touched upon, and in the present book almost totally ignored.

1 The Russian Writer in Context

With its conversion to Christianity at the end of the tenth century, Kievan Russia – known as Rus'* – became one of the important centres of medieval Christendom. Even though by virtue of its geographical position Kiev was constantly threatened by the Asiatic hordes, it became a major bulwark against the infidel, and was anything but a backward country. Its court was linked with nearly every royal lineage in Europe, and Rus' was famed among the composers of the *chansons de geste* for its heroic qualities. As well as this, Kiev had become an important trading and cultural centre, with links in every direction : Constantinople and Asia Minor to the south and east; Poland, Galicia and the Danube to the west; and the Baltic to the north. In keeping with its importance in most other respects, Kievan Russia also produced literature to equal anything of the European early middle ages. Its *Chronicles* have been reckoned superior to any of their Western counterparts, in their vividness and in their attention to historical consistency; and the *Lay of Igor's Campaign*, recounting the defeat and capture of Prince Igor by the Polovtsian tribe, (best known in the West through Borodin's opera *Prince Igor*), stands out as a jewel, brimming with humanity, grace, pathos and vivid poetic imagery, and comparable with the *Chanson de Roland* or *The Battle of Maldon*.

Kiev was already in decline when the city was captured by the Mongols in 1240. There followed a 'dark age' which lasted for over two hundred years. At the end of this period

* pronounced 'Rooss'.

there emerged a new Russia, based not on the tolerance and
free spirit of the long destroyed Kiev, or even on the still
thriving mercantile, democratic city of Novgorod, but on the
centre of monastic theocracy, Moscow; hailed as the 'Third
Rome'. It is undeniable that it was the growing strength of the
Russian Orthodox Church which brought Russia back to political identity, but the price for regeneration some would
consider too high. Byzantium had fallen and, when the Mongol
domination of Russia was finally overthrown in 1480, the
new rulers of Moscow took over the titles and prerogatives
of the Byzantine Emperors, calling themselves Tsars (i.e.
Caesars). Iván IV, known as the 'Terrible' (1533–1584), set
about building a monastic civilization. It has been estimated
that, between 1300 and 1450, as many as 180 new monasteries had been built, and, by the end of the sixteenth century,
a further 300 created. One interesting feature of this first
Muscovite period is the beginning of the unresolved conflict
between West and East which has lasted, with only minor
interruption, down to our own day. The Western menace,
democratization, human rights, were just as much issues in
sixteenth century Russia as they are in the Russia of Brézhnev
and Kosýgin.

The seventeenth century began with a period of civil and
religious strife, known as the 'Time of Troubles', and a foreign
invasion by Poland and Sweden, culminating in the Great
Schism, which grew out of the conflict between three contend-
ing powers: the secular power of the Tsar, the attempt by
Patriarch Níkon to convert the State into a Theocracy, and
the opposition to change or reform by the fundamentalists,
later know as the Old Believers or Schismatics. Níkon failed,
the Old Believers were bitterly persecuted, Church was sub-
ordinated to State, and Russia was well on the way to becoming a European power. During the whole of the period, from
the foundation of Muscovy to the end of the seventeenth
century, the cleavage in literature between the folk tradition
and the tradition of letters, based on Church Slavonic, was
retained. The period saw important additions to both traditions. One of the most important works is the autobiography
of the Archpriest Avvakúm (1621–1682), the leader of the

Schismatics. Avvakúm was twice exiled to Siberia, incarcerated in solitary confinement for fourteen years, yet never gave up inveighing against corrupt practices of clergy and public officials, even under torture, and was finally burnt at the stake. Avvakúm is a Russian version of Bunyan, standing in similar relation to the Schismatics; but the Russianness that literally glares out from the pages of his writings is the very essence that we find distilled down through the generations, appearing in people as diversely Russian as Bakúnin or Tolstóy, and in writers of our own day.

It was but one step, even if a big one, to the reforms of Peter the Great (1682–1725). Westernization in no small way had begun in the reign of Borís Godunóv a century earlier, and had developed apace throughout the following century especially under his father, Aléxis. Peter the Great simply pushed the process to its logical conclusion, even if the measures he adopted were usually drastic. The sweeping changes, which included the wholesale secularization of the State, the introduction of European arts, science, and technology, were symbolized by the creation of the city of St. Petersburg (now Leningrad) on the marshy banks of the river Neva. In Púshkin's words, put into mouth of Peter (the 'Bronze Horseman') himself:

Here we are destined by Nature
to cut a window into Europe,
to gain a firm foothold on the sea.
Here, over waters new to them
Ships of every flag will come to visit us
and we shall make boundless merry.

Peter's reforms and innovations have been criticized for their perverse haste and skin depth. To be sure, Russia had become not long after the end of Peter's reign a great European power; and the new capital, St. Petersburg, was now the symbol of renovation. Foreign manners, tongues, and techniques, German bureaucratic machinery, and the tone of the French Enlightenment had been taken over wholesale. The new climate produced an aristocratic intelligentsia; soon the most precocious in Europe, yet reared in a vacuum. But the

Peter the Great of letters and learning was not the Tsar himself, but Mikhaíl Lomonósov (1711–1765), a Russian of peasant origin from the far north. Having managed to gain entry into higher education in Moscow, he went on to win a scholarship to Germany. He returned to Russia in 1741 a scholar of some eminence, a scientist, polymath, poet, and historian. Lomonósov was not the only innovator of the period – and I shall be dealing with some of the others later on – but he was undoubtedly the most influential. His chief importance in literature is that he formulated three styles: a 'lofty' style for heroic and solemn subjects, based on Church-Slavonic; a middle style for general literary purposes; and finally a 'low' or colloquial style for comic and everyday situations. Lomonósov's secularizing of the language was of great importance for Russian poetry.

Under the reign of Catherine the Great (1762–1796), European influence became a flood; particularly French influence, which reached the pitch of Francomania. It is well-known that Catherine herself conducted a correspondence with Voltaire; and she even had the writings of the French Enlightenment published by direct government subsidy. Despite everything, the net result of her reign was the strengthening of centralized political power and a vast increase in the wealth of the nobility. A reign that had begun under the spell of Montesquieu's *Esprit des Lois* terminated in disenchantment under the sinister shadow of the French Revolution, and ultimately in political and economic absolutism of a rather permanent kind. But it was Catherine who completed the secularization of Russia. In the words of a recent historian* 'Catherine substituted the city for the monastery as the main centre of Russian culture'. The Petersburg that haunts many a Russian writer's pages in the following two centuries and which Dostoevsky's Man from Underground calls 'the most abstract and premeditated city in the whole world' is largely hers, not Peter the Great's. It is from this time too, that the sense of alienation among Russian intellectuals dates. And it is here also that we find the first signs of the gulf between the intelligentsia and the philistines, which is to become a

* James H. Billington. *The Icon and The Axe.*

characteristic pattern of Russian cultural life down to our own
day; the philistines being backed every time by the ruling
élite: Tsarist, Leninist or Stalinist. The crass facetiousness
and gratuitous anti-intellectualism of recent hard-liners like
Kóchetov and Shevtsóv finds a precedent in comparable pieces
turned out during Catherine's reign. This means of course that
the era had its Sinyávskys and Daniéls. It was three writers
of this age who among them set the various keys for Russian
literature down to the present: Fonvízin (1745–1792), who
in his satirical play *The Adolescent* undermined the fabric
of Catherine's imported aristocratic cadres; Radíshchev (1748–
1820), a daring critic of almost everything that the Russian
pseudo-Enlightenment stood for, and who paid for his views
on serfdom by a death sentence commuted to hard labour in
Siberia; and Skovorodá (1722–1794), poet, mystical philosopher and wanderer, whose work has reminded some of
Blake, not only in manner and style, but in his grass-rooted
opposition to the new society that was growing up in Russia.

The late eighteenth century was also the period when literature and thought became subservient to autocracy. From the
very beginning the interest taken by the monarch and government circles in literature looked ominous. Certain features of
the early trend to subjugate letters to State ends prefigures
the policy advocating socialist realism in the modern Soviet
State. Even as long ago as Catherine's time, most Russian
writers were State officials of one sort or another. Assertions
of independence were not only not favoured, but viewed with
alarm. As one recent writer has aptly put it*: 'A book of
portraits of eighteenth-century Russian writers would have
shown many high officials in brilliant uniforms covered with
medals and decorations'. The Soviet Writers' Union which
exerts such a tyranny over the Russian literary scene today is
hardly more than an old phenomenon in new guise.

The first quarter of the nineteenth century is one of the
most absorbing and complex periods in the history of Russia,
culturally even more than politically. These twenty-five years
coincide almost exactly with the reign of Alexander I, the
various phases of which reflect in an uncanny way the succes-

* Marc Slonim: *The Epic of Russian Literature.*

sive predominance of various intellectual and religious trends, too numerous and many-sided to go into within the short space of this introduction. The first half of Alexander's reign up to the defeat of Napoleon, was the most liberal period ever experienced in Russia, and the reforms contemplated brought constitutional government and the abolition of serfdom at least within sight. The reign ended in a phase of marked reaction, politically directed by the brutal Arakchéyev, who had in mind to turn Russia into a vast military barracks, whilst the Tsar had become maniacally engrossed in mystical Pietism. The reader's best available recreation of the climate and events of the period is Tolstóy's *War and Peace*, yet even this is only one side of the picture. Western and Russian philosophical, mystical, political and aesthetic ideals found themselves all on the boil together; and it is almost impossible to pick out a single contemporaneous European development which did not produce some effect, direct or indirect, during this period. Probably the most important formative influence among the intelligentsia was 'higher order' Freemasonry, – indeed the term 'intelligentsia' was first used by Schwarz a German expatriate freemason. Most thinkers and writers in Russia, native or foreign during this period, whatever their personal beliefs, were members of higher Masonic orders. Political reform, the pursuit of perfection, the search for spiritual truth was blended into a common striving. The movement in Russia has been accurately characterized as follows: 'Though Masonry was formally neither a political nor a religious movement, it had a profound influence in both these areas. . . . The lodges filled for the culture of aristocratic Russia something of the role that had been played by the monasteries of the culture of Muscovy. They provided islands of spiritual intensity and cultural activity within a still bleak and hostile autocratic environment'.

This 'Alexandrian age' produced a wealth of literature. Also this period witnessed the formation of a unified literary language; mainly the work of the writer and historian Nicholas Karamzín (1766–1826). Karamzín evolved a natural prose style which could stand up to European comparison, criticized though he was for introducing along with non-

Russian features of style certain mannerisms that the Russian language could well have done without. The age too is rich in poetry, poetry of a new stamp, incorporating the best of European genres with a new indigenous note. This was a generation that produced a Russian literature that was a literature in its own right, with its own taste, its own norms and its own preoccupations; a true base for the line of giants that begins only in the next generation starting with Púshkin and Gógol. It is a pity that the writers of the age, even the major ones, are hardly known in the West, owing to inadequate or to a complete lack of translations. Perhaps we shall have at least some of these in the coming decade. If so, they will reveal just how unjustifiable is the scant treatment devoted to these writers in the various sections of this book.

When Alexander I died in 1825, hopes were raised that he would be succeeded by the Grand Duke Constantine, formerly an active Freemason and a known liberal. But when it became clear that the successor was to be his brother Nicholas, a narrow military disciplinarian reared in the worst Prussian traditions, the Army commanders who had gathered on the Senate Square for the purpose of taking their allegiance to the new Tsar staged a demonstration which ended in disaster. Hundreds were arrested and deported, and five of the ring-leaders were hanged.

Those behind this ill-starred mutiny became known as the Decembrists – named after the month in which the demon-stration took place. At that time to be a member of the intelligentsia inevitably meant being a Decembrist. So, at one fell swoop a whole generation was obliterated. The only ones to have escaped were the under-age, or those already in exile, like Púshkin. Along with the activists went a host of writers, poets, and social thinkers. Alexander Hérzen who was only thirteen at the time has described the aftermath: 'The years following 1825 were horrible. It took ten years for society to regain consciousness, in what had become an atmosphere of slavery and persecution. They had been overcome by a sense of profound hopelessness, a general feeling of collapse.... There was hardly a single family of the nobility who did not have a relative amongst those deported, and hardly one of them who dared to wear mourning or express their grief.'

The intelligentsia at that time were a small enough minority even without decimation; all of them put together would hardly have filled an English stately home. The overwhelming majority of their fellow noblemen were philistines more or less, and a proportion condoned and sometimes indulged in barbarities, which make their Western European counterparts seem like devotees of sweetness and light. December 1825 left only a sense of alienation, which was immediately transmitted to the rising generation. The Romantic idealism of the Decembrists gave way to radical scepticism and trauma, with symptoms not too different from those evident in the West in our own day. The poet of the new generation, Mikhaíl Lérmontov, recreates the climate in terms far remote from any romantic attitudinizing, no mere echo of Byron, Musset or Heine:

I view this age with sorrow and dread
    And see its future empty, dark and bare;
Crushed by a load of doubt and knowledge dead,
    It grows toward age, inert and unaware. . . .
We hate or love as whim or chance controls,
    And make no sacrifice to either mood;
And something strange and cold reigns in our souls,
    Even when passion rages in the blood. . . .

Soon, soon forgotten we pass, a weary lot,
    Over the world, and leave no sound or trace;
Nor to the age bequeath one fruitful thought,
    Nor strike one native chord to mark our race. . . .

Censorship after 1825 was total. 'Orthodoxy, Autocracy and Nationality' was now the government's triple watchword. A police state was already in the making. A particularly sinister form of repression, only recently revived under Khrushchev, was the charge of insanity. Tsar Nicholas personally ordered his police chief to have Lérmontov mentally examined after the publication of his courageously vehement poem in which he had denounced those responsible for Púshkin's death, and accusing them of engineering the duel in which the odds would obviously be weighted against the poet. Another key figure of the period, Peter Chaadáyev was officially declared mad for publishing his epigrammatic condemnation of Russian atavism and backwardness. 'Everything in Russia is ephemeral', he claimed, 'We are like people billeted out. Even amidst our families we are little better than strangers In our towns we have the appearance of nomads. And even nomads are more attached to their deserts than we are to our cities.'

Among the new generation that had grown up under the crushing burden of this period, attitudes were correspondingly extreme, outlandish and overgrown. It is this age that set the tone and mood of much of the Russian literature of the nineteenth century known to English readers. One should not forget though that this was something quite new even for Russia; and this generation was as different in ideals and temper from its fathers as could be imagined. Five of Russia's greatest novelists passed their early years in this grim period: Gógol, Dostoévsky, Leo Tolstóy, Turgénev, and Goncharóv. The age also produced two great political and social thinkers: Belínsky and Hérzen; the latter great enough to be considered among the greatest political thinkers of the nineteenth century.

Not all were able to suffer the oppression of these years. Hérzen, writing about the untimely death of the superb poet Venevítinov at the age of twenty-two, says, 'Venevítinov was not cut out for existence in this new Russian atmosphere. You had to be of a different stamp to endure the atmosphere of that grim period. . . . You had to accustom yourself to insoluble doubts, to the bitterest kind of truths, to your own impotence; to constant daily insults'. For different reasons, Hérzen himself was forced into emigration: to London, from where he directed the education of yet another, even more radical generation of the Russian intelligentsia through his journal The Bell. Generally these years produced a Hamlet-like disorientation in those who could survive; but it also produced one of the most dedicated revolutionists of all time: Michael Bakúnin, a Che Guevara with nine lives.

A recurrent figure in literature of the period is the so-called

'superfluous man'. Almost every major writer has engendered
his own particular version of this prototype. Perhaps the
clearest, because most conscious, example is the character
Béltov in Hérzen's *Who is to blame?* written in the early
forties. Béltov is supposed to have been a completely western-
ized intellectual, stuffed with all the most worthy ideals of the
age. As a result, his every contact with the Russian reality
turns instantly into disillusionment. Béltov discovers himself
to be 'a wanderer about Europe, a foreigner at home, a
foreigner abroad, an aristocrat by virtue of his refined way of
life, yet a man of the nineteenth century by conviction.
How could provincials be expected to welcome him?
He could not share their interests, and they hated him, realiz-
ing instinctively that Béltov was a protest, a condemnation of
the lives they led, and a living objection against its very order'.

But not all was disillusion and defeat. A new spirit was
astir. Chaadáyev who had condemned so much of his country's
shortcomings was to become the spokesman of the new
messianic ideal. Russia's destiny, he believed, was to bring to
the world a great new idea, and to restore the dying spirit of
the West: 'We are an exceptional people. We exist only for
the purpose of administering some important lesson to the
world. But who knows what miseries we shall have to endure
before our destiny is fulfilled'; 'I am convinced that we are
destined to resolve the major part of the social problems existing in the world, to put the finishing touches to ideas which
took root in older societies, and to make valuable pronouncements on the various serious questions which occupy mankind.' If Chaadayev was not a madman, he made a very fair
prophet. Compare Pasternák's remarks on the Russian Revolution addressed to his readers abroad in a New Year message in
1957, not long before his death: '... And there is one more
thing that you have to thank us for. However great the difference between us, our Revolution set the tone for you as well:
it filled the present century with meaning and content. It is
not only we – our young people – that are different: the very
son of one of your bankers is no longer what his father and
grandfather were. ... And it's us you have to thank for this
new man, who is present even in your ancient society, us you

have to thank for the fact that he is more alive, more subtle and more gifted than his pompous and turgid forebears, for this child of the age was delivered in the maternity hospital called Russia.'

The greatest idea to emerge from this 'generation on trial' typically had its origins in imported Western philosophy, in particular in the philosophy of Schelling; as well as in a subsequent reaction to Hegel in the work and activity of Vissarión Belínsky. Belínsky embodied all that was best in the Russian intellectual. 'For me to think, feel, understand and suffer are one and the same thing' was Belínsky's life view. Out of his violent reaction against Hegel emerges the value and inviolability of the individual. No ideal, no culture, no perfection is worth anything if it is erected on the suffering of even a single victim: 'Most humble thanks, Mr Hegel. I bow before your philosophic nightcap. But, my respect for your philosophic philistinism notwithstanding, I must respectfully assure you that even if I succeeded in crawling up the developmental stairs to reach the topmost step, I would endeavour even there, to take into my reckoning all the victims of history, all the victims of misfortune, of superstition, of the Inquisition of Philip II; and so on – and if I failed I would hurl myself headlong from the top. I have no desire for happiness on any other terms, and I need to be given guarantees concerning the fate of every single one of my fellow men'. It is this idea that may in time to come seem the most significant political philosophy to come out of Russia. Belínsky's is no mere libertarian premiss, but an idea with force and passion behind it. Hérzen, some time after his own disillusionment at the outcome of the revolutionary episodes of 1848, clearly foreseeing the erosive threat of the modern totalitarian state, and insisting on individual human worth in face of the irrational state political machine, wrote: 'The liberty of the individual is the greatest thing of all, and it is on this and this alone that the true will of the people can develop'. Belínsky's idea is probably more familiar to readers through *The Brothers Karamázov*, but it is an idea that has worked powerfully on nearly all Russian writers and thinkers down to our own day, and finds its fullest maturity in Russian dissident writers of our own day.

If the whole world is doomed eventually to drift into totalitarianism, resistance movements of tomorrow will find more ready consolation in the work of Belínsky's heirs, especially Pasternák and Solzhenítsyn, than in almost any writer of the West.

Russia's defeat in the Crimean War (1853–56) opened the eyes of all but the most rigid conservatives to the many shortcomings at every administrative and political level. The accession in 1856 of Alexander II, a liberal, relatively speaking, coincided with a radical sharpening of the ideological climate, inaugurated by the so-called generation of the sixties, most of them barely out of the classroom. The importation of Western technology and industry symbolized above all by the railway, was accompanied by even less discriminate absorption of the most modern Western social, economic and political theories. The British Utilitarian Radicals came in along with the positivism of Comte, and the left-wing Hegelian theory of Stirner and Feuerbach.

The new generation had been fashioned during the particularly harsh repression of the last days of Nicholas I's reign (when the police state came really into its own) in the wake of the alleged Petrashévsky conspiracy, in which a number of prominent intellectuals and writers including Dostoévsky had been implicated. It is hardly surprising that the new generation, out to make the most of the new liberalization, turned out to be iconoclasts, debunkers, and intellectual anarchists of every hue. Turgénev coined the label 'nihilist', and his character Bazárov in *Fathers and Children* was meant to embody the ideals of this generation: anti-aesthete, anti-metaphysics, protagonists of the natural sciences. Bazárov himself dies from an infected cut after carrying out an autopsy. His generation were generally from a new class, the sons of professional people in the main. The non-aristocratic backgrounds of these *raznochíntsy** created yet a further barrier between them and their elders.

In the manner of their teacher Hérzen, whom they were soon nevertheless to reject for not being militant enough, they had passed in their student days through the agonizing phase

* men of various ranks.

of 'positivist disillusionment', a panacean remedy for most of those 'accursed questions' over which the Russian intelligentsia had laboured since its beginnings. This could be seen in simple terms as a turning away from German ideals to Russian facts. For Chernyshévsky (1828–1889) civic concern, social utility and social processes were the only fit goals of philosophy; the rest was bunkum. Anyone devoid of social awareness was capable only of triviality or vulgarity. It was considered better to leave someone totally uneducated than to educate him in the wrong way, without inculcating common sense and a pragmatic turn of mind. Art was considered unnecessary except when it could be put to use; the hardworking local midwife was of more value than Mozart or Raphael.

The new-style radicals were not without their opponents. The most telling critique of their monstrous utopia, symbolized by the Crystal Palace, and the ant-heap mentality, is Dostoévsky's *Notes from Underground*, originally conceived as devil's advocacy to Chernyshévsky's major premiss, the ultimate predictabilty of human actions and motivation.

By the sixties it had become the custom for writers to concern themselves, directly or indirectly, with social problems. Even as far back as the early 1840s Gógol had upturned some rather revealing stones in his *Government Inspector* and *Dead Souls*, and had, unwittingly it seems, set a fashion for the cult of the underdog in his famous short-story *The Overcoat*. This was followed three years later by Dostoévsky's first published work *Poor Folk*. In addition, in the late forties, interest in the lot of the peasant was aroused by Turgénev's *Hunting Sketches* and Grigoróvich's *The Village*. By 1856 there was hardly any writer who kept clear of social questions. Turgénev's novels, spanning some twenty years, are a record of many of the attitudes co-existing during this period; and even Dostoévsky, after his return from Siberia, was at first directly concerned with the underprivileged. The only prolific poet of the time, Nicholas Nekrásov, a kind of Russian Victor Hugo, was acclaimed 'civic' poet.

The sixties bore fruit only *after* the curtain of repression came down once more, with the attempt on the Tsar's life in 1866 by a member of the first generation of militant revolutionaries in Russia. Although Alexander II had introduced a number of reforms, including two of extreme importance – trial by jury, and the emancipation of the serfs – the expectations that these years had produced outstripped the pace at which reform could proceed. Out of the positivism, nihilism, and European radicalism of the sixties; as well as out of Slavophilism, which had in its later stage taken on a political-economic shape; out of Herzen's 'Russian socialism'; and even indirectly out of a revival of concern for the Old Believers, and the movement called autochthonism, to which Dostoévsky adhered, there began to emerge a general political and cultural trend, whose central core was known as Populism.

It is the Populists who dominated the seventies, and their founder was Lavróv, who claimed that every educated man had profound obligations to the common man, the pillar supporting all that was possible in the way of enlightened and artistic endeavour. Anyone who considered himself a member of the intelligentsia had an obligation to repay his debt to the people by taking part in the foundation of a social order capable of providing cultural and welfare amenities for everyone instead of for a privileged minority.

Populism was an immediate success in that it attracted many people of both sexes and every political shade. A massive 'crusade to the people' was planned and thousands recruited. Going from village to village they took every kind of manual occupation they could find, working as labourers, hospital orderlies, and factory operatives. It was out of this ferment that the first terrorist organizations grew, first *Land and Freedom* and later the extreme and fanatical *Party of the Popular Will*.

It is to these years that we look for those towering masterpieces of the Russian novel: Tolstóy's *War and Peace* and *Anna Karénina*, and Dostoévsky's *The Devils* and *The Brothers Karamázov*. The sixties and seventies were the great age of Russian prose, teeming with a host of minor writers, some of whom are not really minor, but only so by comparison with the giants. In a very real sense too, the great novels were the fruits of this age, without them being any the less works of art in their own right; whether the social connection is obvious in the case of Turgénev's *Virgin Soil* and Dostoévsky's *The Devils*, or not so obvious as in the case of *War and Peace* and *The Brothers Karamázov*. Russians have seldom, if ever, been given to writing in a vacuum; and their greatest work has always been achieved as if by some resonance or reaction to social and political currents. The astonishing thing is that the bad product one might expect in abundance, is in fact rare: a failure like Chernyshévsky's *What is to be done?* is the exception, not the rule, as far as the major, and many of the minor writers are concerned.

Drafts for constitutional reform had been prepared, and were being noised abroad, when barely a month later all was cut short by the attempt on the life of Alexander II, this time successful. It has been confidently predicted, and not only by prophets, that, had constitutional reform came about, the course of Russian history would have been entirely different, with a constitutional Monarchy and a democratic form of government. Instead, effective power was now seized by another extremely able and formidable figure, an apostle of autocracy, among the bleakest reactionaries in Russian history. This man, Pobedonóstev, seems to symbolize the unrelieved pessimism of the remaining decades of the century. His 'reign' ended only in 1905, with the abortive Revolution of that year. Pobedonóstsev was a superbly educated philistine, with a sophisticated but totally negative attitude towards social change. Education was in his view a dangerous thing except for a tiny élite; for the rest only Orthodox official religious indoctrination was permissible. He ruled Russia like some eccentric, but fanatical and illiberal, don, devoting his spare time to such tasks as the translation of Thomas à Kempis. His only opponent was that supreme Populist, (without any direct affiliation to Populism as such) Leo Tolstóy. Tolstóy carried populist ideals to their logical conclusion, advocating complete identification with the people, renouncing every form of coercion, and finally giving up art and even family life in his search for moral truth and justice. The frustration of the politically active, all of whom were forced to choose between emigration or Siberia, is to be found nowhere better than in Conrad's *Under Western Eyes*. The general mood of the era, some think, is most poignantly distilled in the later plays and stories of Chékhov, where repression seems to have seeped through into people's everyday sentiments. 'I am in mourning for my life' are Masha's opening words in *The Seagull*.

The literature of the end of the century was, with few exceptions, turned away from social and political issues, and along with a generation of philosophers the writer became a prophet of a new idealism. A new conflict of generations arose. The new generation which found itself straddled along 'the boundary between two centuries' rejected the scientific materialism and ,rationalism of its parents, aghast at the general swing towards mysticism, occultism, aestheticism. The idols were Dostoévsky, Schopenhauer, Nietzsche, and right in their midst the religious philosopher and visionary Vladímir Soloviév,* the Russian prophet of Antichrist. Soloviév in his youth had known Dostoévsky, and they had influenced each other profoundly. The work of Soloviév's later years evolved in the shadow of Dostoévsky's work, and out of it emerged a small constellation of poets: the Symbolists and Decadents. The return to poetry is unannounced and sudden. Back in the forties poets had dropped out of fashion. Since Lérmontov, there had been only three poets of significance: Nekrásov, mentioned earlier; Fet, an isolated later Romantic; and Tyútchev, a great poet who foreshadowed the Symbolists, still largely undiscovered long after his death. From now on poets multiply. Original and very different each from the other, most of them are experimenters and innovators, all 'changing the poet's vision of things', at least one of them, Alexander Blok as great as any poet Russia had yet known.

The generation that followed the Symbolists and Decadents – the generation that came to maturity in the years immediately preceding the Bolshevik Revolution of 1917 – was to be still more remarkable. This new generation produced not only poets who are among the wonders of modern poetry, but also artists in other spheres like Kandínsky and Chagáll, Prokófiev and Stravínsky, Diághilev, Meyerhóld and Eisenstéin. The young poets, dissatisfied with their elders' obscurantism, lack of clarity, and divorce from reality, sprang up under a range of different banners: Acmeism, Futurism, Imaginism,

* pronounced Solovyóff.

Constructivism, Formalism; but all of them strikingly marked out as individuals, and among them figures of genius, some of whom are still barely known in the English-speaking world for lack of translations. A new prose was making its appearance too. Some of it was the work of those who were also poets, but there were also three remarkable prose writers who appeared in the early post-revolutionary years: Isáac Bábel, Borís Pilnyák and Evgény Zamyátin. This was a tragic generation. None of its oustanding representatives was able to come to terms, partly or at all, with the new totalitarianism, and those who lived into the thirties, became victims of the Stalin terror. Of the poets, Nicholas Gumilyóv was shot as a counter-revolutionary in the period immediately following the Civil War. Sergéi Esénin, Vladímir Mayakóvsky and Marína Tsvetáyeva all committed suicide. Osíp Mandelstám along with Bábel, Pilnák, Meyerhóld and Eisenstéin and others disappeared during the Yezhov Purge. Zamyátin and many others were early driven to emigrate. Only Borís Pasternák and Anna Akhmátova remained, and even they were dishonoured; Pasternák at the very end of his life, following the publication abroad of *Doctor Zhivago*. No age in the whole of human history has known such loss.

Populism, nurtured in its later phase by Mikhailóvsky (1842–1904) was the only important political movement in Russia at the time when Marxism was imported from the West. In the spirit if not the letter of Belínsky, Populism had insisted on the freedom and value of the individual. Marxism on the other hand was concerned only with the dynamics of history and class struggle. The historical background to the emergence of Marxism in Russia is far from obvious, still leaving some ground for speculation. Little headway was being made by the Populists, however, and the Marxists had in their ranks not only well-trained agitators but also brilliant charismatic figures. The Marxists also brought about a switch in attention from the peasant to the industrial worker.

By 1905, the year of the first Revolution in Russia, Marxism had already split into factions. Lenin and his Bolshevik splinter-group had been impatient with various points of Marxist theory which they thought not entirely applicable to

Russia as it stood. They changed the theory. Marx's teaching on the class struggle, Lenin believed, leads of necessity to the recognition of the political rule of the proletariat, and to the 'dictatorship' of the proletariat. The overthrow of the bourgeoisie could be achieved only by the proletariat taking over the apparatus of the State and State power. The bourgeois machine had to be taken over and transformed to meet socialist ends, until a time was reached when the State could be let to wither away. Lenin's preoccupation with the dynamics of the moment and his impatience with theory which seemed to lag behind concrete demands led him and his Party into a doublethink which released the catastrophe of Stalinism, and the Stalinist revival of the present time.

Much was learnt by the Bolsheviks from the events of 1905, and many of those who were not even Marxists were disappointed by the outcome, not so much, in the form that it took – a sham constitutional government – but in the promise of a new era which turned out to be its own caricature. Among the Marxists there was a powerful messianic element, a prophetic belief in the possibilities of the future, and the ideal of a genuine proletarian culture; but there were also the seeds of the opposite: the old familiar philistinism, this time founded on the masses' 'stupefaction from the narcotic of mass culture' as one outspoken critic in the Soviet Union has recently put it. Even Lenin himself was not free from philistinism, and, under his successor Stalin, the reverse of the ideals upheld by Trotsky, Mayakóvsky and many others was established. The masses, far from being transformed, became the object of pseudo-culture for the cynical purpose of creating that class Marx or Lenin had never dreamed of – the New Class. October 1917 was the beginning of a new era; not Trotsky's cultural transformation of mankind long-lasting, but the coalition of Police and Party rule.

The first years following upon the Civil War were by no means the worst, and by comparison with certain periods of Tsarist rule, they were relatively mild. Fortunately Lenin did not press his own judgments in literary matters; instead he left the responsibility to Lunachársky, a benevolent if not always very imaginative controller of the Arts. Thus the twenties despite strict censorship became the heyday of modern Russian prose and poetry: Mayakóvsky, Zamyátin, Mandelstám, Bábel, Pilnyák, the early Pasternák, Shólokhov and many others. Lunachársky's supremacy ended in 1929. It was in this year that the fanatical Association of Proletarian Writers (R.A.P.P.) forced a showdown with the rival All-Russian Union of Writers in which both Zamyátin and Pilnyák were prominent figures. The accusations against Zamyátin and Pilnyák – that they had evaded censorship by publishing abroad – are a direct antecedent of those numerous show trials of recent years. The difference was that at that time Stalinism had not yet taken firm root, and these writers were able to prove their innocence. This did not prevent their being pilloried on another score, that of being anti-Soviet. They were 'purged' along with the ranks of the All-Russian Union of Writers. Zamyátin was granted permission to emigrate, whilst Pilnyák publicly recanted only to be arrested a few years later during the Terror.

From 1929 onwards down to the present day, the Russian writer becomes a barometer of political rivalries and internal balance of power. In 1932, R.A.P.P. was dissolved and replaced by the Union of Soviet Writers, which has become and remains even now the writer's worst enemy. Ironically, the fanatical, extreme left-wing Marxists of R.A.P.P. were not at all to Stalin's liking. The writers now in favour would have been branded ten years earlier as reactionary bourgeoisie. Also in 1932 appeared that most bourgeois literary method of all time – socialist realism. This dogma in the formulation of which Górky seems to have played an important part – conforming as it does to Górky's classical realism and meeting with Stalin's own taste for boorish vulgarity – was imposed with varying degrees of ferocity and fanaticism, except during the war years, from that time until the death of Stalin twenty years later; and still manages to survive in spite of one onslaught after another. Sinyávsky described it as 'neither classicism nor realism. It is semi-classical demi-art of a none too socialist demi-realism'.

During the growing terror of the mid-thirties, culminating

in the Yezhov 'purge' of 1937, writers either had to comply fully with the policy of socialist realism, or had to cease writing altogether. Those who continued to write according to other canons, and even some of those who had stopped, disappeared during this time. The magnitude of the slaughter can be gained from the figure of 1,200,000 party members alone arrested during 1936–39. Of these about 600,000 are known to have been shot – a merciful death compared with the fate of the half million others who died in the lumber camps of disease and starvation. A mere 50,000 survived and were 'rehabilitated'. Evgénia Ginsbúrg who has with artless frankness described the unimaginable horrors of the beginnings of twenty years' solitary imprisonment and hard labour in her book *Into the Whirlwind* was one of the few. Most writers became collaborators, many of them outright opportunists.

Whatever respite had been brought by the war years was brutally cancelled out by the post-war terror since known as Zhdánovism, a campaign directed against an alleged Western bourgeois influence, and attempts to undermine socialist realism. These were the years when for the first time in Russian historical memory literature along with the rest of the arts virtually ceased to exist. It was also the time when those who had fought bravely in the war were sent indiscriminately along with proven traitors to the arctic wastes. Only a small proportion lived long enough to be rehabilitated; including, unluckily for the Kremlin eminences, Alexander Solzhenítsyn, that remarkable, devastatingly articulate, and courageous writer, whose first published work *A day in the life of Ivan Denisovich* was 'used' by Khrushchev in his destalinization campaign.

The death of Stalin in 1953 brought an end to the worst rigours of Zhdánovism, and there ensued a brief 'thaw', symbolized by Ehrenburg's novel with this welcome word as its title. 1954 held a promise of things to come, the tip of an iceberg of fresh writing, provoking the wrath of the hard-liners and bringing the brief thaw to an end. Khrushchev's move to pin his own aggrandizement on an anti-Stalinist policy – first made known in his famous secret speech at the Twentieth Party Congress in 1956 – raised hopes for freedom. People who had

feared that twenty-five years of oppression had stifled everything, were at the time not only heartened by the appearance
of a new generation of poets and prose writers, but were
astonished by the daring modes in which they expressed themselves. Socialist realism, despite Khrushchev's warning to them,
was practically swept away; and the more important Russian
writers were back once again among the world's greatest. The
flood began with Dudíntsev's *Not by Bread Alone*, and later produced Yúri Kazakóv, Vladímir Tendryakóv, Solzhenítsyn,
Abrám Tertz (Sinyávsky), and the poets Evgény Evtushénko,
Andréi Voznesénsky and a host of others; and of course that
'delayed action bomb' as if from the past, Pasternák's *Doctor
Zhivago*. And by some irony, the new Russian writer has become
more important politically than at any time since Púshkin's day.
The party bosses and their cultural fellow-travellers' fear
for him is more than matched by the fearlessness of those
who have actually or spiritually survived the concentration
camps and have passed beyond fear. In the words of one of
Solzhenítsyn's prison characters in *The First Circle*: 'You can
tell old You-know-who – up there – that you only have power
over people so long as you don't take *everything* away from
them. But when you've robbed a man of everything he's no
longer in your power – he is free again.'

During the past decade the misgivings of those who lived
through the Stalin era have returned. These fears suddenly
deepened early in 1966 with the now infamous trial of
Sinyávsky and Daniél and further trials since. Although in
many ways it is a repetition of the Zamyátin – Pilnyák
frame-up which ushered in the terrors of the thirties, in other
ways the Sinyávsky–Daniél 'trial' was even more sinister.
The political cynicism behind the former was obvious and
foremost. In the series of 'trials' which began with the
Sinyávsky – Daniél indictment there is crude political motive
too, but there is an even more formidable tyranny, that of
philistine public opinion. A protest demanding the release of
Sinyávsky and Daniél was signed by forty-nine prominent
writers in the West, the Western Communist press roundly condemned it, and even outside the courtroom in Moscow an un-
precedented demonstration took place. A member of the crowd

ture, but all literature mark! Andréi Sinyávsky was already
known for his freshness and originally as a critic, especially for
his introduction to Pasternák's poems published in *Novy Mir* in
the year of his arrest, and it only became clear at the 'trial' that
he was the writer Abrám Tertz, who had published several important novels and stories abroad. Yúli Daniél had been working
gathered outside was reported as saying : 'There has never been
anything like it in the history of literature,' – not Russian literature, but all literature mark! Andréi Sinyávsky was already
known for his freshness and originally as a critic, especially for
his introduction to Pasternák's poems published in *Novy Mir* in
the year of his arrest, and it only became clear at the 'trial' that
he was the writer Abrám Tertz, who had published several important novels and stories abroad. Yúli Daniél had been working
mainly as a translator but had published several scurrilously
satirical pieces abroad under the name Arzhák. The evidence
brought against these writers, both of them convinced social-
ists, included not only the obvious one of carrying out anti-
Soviet propaganda. Their frame-up also included remarks made
by the purely fictitious characters in their own books. The
ludicrous highpoint was reached when Daniél, himself a Jew,
was accused on trivial internal evidence of anti-Semitism.
Both writers received extremely severe sentences, Sinyávsky
seven years' hard labour, and Daniél five. After sentence was
passed Sinyávsky made a final plea, a brave but calm reply
which quietly in turn put the entire political-legal machine on
trial: 'What makes my defence difficult is the peculiar atmosphere which has been created in this courtroom. . . . The
Prosecution has created in effect a wall of deafness through
which it is impossible to get any truth. . . . It has succeeded in
creating a curtain, a particularly electrifying atmosphere
which destroys reality and carries us into the grotesque: as
in the works of Arzhák and Tertz. It is the atmosphere of a
murky anti-Soviet underground hidden behind the bright faces
of the candidate of sciences Sinyávsky and the poet-translator
Daniél, who hatch plots, nurture plans for terrorist acts,
pogroms, assassinations, assassination and more assassinations. . . . It is difficult to break through this atmosphere – no
arguments, however circumstantial, about the nature of the

creative process, are of any avail here. . . .'

Public opinion did not triumph as it had in the case of Bródski, two years previously. And what some had hoped would in the course of time come to be recognised by the perpetrators of the trial as a blundering political and judical miscarriage proved to be only the beginning. Sinyávsky's story *The Trial Begins* was truly prophetic. Yúli Galanskóv, Alec Ginzbúrg, and other intellectuals and writers since, were 'tried' and given savage sentences. There have been recent Stalinist-type putsches also against Soviet minority nationalities, as well as an ominous recurrence of anti-Semitism.

The poet Andréi Voznesénsky, long acclaimed by many as a modern successor to Púshkin, has been attacked and finally silenced completely: 'My fellow poets, members of our federation, will write the poems I am not writing. . . .' Matters have been brought to such a pass that there is at the moment of writing no Soviet writer with a reputation abroad who has not been disgraced or silenced in one way or another. Among the more vocal dissenters is Andréi Sakhárov, probably the Soviet Union's most important nuclear physicist and believed to have played an important part in the development of the hydrogen bomb. For him the situation developing in his own country is one that is developing in many parts of the world; the disease and the cure are he believes universal. Nevertheless his essay on intellectual freedom specifically condemns events at home: 'Was it not disgraceful to allow persecution, in the best witch-hunt tradition, of dozens of members of the Soviet intelligentsia who spoke out against the arbitrariness of judicial and psychiatric agencies, to attempt to force honourable people to sign false, hypocritical "retractions", to dismiss and blacklist people, to deprive young writers, editors, and members of the intelligentsia of all means of existence?'

But for all that the scene emerging in Russia today retains a traditional dimension of magnificence and epic grandeur. Persecuted as he is, the Russian writer is not some idle passing fancy of a jaded reading public, but a figure such as writers have ceased to be elsewhere. Whether silenced or in prison, his voice is still to be heard. The politicians are afraid, sometimes to the point of panic. The Russian writer is the small but brightly burning flame of a great culture whose conflagration centuries of autocratic rule have never succeeded in stamping out. Though for many a contemporary Russian writer the Gutenberg era has ended, *Samizdát* ('do-it-yourself' publication relying on multiple typed copies) continues to flourish. In this context we come to see that such men as an unnamed Soviet literary critic who handed over a manuscript for publication in the West are no victims of egotism or self-delusion but people who are prepared to perish for their ideals and for their own country: 'I see no possibility of publishing it here. If I publish it abroad they will arrest me. If they arrest me, I will not survive (he had a weak heart and damaged kidneys from an earlier arrest in Stalin's day). I do not want to die, I'd much rather live. But I am perfectly willing to die for my book. So go ahead and publish, but for heaven's sake see that it is published correctly.'

2 Poetry

We have already seen that the poetic tradition in Russia is both ancient and prolific. In various distinct genres – the epic ballads or *bylíny*, the lyrical songs, and the liturgical poems – the tradition goes back to the Middle Ages, to a time when epic and ballad flourished from the Atlantic to the Urals. Russian oral literature has created and preserved some of the finest specimens. For reasons of history Russia had no strictly *written* poetry until the early eighteenth century. It is typical nevertheless that, before as few as four decades had passed, Russian verse writers—and they cannot all justifiably be called 'poets' – had experimented with just about every style known to Europe, ancient or modern. Sometimes, even when not overly original, these creations breathe a freshness which was seldom attained even by their foreign models. They have the feel and smell of newly carved wood. Modern Russian poetry's founder was Prince Kantemír (1708–74). The Prince was a Russian diplomat in London when he published his *Satires* (1750), a work which gave Russian letters a secure foothold, as well as a distinctive character, within the European mould.

With this brilliant apprenticeship, it is hardly surprising that at least one major poet had emerged before the end of the eighteenth century. In fact the first of a long line also happens to be one of Russia's greatest, although not recognized as such in his own lifetime. Gavríl Derzhávin (1743–1816), a half Tatar from the lesser nobility, rose to a position of eminence both as administrator and court poet during the reign of Catherine the Great. The reader of Derzhávin cannot fail to be impressed by the sheer range, the virtuosity. He may recognize the nature mysticism and the ecstatic note of Klopstock, and may sometimes be reminded of Gray or Collins. But he will not miss the individuality and freshness, the unmistakable Russian flavour, with all the classical forms turned wild and loose. My favourites among Derzhávin's poems are not his more celebrated and grandiose ones like *The Waterfall* or *God* (a poem widely known outside Russia at that time on account of its Deistic inclination) but the more intimate poems of his later years composed after his retirement to his country estate.

The early years of the nineteenth century bring with them a flood of poets the best of them remarkable enough to be compared with their better known European contemporaries. Among them was Vasíly Zhukóvsky (1783–1853). Zhukóvsky besides being an important poet in his own right was also a prolific and a great translator, and it was he who set the tradition by which Russia's foremost poets have generally been superb translators as well. It should not surprise us that Zhukóvsky's poetry reflects the prevailing pre-Romantic moods of the day. Zhukóvsky's highly polished, mellifluous verse owes a good deal to the Germany of Goethe and Schiller as it does to the English poets: Gray, Southey, and especially Scott and the early Wordsworth. Poets like Púshkin were able to start where Zhukóvsky left off, with an enormously wide repertoire of possibilities at their elbow. Another important figure at this time was Konstantín Bátyushkov (1787–1855). While Zhukóvsky had been busy acquainting Russia with European currents, Bátyushkov took in the Italian Renaissance, and the poets of Rome and Greece. Bátyushkov's 'classical' diction reminds us of the miraculous timelessness achieved by Goethe and Hölderlin (and like Hölderlin Bátyushkov was to spend the last thirty years of his life insane); this diction became the model for Púshkin's elevated mode.

Alexander Púshkin (1799–1837) is for Russians what Shakespeare is for us. Forty years after Púshkin's death, Dostoévsky said: 'Everything we have comes from Púshkin.' Writing about Púshkin then is a forbidding task, and there seems to be no way of avoiding upsetting experts and vener-

ators alike. That is only a part of the difficulty; for whereas
Shakespeare survives translation, Púshkin's poetry loses
virtually everything. Púshkin has often been compared to
Mozart. And in Mozart tonality, medium, instrumentation,
even key, are crucial. Translating Púshkin is something like
transcribing Mozart's piano concertos for guitar, or the symphonies for brass band. In Púshkin language and composition
are one, for in a very real sense Púshkin and the Russian
language had become inseparable. Besides giving the Russian
language its present shape and its immense range Púshkin
'undulating and slashing through verse melodies the likes of
which have never been known before in Russia' spun out of
this language a wealth of worlds and people, real and fantastic,
a whole anatomy of the human heart. This does not mean that
all in Púshkin is lofty or intense. On the contrary, Púshkin
like Mozart perpetually parodies himself as well as his characters; not grossly, but affectionately, even if devastatingly. All
the fun and humour is never far from grief, though a grief
which is not personal but common to every man. Elegant
miniatures keep company with lofty elegiacs; lampoons and
give-away pastiche with the most incisive and courageous
utterances of all time; and we slip from farce into the eerie
world of faery. As Nabókov not so long ago put it: the reader
is able to revel in all the tomfooleries of genius. The great
achievements of those who follow Púshkin – poets and novelists alike – we find them all there, and often much more than
in embryo.

Púshkin was no aesthete or literary dandy. Uncommonly
outspoken, contemptuous of authority and the quiet life,
Púshkin was politically one of the most dangerous, if not *the*
most dangerous, figures in post-Decembrist Russia. Nicholas I
considered Púshkin too explosive for anyone to handle but
himself. Accordingly he appointed himself Púshkin's personal
censor. But in spite of all this Púshkin never stopped defying
authority and was in consequence obliged to spend much of
his life in exile. His taste for danger led to his own demise
in a pistol duel.

None of the categories – classical, romantic, realist, or any
other – fits Púshkin even remotely. The dimensions are far too

many. In his early twenties Púshkin like many another of his
generation had been influenced by Byron. This phase was
short-lived, as a remark he made a few years later shows:
'Byron conceived and lived only one character – himself.
Byron took a one-sided view of the world and human nature,
then turned away from them, and became immersed in his
own self.' With Púshkin a character, a mood or situation is
never predetermined. The reader is never in a position to
specify at a particular moment: 'so this is what it all means.'
Instead he finds himself in a hall of mirrors. Relationships,
happenings are never fixed, but change according to the
perspective of the reader, along with the poet and his
characters.

Púshkin was barely out of school when his mock-heroic
Ruslán and Ludmíla brought him fame. By that time controversial verses of his were already circulating in manuscript
(no new phenomenon in Russia!), and even at thirteen years
Pushkin had referred to himself as 'a disciple of Voltaire speaking the Moscow dialect'. One of these ditties, a scurrilous
lampoon directed at Tsar Alexander, got him into very serious
trouble. Siberia had been rumoured, but in the event Púshkin
was 'exiled' by the usual method of enforced military service,
and spent the next four years cooling his heels in various parts
of southern Russia. Hérzen, in an attempt to convey the extent of Púshkin's influence at this time says: 'There was not
a single young lady with even a modicum of education who
had not learnt his more dubious works by heart, and not a
single army officer who did not carry a copy in his knapsack,
nor for that matter any priest's son who had not made at
least a dozen copies of them.'

As well as being Russia's greatest poet, Púshkin is also its
Hans Andersen. *The Golden Cockerel, The Tale of Tsar Saltan,*
and other tales in this vein, are beloved of children and
adults alike. They are remarkable as literature and among
Púshkin's best works. They are based on the long tradition of
the Russian fairy story but, besides this, they glitter with
parody and wit, and with kaleidoscopically shifting glimpses
of Púshkin's vision of faery. Not only do these tales – to adapt
Tolkien – 'open a door on Other Time, where we stand out-

side, if only for a moment, outside Time itself, perhaps' but we also sense that the world of everyday has been dissolved and recast. The real secret of their intoxication is their marvellous verse diction and Púshkin's own unique manner of using language for blending styles. It was this latter secret that the great prose writers who came after him, especially Gógol and Dostoévsky, came to learn. The most remarkable thing in Púshkin is his 'wizardly' prologue to *Ruslán and Ludmíla*. Búnin said of these lines that 'they poisoned him for the rest of his life'; 'What nonsense it would seem – some curved sea-shore that has never existed anywhere, some "learned" cat that for no earthly reason came to be there and – heaven knows why – is chained to the oak tree...' But then evidently the point was in its being nonsense, an intoxicated vision, something totally absurd, unreal, not anything reasonable or real.

It is an extraordinary fact that in his youth Púshkin knew Russian only as a second language. His elders and peers alike spoke mostly French, and what Russian they did use was adulterated and unidiomatic. In a letter to his friend Chaadáyev, Púshkin writes: 'I shall address you in the language of Europe (i.e. French), I am more at home in it than ours.' Even admitting the ironic overstatement, we must realize that Púshkin worked hard to learn his Russian anew – from country folk and street traders. A particularly special influence was his nanny, an ordinary countrywoman, to whom he became closely attached during the time he was obliged to stay on his mother's estate at Mikhailóvskoye. For up-and-coming writers Púshkin had this piece of advice: 'Listen carefully to the speech of ordinary people. You will be able to learn a lot more from it than from our journals. Read the popular fairy tales to find the real qualities of the Russian language.'

Like Chaucer with English, Púshkin succeeded in creating an integrated Russian style and language. He mingled dialect, colloquialism, gallicism, archaism, every possible resource of the language, sifting them carefully, giving them exactly the right weight, and then using them with perfect precision. Even though Púshkin managed to graft a large part of the expressive

possibilities of other European poetic languages on to the
Russian language, he had never known Europe at first hand
and never once visited any European country. He had wanted
to, but permission to travel abroad had always been refused.
Belinsky described the effect of the young Púshkin on his
contemporaries: 'He was like some sorcerer, capable at one
and the same moment of drawing laughter and tears from
us, playing upon our emotions exactly as he pleased. . . . Russia
had never before heard such songs as these. How avidly she
drank them in. It is little wonder that every nerve in her
being quivered at the sound of them.'

Threading its way through Púshkin's life is the novel in
verse *Evgény Onégin*. An entire chapter devoted to a work
of this order would amount to little more than a footnote;
and even Nabókov's recent four-volume commentary is
limited in its exploration. Púshkin started this novel at the
age of twenty-three at a time when he was a fashionable
political nuisance, and completed it almost ten years later.
These were years intensely lived, sufficient for several life-
times. All the more amazing then the perfection of *Evgény
Onégin*. Like *The Ancient Mariner* or *Ulysses*, this novel in
verse is an entire poetic universe. Every stanza, every line,
every nuance is echoed and counter-balanced; and the art is
such that the removal of a single phrase could shatter the
entirety. But there is much more besides. Nabókov has
described the novel as 'a series of bright, open rooms, through
which we may pass freely, taking a look at everything inside.
But in the very centre of the building is a secret place. The
door is locked, we look through the window and inside are
all kinds of mysterious things.' This 'secret place', a lurking
surreality, is packed away behind the least suspecting pecca-
dilloes. This faery meaning binds the many different elements,
and gives them their particular transformations, spellbinds
them. In one of his poems Púshkin wrote: 'In the world exists
a heart, and it's there I dwell.'

The reader who knows no Russian could easily be disappointed. The mercurial texture, the distant music, the strange
shifting light cast by the diction all vanish in translation.
Even the narrative ingredients look unpromising. The central

characters are Onégin and Tatyána. The novel begins with
Onégin, and we could easily forget that we are not reading
Byron's Don Juan. Onégin when we first meet him is a bored
youth, a dandy, a fledgeling of the Westernized aristocracy.
But it is upon Tatyána that Púshkin lavished his poetic wealth.
Tatyána stands in relation to Russian literature, like Gretchen
to German or Beatrice to Italian literature. Surprisingly, she is
the spiritual child of the eighteenth century sentimental novel.
But this is no more than a superstructure which stands in
curious contrast with her weird true nature. Tatyána the
drawing-room dreamer is a child of the elves as well –
'Sauvage, silent, timid. . . . In her own family she seemed a
strangeling.' Only as the novel grows does this strangeness
become dominant. Onégin first meets Tatyána at the country
home of his friend's (Lénsky) fiancée, and it is in Onégin
that Tatyána in accordance with the prescriptions of her
'sentimental education' finds her destiny. It is only in the
hobgoblin depths of her queer dream that Tatyána finds the
true nature of her love; only then that it becomes real beyond
her comprehension. Built around the mystery of Tatyána, the
novel moves through all the registers of human love.

Púshkin's work on Evgény Onégin had been interrupted
more than once, and at the end of Part Six he announces
that although he is still fond of Onégin he is in no mood for
him. Púshkin had already completed his first term of exile
when, for a most trivial passing remark in a letter, he was
exiled a second time. Púshkin was to be confined to his
mother's estate, and his father was appointed his guarantor.
Imprisonment or hard labour was preferable to this humilia-
tion. These two long years of confinement at Mikhailóvskoye
form a watershed in Púshkin's life. They dampened the bright
wit of his early years, and left spleen in its place (an affliction
which at the height of a severe cholera epidemic Púshkin
claimed to be worse than cholera itself). The Russia he had
loved and still loved so dearly had already become a vast
prison. The events of those years, the savage crushing of
the Decembrist movement, the blanket of fear and uncertainty
proved almost too much even for a man like Púshkin. He
was allowed to return to the capital in 1826, and found the

city a desert where everything had withered. Púshkin was no longer lionized, and his popularity was never regained in his own lifetime.

When we meet Tatyána again she is 'no longer the crushed lover. She is married and a doyen of the Petersburg aristocracy. Onégin is under her spell; her remoteness a terror and a fascination for him. There is something forbidding about this 'inaccessible goddess', and she now reminds us of those other fearsome creations of Púshkin – Rusálka and Cleopatra.

Almost nothing has been said here about Púshkin as poet. To give any idea of his range even with the best of translations would still be an impossible task: the odes which equal those of Keats and Shelley; the love lyrics; the grandeur of the Caucasian poems, in which poet and scene are welded into a single medium; the Russian rhythms and music of the ballads; the cosmopolitan wit; the foreboding of the 'personal' poems.

The mood of composition was a thing miraculous. Without warning the spell was upon him – 'I am visited by an invisible swarm of guests.' The rhythms began flowing and bursting all around. In this one-act verse play *Mozart and Salieri* (based on the then current rumour that Salieri, a minor composer, had poisoned Mozart out of jealousy), Púshkin portrays Mozart as someone totally unpretentious, unable to take his own art seriously, absorbed in his own children's games. Salieri's morbid self-appraisal is contrasted with Mozart's ingenuousness. With Mozart music was just something that happened. He had no need, no idea even how to reflect upon the divine madness. Like Púshkin he experienced it firsthand.

Lack of space obliges me to pass over a number of poets who are lesser only when put beside Púshkin: – Evgény Baratýnsky (1800–44), a poet of pessimism and the human condition; Dimítri Venevítinov (1805–27), another introspective poet who, had he lived a few years more, might have become one of Russia's greatest; Alekséy Koltsóv (1809–42), best known for his peasant lyrics; Nikolái Yazýkov (1803–46), a poet of Bacchic revelry, whose 'crackling and clicking' foreshadows modern poetry. That brings us directly to Lérmontov.

Mikhaíl Lérmontov (1814–41) is surely one of the
wonders of literature. We are dealing with a very young man
killed in a duel at 26; a poet and prose writer of such range
and originality that his work even today has not yet been
fully evaluated. Twice exiled, Lérmontov (his name was a
Russianized version of Learmont, the surname of a Scottish
ancestor) spent the greater part of his mature years travelling
back and forth to the Caucasus – no mean journey in those
days – or on active military service under the worst possible
conditions. At a time when Púshkin was the undisputed
master, Lérmontov, at first his close disciple, was already
taking Russian poetic diction beyond anything even Púshkin
had imagined. Without knowing it Lérmontov was busy
laying the foundations for the next golden age of Russian
poetry at the turn of the century. Less than one year older
than Keats at the time of his death, Lérmontov not so much
astonishes as bewilders; especially if we reckon up the mass
of circumstances which run directly counter to anyone becoming any kind of poet. The advice he usually received was
discouraging, and his army comrades could tell him only to
'pack it in'.

There is no poet more precocious than Lérmontov, not
even Rimbaud. At sixteen Lérmontov was writing strangely
symbolistic lyrics for which there were no obvious models
in Russian literature at that time. Lérmontov was original
despite himself and worked up a natural resistance against
Romantic lyricism and the notion of poetic inspiration. The
things he had to say were limitless, and he regarded the saying
of them as more important than the vehicle itself. Also there
was the premonition, as with Keats, that time was not on his
side:

'I began early, and shall finish early,
Very little will be achieved.
In my soul the weight of shattered hopes
Lies as in the ocean . . .
Who will give the world my thoughts
I – or God – more likely no one!'

A reader's first impression of Lérmontov can be one of

prevailing gloom and morbid introspection. This is a mistaken impression. His acute awareness of his own isolation cannot be denied; but self-pity there is none. Rage and despair were pointless, he believed, and the inevitability of things was to be marvelled at:

'I go on my way alone.
From life I want nothing
and have no regret for what's past.
I long only for freedom and rest,
for sleep and oblivion.'

Lérmontov had discovered very early his own method of disenchantment. Like most of his generation, he had come under the influence of Schelling; but what attracted him most about this philosopher was his theory of the will and evil – the principle of human suffering arising from the coexistence of holiness and wickedness in the human heart. Lérmontov's concept of evil is poles apart from the Marquis de Sade's 'evil as a universal principle'; a purely necessary, automatic evil. There is nothing morbid or mechanical about Lérmontov's principle, a fact which sets him apart from the other Romantic connoisseurs of evil. His long poem *The Demon*, which took nearly eleven years to complete, is the portrayal of a new kind of Satan – not Milton's rebel, nor Goethe's urbane Mephistopheles, but an anguished, lonely, bored Satan. The experimental Russian painter Vrúbel became obsessed by this demon of Lérmontov's and created a series of representations which took him through to his own insanity (the most famous of these paintings is Vrúbel's *The Demon Prostrate*). Moreover, Lérmontov's demonic figure haunts Russian literature right down to the present day.

Lérmontov cannot extricate himself from that 'stupid joke' life, and is forced to let himself be dragged along by its weight and pain. He warns the purveyors of pathos that their cries of anger are ridiculous; they are merely 'waving their tinsel swords in some silly show', flaunting wounds 'that rot the soul beneath'. Lérmontov's sense of alienation is unlike anything belonging to his own time, and anticipates Schopenhauer and Baudelaire.

The personal poetry is so unlyrical that it resembles prose. And yet, the diction, the rhythms and metres, even the layout, are such that nothing can be displaced since they are exactly equal to the sense and mood. This anti-lyricism is even more evident in the Caucasian poems. These were written in the period of enforced military service, which was his punishment for having published a white-hot condemnation of those conspiratorially responsible for Púshkin's death. It was in the Caucasus that Lérmontov discovered nature, a discovery peculiarly his own. His is not nature reflecting man, with poetry as its medium, but the other way round. With Lérmontov it is as if the poet runs in nature's veins, as if nature inhabits the poet whilst remaining its own intractable self. That is why the great poems built around natural imagery affect us so powerfully, and so strangely. At one and the same moment Lérmontov uses an image to symbolize his own mood or lot, yet has the same image gather pathos carrying us right away from the poet. The wanton human destruction of a tiny oasis of palm trees becomes a symbol of the poet's own fate, but it is not his fate so much as the obliterated lives of those trees we actually lament. This was Lérmontov's most important discovery, one that has been handed on to future generations of poets. It is probable that Russian poetry would have developed very differently without it.

There is no more undiscovered poet in Russia than Lérmontov. Alexander Blok writing in 1920 was convinced that an evaluation was overdue: 'About Lérmontov almost nothing has been said – there is only silence and still more silence.' The insights gained in the fifty years that have elapsed since then have brought that goal only a little nearer.

Equally great but worlds apart stands another lonely figure Fyódor Tyútchev (1803–73). A symbolist poet ahead of his time, outdoing the Germans in profundity; a writer of love lyrics of unsurpassed candour and freshness; one of Russia's foremost nature poets; and subsequently an embarrassingly bad jingoist versifier, Tyútchev was several distinct poets rolled into one. This oddness is carried over into his life which, if anything, is an even greater bundle of contradictions. Tyútchev was a Slavophile who could not bear to live for

long in Russia; a man who opposed Western ideals, but spent
his happiest years and the greater part of his adult life in
Europe; a lover of the social round who on the whole did not
much like people; an advocate of State theocracy, yet himself an unbeliever; and a nature poet who was easily depressed
by the countryside. Besides this, Tyútchev was a reluctant
poet, composing verses inadvertently. One of his friends said
of him that 'he did not understand what it meant to write
poems; they created themselves. . . . He threw them down on a
piece of paper; then, forgetting all about them, let them fall
on to the floor, and his wife would pick them up.' Many of
Tyútchev's poems would have been lost had not friends and
scholars seen to their posthumous publication. For reasons
like this, coupled with his lengthy and virtually uninterrupted
sojourn abroad, Tyútchev remained practically unknown
during his lifetime. His published poems appeared in obscure
journals, and even when this was not the case he insisted on
signing himself 'F.T.' Tyútchev came into his own more than
a decade after his death, when his full significance was recognized first by Vladímir Soloviév, and afterwards by a whole
generation of Symbolist poets.

One of the few contemporaries to appreciate Tyútchev
was Dostoévsky. The reason is no doubt partly that they
had so much in common. Both wrote without complete conscious control, by some inner compulsion; both were enigmas,
for themselves as well as for others; and perhaps most signifi-
cantly of all, both were endowed with insight into meanings
of existence none had so far explored. The last word on either
writer is still wanting.

To illustrate Tyútchev's oddness, I will take his work as
translator. In the first place, Tyútchev was not really a translator at all; he was a 'transmuter'. He transmuted the most
diverse styles, even Goethe, into his own unique and distinctive
style, a style which none the less eludes analysis. Many of his
'own' poems (and it is doubtful if Tyútchev always recognized the existence of a boundary between translation and his
own creation) contain strangely transformed images and
themes of works he had been familiar with as a boy. This
transmutation extended to philosophy, even to the nature

philosophy of Schelling which he digested but largely rejected. In that this transmutation was entirely unconscious,
Tyútchev once again resembles Dostoévsky.

A few pages can convey no adequate idea of Tyútchev's
achievement and poetic quality. Tyútchev was the first poet
in Russia to capture the paradisal essence of leaves in springtime, of rock and running water. He not only discovers the
universe in a flower, but enables us to penetrate the essence
of this discovery. Tyútchev turns night into the Garden of
Eden with the vault of heaven peering wanly down at the
peopleless earth fast in its sleep of iron; only here and
there a pale birch tree, a piece of shrubbery, or grey moss
disturb the tranquillity, like fevered dreams left over from
the daytime – 'The abyss with all its misty dread exposed to
our sight; and there are no barriers between us – that is why
night is so terrible to us!' The hundred-eyed beast of the
firmament, the stars in all their glory stare down at us mysteri-
ously from out of the fiery depths of space – 'and we were
floating there surrounded on all sides by this blazing chasm'.
There is a mysterious agitation about Tyútchev's stillness, and
this stirring is life in things and life in the poet at the same
instant:

'everything was so calm
so dark and peaceful things had ever been!
The fountain gurgled; still and graceful
a neighbouring cypress looked in at the window.
Suddenly all was confusion – a convulsive tremor
ran along the cypress branches ...
The fountain fell silent – and some sort of strange babbling
as if through sleep murmured incoherently.'

The agitation is the counterpart of the evil flowing in the
poet and his mistress as it suddenly crosses the threshold. At
such moments the boundaries are dissolved between outer and
inner. The poet stands spellbound – 'the invisible mysterious
evil poured out in everything – in flowers, in the clear glasslike
spring'. Man's love for woman that produced some of
Tyútchev's finest verse was essentially evil.

Tyútchev's reality was nature, not that of everyday life; and

man was 'merely nature's dream'. The world which beckoned
púts us in mind of Baudelaire's L'Invitation au Voyage. Take
for instance Tyútchev's early poem Dream at Sea:

'The winds answered, the waves sang –
Deafened I flew in a chaos of sounds,
Above the chaos this dream of mine was borne,
Sickly bright, magically silent,
It lightly blew over the sounding darkness.
In rays of fever it opened up its world –
The earth grew green, the skies filled with light –
Labyrinthine gardens, palaces, colonnades;
And crowds in silence thronged.
I made out many an unfamiliar face,
Beheld enchanted creatures, birds of mystery . . .'

During the second half of the nineteenth century poetry was
out of fashion. Writers like Turgénev or Chékhov, even when
they felt the need for poetry, invariably chose the medium
of prose. An exception is Afanásy Fet (1820–92). Fet serves
as a bridge between the Romantics and the modern Russian
poets. But times were inauspicious, the critics scathing, and
Fet (for a period) abandoned poetry altogether for the life of
a tough, business-minded landowner. Paradoxically this did
nothing but strengthen his art. Besides creating some of the
loveliest of all Russian lyrics, Fet was also a great translator;
his translations of Heine many a time rivalling their originals.
Although a slighter poet than Tyútchev, and narrower in
range than the Symbolists who came after, Fet is like no other.
Fet is the poet of springtime, of the May night of palpability;
but his spring embraces autumn, and his concreteness is time-
less and transparent. And there is the Unknown Woman too,
who later haunts the poetry of Alexander Blok. In the
moonlit park, in the movement of a willow, her presence
is revealed in the 'breathing' of all poetry and things of
beauty; it is also she who makes us pity all this beauty around
us. Fet was no exalted visionary, and was able to content
himself with what he once described as 'the obscure ravings
and the confused aroma of the grass.'

In the last decade of the century came a vigorous revival
of Russian poetry. Very soon there was a cluster of poets,
nearly all of them important, and variously known as Symbolists or Decadents. Between the two schools the dividing line
is none too clear, although both are a product of a common
intellectual climate generated by a curious assortment of
Russian writers and thinkers. Among the latter were the visionary philosopher and theologian Vladímir Soloviév; two
who have latterly been hailed as Existentialists, Nikolái
Berdyáev and Leo Shestóv; the exalted but vapid Dimítri
Merezhkóvsky (particularly influential as the prophet of the
coming Apocalypse); and Vasíly Rózanov, a writer in some
ways very close to D. H. Lawrence. Two further decisive
influences were Nietzsche and Schopenhauer. 'Decadence' in
part originated in the aestheticism of Merezhkóvsky, in his
sense of impending catstrophe, of a civilization drawing to its
close; the oppressive and at the same time exalted awareness
of being the last of a series. The Decadents believed that the
twentieth century would be a time of chaos, alienation, uncertainty, dissolution, and of terrifying and undreamt of innovations and discoveries. For them all traditional bonds and
limits were cancelled. Nietzsche bolstered their anti-ideals;
beauty and evil, sex and religion, God and the individual
became merged. Theirs was Merezhkóvsky's prescription:
'In pursuit of the new Beauty we break all commandments,
we transgress every limit.' 'Symbolism' by contrast seemed
more positive. It was based not so much upon the decadent
symbolism of Mallarmé but upon an indigenous Russian
mystical strain. Their inspiration was drawn originally from
Soloviév, himself a poet besides a philosopher; and it was
he who had convinced them that poetry was before everything
else the vehicle of prophecy and an emanation of a super-
natural presence. The Russian Symbolists shared the
apocalyptic forebodings of the Decadents, but they cultivated
their aesthetic to the point of religious affirmation. According to the Symbolists the foremost task of the poet was to
become a high priest or a medium.

It frequently happens that great innovators are eclipsed
by those who follow in their wake. Such was the case with

Valéry Bryúsov (1873-1924). Reading Bryúsov gives one an
uncanny sensation. One catches echoes of many a later Russian
poet: Blok, Tsvetáeva, Pasternák. This should not really surprise us since it was Bryúsov who roughed out the framework in which modern poetry could grow. Bryúsov is the
Eliot or Pound of Russian poetry. On a quite different level
Bryúsov was also a charismatic figure, a new Magus. Blok
described him as 'a hypnotist, compelling one to serve him.
He hypnotized me for a very long time...' Bryúsov himself
was explicit about the purpose of the new poetry – 'to
hypnotise the reader, to create within him a certain state of
mind'. Bryúsov's most revolutionary collection of poems Urbi
et Orbi Blok compared to the springing of tiger from its jungle
lair 'striking terror into us with the aspect of some dread
Magus'. Many ideas current at the time were taken to their
furthest reduction. Schopenhauer for example had claimed
the world to be merely our representation; Bryúsov insisted
that the world is our creation. And with characteristic para-
doxicality Bryúsov's philosophy of the moment was based
only on the future not the present. Although not himself a
Symbolist, Bryúsov denied the possibility of any poetry which
was other than Symbolist, and went on to assert that life and
the world are no more than material for putting words together with. With supreme eclecticism he managed to assimil-
ate all the most essential characteristics of all previous literary
trends; though according to Gumilyóv 'he added something
quite new to them, and caused them to burn with a new fire,
making one forget their original impetus.'

To reach the three most important poets of the period I
am obliged to pass in unseemly haste over poets who are far
from minor. Nothing will be said here of Konstantín Balmónt
(1867-1943) one of Russia's great virtuosos, who once
described himself as the exquisite flower of leisurely Russian
speech; or about Fyódor Sologúb (1863-1927) or Iván Búnin
(1870-1953) (although I shall be touching upon their prose
work in a later section). My survey also excludes Innokénty
Annénsky (1858-1909) a poet of immense subtlety, once
characterized as 'a Verlaine in Saturnine mood'; and a number
of others whose names are not even mentioned.

The first of the three – all Symbolists – wrote under the pseudonym Andréi Bély 'Andrew the White'. Andréi Bély (1880–1934) started life as a scientist, and began writing poetry in that eschatologically critical year 1900, the year in which the 'boundary between the two centuries' was forebodingly crossed. Soloviév's aesthetics, the lucubrations of Schopenhauer and Nietzsche, and Fet's haunted landscapes were the early formative influences. Bély's first works were prose poems which he called 'Symphonies'. Uneven in quality they may be, but these pieces contain some startling flights of imagination. Inspired by Nietzsche's Zarathustra they are nearer to James Joyce or Paul Valéry. The later poems exhibit the same unique blend of mysticism, dissonant tonality, and parody; and the verse technique of *Gold in Azure* and, later *Ashes* takes Russian poetry slap into the avant-garde of world literature. Behind them was Bély's credo that art needed to be transformed into life, and life in turn into religion – a theurgical view. The Word literally had to become flesh; the only form of art possible was Symbolism therefore. Searching for an 'emblematics of meaning' by way of an extensive exploration of every form of knowledge from philosophy and history to the natural sciences, Bély came up with the view that natural phenomena yield only symbolical forms and solutions, and that life itself is reducible to a system of such symbols – 'A jewelled dawn is no higher thing than a pub, because both are equally symbols of a common reality.'

The second of these three Symbolists, and a poet not to everyone's taste, is Vyacheslàv Ivánov (1866–1949). Most of Ivánov's life was spent abroad: as a young man he had lived in Germany, studying Roman archaeology under Mommsen, and subsequently becoming addicted to Nietzsche. The years he spent in Russia spanned the nineteen years from the upheaval of 1905 until shortly after the Civil War. Although he lived for another twenty-five very active years, Ivánov was already living in a kind of home for distinguished old elephants when, in 1924, he eventually decided to leave Russia. Because Ivánov was a brilliant classical scholar as well as a poet, his poetry is steeped in Hellenic tradition. He shunned modernism in any form, and his own diction stems from early

Russian poets, from Derzhávin and Bátyushkov, by way of Tyútchev. Ivánov's work is only incidentally Symbolist, and is the embodiment of his own Dionysian thesis that poetry is the stepping out from the temporal into the eternal. If Sir Maurice Bowra is right this puts Ivánov in line with the Greeks: 'True to the Greek tradition, Ivánov regarded the task of poetry as a search for an unchanging reality behind the veil of changing appearances. By creating the poet reveals, and what he reveals is the essential nature of the universe.' The early collected poems *Pilot Stars* (1903) and *Translucency* (1906) happened to be in tune with the mood of the day, and before very long Ivánov was recognized as a leading figure in the poetic revival. When they returned from abroad Ivánov and an equally dazzling wife inaugurated their weekly gatherings, their famous 'Tower', which became the centre of gravity for the new generation of writers. When not outstanding, Ivánov's poems strike one as dry and laboured; a factor that could fairly be ascribed to the poet's failure sometimes to project the richness of his own interior world and of the semantic content of a language that occasionally borders on cliché. But at its best, Ivánov's poetry is among Russia's finest. Poetry had become for him the expression of a mystical religion, and of the belief that he was its high priest. At its least compelling, his verse abounds in those 'wearisome, sentimental and vapid thoughts that Blok supposed no one adopting a stance like that of Ivánov could avoid. Occasionally though there are moments of dizzy profundity. The collection of sonnets *De Profundis Amavi* (*Out of the depths I have loved*) written upon the death of his second wife must be among the most moving lamentations of all time.

Easily the most outstanding poet of his generation is Alexander Blok (1880–1921). Like Dante in the *Vita Nuova*, although in a very different way, Blok builds the major part of his work upon the vision of a woman. And he succeeds. His verse contains every cliché of Romantic poetry, but he always manages to transcend what in a lesser poet would emerge as banality, and to sweep up our everyday world into vision after vision. In addition Blok is among Russia's most disquieting thinkers, with all the uncanny insight of a Dostoévsky or a Soloviév. Like Soloviév, and deeply influenced by him, Blok was a visionary, visited by that same mysterious woman; a creation not of the Greek gnostics but of the Russian collective unconscious. Soloviév and Blok were both well acquainted with her perilous ambiguity; yet they preferred the hazardousness of involvement to distant contemplation. The main difference between them was that Blok divided mysticism from religion – 'Mysticism is bohemianism of the soul; religion is being on one's guard'. The mystic needs only ecstasy, and his medium is art. For Blok art was the only truth. He once said: 'I love only art, children, and death.'

Blok could never be described as ivory tower. He lived very close to life, and entered so fully into the moral and politico-historical crises of his day that he developed an uncannily accurate prescience of times to come, right down to the present. At a time when few people could visualize totalitarianism, Blok was able to resolve it into its ingredients and to diagnose the impending sickness. This was not the theorizing of a Nietzsche or Spengler, but the living awareness that came from being a poet in an apocalyptic era. As a poet Blok found himself painfully close to those elemental forces which tear not only a single individual but an entire nation into disorganised fragments. Poetry, it seemed to him, was a kind of violence committed by unknown forces against the poet. These forces are coiled up within the poet and he is at once their tool and their victim. Poetry was no noble calling but a mark of weakness, condemning the poet to ineffectuality and powerlessness.

It is beyond my powers to convey to the reader the marvels of Blok's poetry. He loses almost as much in translation as Púshkin. And even with the perfect translation it is doubtful if the symphonic quality of the whole of a particular cycle would remain (Each poem is linked to the rest by diction, tone, mood, rhythm, and every possible verse dimension, and to pick out a single poem is like dislodging a gem from its setting). The presence of the 'Unknown Woman' is sensed from the outset. Her mysteriousness seems like the Russian language itself. Somewhere behind the scenes 'someone is

whispering, and laughing . . .' She reflects the poet's own
divided self. He buries himself ecstatically in the sights and
sounds of an ancient cathedral church, in the very prayers.
But he cannot escape from his other nature which mocks
him through the prayers, through the flickering of the candle
flames. His sinister-divine 'companion' pursues him into the
murky reaches of the city:

'Every evening – punctual as a guest
(This couldn't be some dream)
The figure of a girl, swathed in silk
Crosses the misted window-pane.

She edges through the drunks that fill the room,
Is always by herself, totally alone,
And breathing mists and perfumes
She settles by the window . . .

Bewitched by this strange presence
Gazing into her dark veil
I see an enchanted shore
and enchanted distances.

Vague mysteries for me to keep
And someone's sun to tend
The tart wine has entered
Every convolution of my being.

Those drooping feathers
Quiver in my brain,
And on a faraway shore
Flower blue fathomless eyes.

In my soul is buried treasure
And the key to it is mine! . . .'

Far from the city, the Beautiful Lady is transformed into the
Night Violet, a flower of the wild forest marshes. She is in
the snowdrifts too; in the howling of the winds and the merciless lashing snow – 'No, I won't open the door for you. Never!'
Even though the Unknown One is enthroned in the same
starry heaven – 'when you and I meet, there are inescapable

eyes – the snowy depths break up, and lips come close . . . The
heights. The depths. A snowy silence. And you, you are silent.'
Her presence is something to dread – 'Listen, heart, that light
step behind us. Heart, do you see? – Some one has given me
a sign, a secret sign with her hand.' In the end she resembles
'a diabolical fusion of many different worlds, especially blue
and lilac-coloured ones. If I had been Vrúbel, I would have
conjured up a Demon; but everyone does what he is cut out to
do.'

Out of Blok's phase of disenchantment emerged the
prophet. In the approaching Revolution (February and October
1917) Blok sensed the same elemental forces running wild
within art and within himself. Paranoia or not, his contemporaries knew well what he meant when he urged to 'listen to
the music of the Revolution'. Blok's greatest achievement of
this period is *The Twelve*, a poem which evokes those fearful
days. It centres around twelve militia men who are transformed by the poet into the twelve apostles, with a down-and-
out Christ at their head. The howls of derision which greeted
Blok's poem were part of the anti-religious hysteria of the
time; it is only in retrospect that it stands out as a landmark
in Russian poetry. Despite obvious differences in mood and
setting, the structure of this poem, its juxtaposition of hetero-
geneous material and styles, popular and impressionistic verse,
its freedom is faintly reminiscent of Eliot's *The Waste-
land*. Blok's Christ is no glorious Redeemer, but a humiliated
figure; and the Revolution is symbolized not by Blood or Fire,
but by Ice. This is the Christ of an icon which the poet once
saw through a cottage window, a poor Christ, wreathed in
simple garlands. Like some artist-beggar Christ created the
world; and the icon, in which the face of Christ and the sky
are one, is a paradigm of this creation, poor as it all is. In
The Twelve we have the icon of a bloodless and frozen God,
more likely to arouse detestation – as it sometimes did in Blok
– than love or pity.

Symbolism lasted little more than a decade. Blok's own misgivings were clear: 'It is as if, when we went up on deck,
we found ourselves in a boundless ocean of life and art,

already very far from land. We cannot as yet make out any
landmarks towards which our dream, our creative will is
drawing us.' Blok's own personal crisis vis-à-vis Symbolism
was due to a realization that he and others like him had fallen
into the trap of treating Symbolism as an end in itself – 'Our
sin is too grievous. From the position in which we find ourselves there are plenty of ways out, but they are all frightful'.
Actually Symbolism was the beginning only. Landmarks
eventually did appear, but it was for the next generation to
make them out, a generation whose early maturity coincided
with the Revolution and the Civil War. There were soon so
many outstanding poets that by the early nineteen twenties
no other country could compete with Russia. Like typical
Russian cuckoos in the nest these new giants were hatched
within the fairly narrow confines of various 'schools'.
It is hardly worth taking up space to go into detailed ex-
planation if only because the products of these schools soon
had very little or nothing in common. There were European
importations like Futurism and Imaginism, and home-made
ones like Acmeism and Constructivism. What use though is
Marinetti's tag 'Futurism' when applied to three poets so
original and vastly different as Mayakóvsky, Khlébnikov, and
Pasternák. Why bother going into the origins of Imaginism
in Wyndham Lewis and Pound, or even into its Russian
manifestations – Mariénhof's 'fornication with experience' or
Shershenévich's $2 \times 2 = 5$ – when the key poet here is Esénin?
And who could have supposed that a label like Acmeism
originating in a chance remark of Vyacheslav Ivánov could
have rallied round it such different people as Gumilyóv,
Akhmátova, Mandelstám, not to mention the lesser figures.

Let us begin with Nikolái Gumilyóv (1886–1921). 'A poet by
the grace of God' Gumilyóv wryly styled himself. He is
still generally thought of as a kind of poet-buccaneer. It is
true that he gloried in war – he was twice decorated in the
First World War with the highest Russian award for bravery
– and that he craved physical adventure, his travels taking
him all over Africa. After the Russian withdrawal from the
War, Gumilyóv thought of joining the Foreign Legion or going
out to join Lawrence of Arabia, but instead returned to Russia

– 'I have been fighting the Germans for three years, and have killed lions. But I haven't met any Bolsheviks so far. Russia can't be more dangerous than the jungle.' But Gumilyóv had not reckoned with the Cheka.* In 1921 he was arrested on the flimsiest of charges and shot as a counter-revolutionary. In keeping with the spirit of those poems he wrote to help his comrades overcome fear, Gumilyóv spent his last hours calmly reading Homer, and stepped out to face the firing squad as though he had been invited to a reception in his honour.

No complete critical study of Gumilyóv is yet available, and much of what has been written about him is misleading. The essential Gumilyóv remains to be discovered. His early work admittedly bears more than a few traces of the French Parnassians, and a few of his early poems are reminiscent of Kipling; but for the real poet we have to look to the collections published at the end of his short life – *The Pyre* (1918) and *The Pillar of Fire* (1921). Among these poems are some of the finest ever written, and they make us rage all the more against his untimely judicial murder.

Gumilyóv is Nietzsche's 'gay philosopher' who has tossed aside all theories and stances – 'Terror, pain, disgrace are beautiful and endearing even, because they are linked so inseparably with the entire universe and with our own creative domination of things. When you are in love with life as with a woman, you don't when caressing her consider where pain ends and joy begins – all you know is that you want things to be as they are.' Gumilyóv's poetry is deeply philosophic, but intense as life. And there is a new music, impossible to describe; depending not on assonance or rhythm, but on some strange quality of the human voice itself:

'I saw the way the night came,
came striding like the colour of heavy hemlocks,
I was afraid.'

It was never pain or death that terrified him, but the wonder of being in the world at all; the awareness that, in spite of his childish conceits and bravado, civilized man 'has scarcely more than a precarious foothold and a pitifully inadequate

* The Secret Police under Lenin.

conception of his true nature. The world is very far from being completely discovered, and there are physically existent beings and powers we know nothing about. Civilized man is blind man. Writing poetry the poet uncovers new and hidden selves, and trains himself to make out the colour of their eyes, the shapes of their hands – an altogether uncanny business. Hence Gumilyóv's realization that the poet is not really of this world at all, but Hamlet-like 'somewhere in the background, in the shadows':

'It's to trees, I've learnt, not us
that life is given in all its fullness.
On this tender earth, sister to the stars,
we are the strangers, and they its real inhabitants.'

We human beings only dream our way through life 'drowsily leafing through the summer, the scarlet pages of bright days'.

'Now I understand. Our freedom's but a light
that bursts forth from yonder.
People and shadows hug the entrance
to the planet's zoo . . .'

We come next to a poet who, thirty years after his death in a concentration camp, remains virtually an unperson – Ósip Mandelstám (1891–1938). Although officially 'rehabilit-ated' a recent entry in a Soviet work of reference concludes with the standard cliché: 'Illegally suppressed, posthu-mously rehabilitated'. And the Russian public is still awaiting even snippets, let alone a complete edition of his writings.

Mandelstám secured a prominent place among the poets of the day with his first book of poems *Stone* (1913). There are plenty of influences: Baudelaire, the Parnassians, poets before Púshkin; and English readers can sometimes catch a passing resemblance to Shelley. None the less Mandelstám's originality is striking. Somehow he managed to go beyond the image as an independent element and to transform it into a world of its own. Monad-like, Mandelstám's image reflects and is reflected by neighbouring images; not sequentially; simultane-ously. Poetic creation is epiphanic, a sudden and unanticip-

ated eruption, an emptying of something from the core of
one's being –

> 'Heavens! – I said, unintentionally
> not thinking what I'd said
> the Divine Name a huge bird
> from my breast had flown.
> Out in front of me a dense mist,
> behind me an empty cage.'

This was no attitudinizing. Mandelstám never failed to be
astonished at what could emerge, and went around reading his
poems to his friends simply to share his wonder with them.

In a bitingly satirical poem Mandelstám referred to Stalin,
the 'Kremlin Highlander' with 'his cockroaches' huge
moustache laugh', and paid dearly for it. It is said that
Pasternák intervened on Mandelstám's behalf, and that Stalin
interviewed him personally. But this did not prevent his
further arrest a few years later at the height of the Purges.
According to one report he spent his last days a half-
demented figure in rags squatting by a garbage heap in one of
the notorious Far Eastern labour camps.

More fortunate or less fortunate, depending on how you
look at it, was one of Russia's great women poets. The lifetime
of Anna Akhmátova (1889–1966) spanned several eras. Her
visit to England not long before her death is still fresh in
many people's memories. And it is from this vantage point,
its incongruity heightened by her Oxford honorary degree,
that we can look back across the 'rehabilitations' – two in her
case – to the Second World War and the siege of Leningrad;
to the Purges and her own private sorrows; and beyond that
again to the dream-like enthusiasm of the pre-Revolutionary
years when art and mania were not always easily disentangled.

Akhmátova lived a series of poetic lives. The earliest collection of poems, one that brought her immediate fame, is
mostly love lyrics, gentle, impassioned, sometimes tinged with
irony, always richly musical. They are addressed to a man:
whether one or several it is impossible to know. If this man
was Gumilyóv, her husband (who incidentally scoffed at
the idea of a woman writing poetry), then he was eventually

disincarnated, for this same figure recurs in her poems right to the end of her life, and definitely not as some sentimental memory. Her earliest poems are minor, and Akhmátova as an old woman, when asked to recite them, would say: 'You can read them for yourselves. I don't like them.' But when we come to what she wrote in the years immediately after the First World War it is an entirely different matter. The cycle *Anno Domini MCMXXI* (1921) is of symphonic proportions, set in contrasting but interrelated keys and moods. And in another collection *The Reed* a few of the poems are comparable to Shakespeare's sonnets. By a hair's breadth of good fortune we now possess a handful of poems which she had published abroad towards the end of her life. They have the simple title *Requiem* and place Akhmátova among the immortals. These poems were composed during the Stalin Purges after her son had been arrested and deported.

During the inter-war years Akhmátova published nothing; she wrote only for herself. But these years in the cocoon were followed by an outburst. Her *Requiem* imbued with all the strength and doom of Greek tragedy is a requiem not for her own son only (for he actually survived by some miracle) but for all those who needlessly suffered at the hands of political cynics and bureaucratic accomplices during those nightmare years:

'They came for you at dawn
Like people come to fetch a corpse.
In the darkness children sobbed
And the candle by Our Lady spluttered.
Your lips turned cold as icons
And that deathly sweat . . . I can't ever forget!
And I, like the streltsy* women of old,
Beneath those Kremlin walls would go and wail.'

The gates of many a Russian Dachau were in Moscow and other cities for all to see. In her 'Epilogue' Akhmátova writes:

'Remembrance day again comes round.
I can see you, hear you, even touch you . . .

* The 'streltsy' were a military caste the members of which were executed by Peter the Great.

Would that I'd remembered each by name.
My list was confiscated. No way of finding out.
For them a shroud I've woven
From wretched words they've never even heard.'

This woman, who had written that if anyone wanted to erect
a monument to her she would agree only on condition that
they put it on the spot where she and thousands like her
'had stood for three hundred hours on end' in front of locked
gates, their wait interrupted only by the 'rumbling of the
black marias', became a living memorial to herself in her own
lifetime. After the war she had been expelled from the Soviet
Writers' Union. 'Half-nun, half-prostitute' was Zhdanov's
coarse and infamous gibe. After this she made public appearances only rarely, and even after her first rehabilitation published very little. The public did not forget her however, and
their affection for her actually increased. Not long before her
death Akhmátova received at least a little of the honour due
to her when she was fully rehabilitated and readmitted to the
Writers' Union.

The poems of Akhmátova's last years are serene, intimate,
and direct in appeal. Her 'other' is now the anonymous reader
with whom she converses at moments in her unique way. In
a poem *The Willow* written in 1940 she looks back in quiet
bewilderment, as if marooned in the past:

'I grew up in dappled silence
in the cool nursery of a young century . . .
I loved the burdocks and the nettles
and most of all a silver willow tree.
Thankfully living out its life with me
with weeping trailing boughs
it covered my sleeplessness in dreams.
Then – inexplicably! – I outlived it.
Nothing but a stump's left jutting out
and other willows converse in unfamiliar voices.'

'I have decided that Russia must be shown through the
eyes of a cow' wrote Sergéi Esénin (1895–1925) a poet of
peasant origin (though of the literate Old Believing peasantry)

who wanted to see the world as simple countryfolk, creatures
of nature, and nature itself saw it. At a time when anthro-
pologists were busy investigating the mentality of primitive
man, this 'poet of wooden Russia' knew all about 'mystical
participation'. Esénin's poetry teems with primitive imagery;
images like 'the wooden clock of the moon' or 'the moon
cleaning its horns in the thatch of some rooftop'. In his
Tale of Petya the Cowherd Petya finds no difficulty in
communicating immediately with his cows, the trees, the
flowers, the moon; and equally they find no difficulty in
communicating with each other. Esénin avoids the convention
of having animals and objects speak, and Petya's 'dreamtime'
– life as tedium and bliss at the same time – is eloquent without any kind of verbal expression. The reader is usually
convinced even when the themes verge on the sentimental
or ludicrous – the birch tree for instance that the poet has
fallen in love with, and what the tree tells him about the
shepherd who had embraced her, bidding her farewell till the
next spring. This kind of material sounds distinctly unpromising until we actually see what Esénin does with it. Only then
do we find that the pathos of nature, as also in Lawrence,
goes deeper than lyricism.

Soviet critics have tended to kick over the traces of
Esénin's notoriety, his 'hooliganism', his alcoholism, his anti-
social behaviour – the inevitable reactions against a society
which appeared to be a living negation of his own poetic
values. It must have seemed to him that Russian poetry itself
was a conspiracy against him. The received styles and conventional approaches to rural Russia were false and alien to him.
'Adjustment', following the rules of the game could only be
achieved at the price of loss of identity; and life became
bearable only among the outcasts and dregs of society – 'I
live as on the open road, belonging to nowhere.' His
'discovery' as the precocious peasant poet only drove him to
rage, and his vaudeville turns in the literary salons, rigged out
in folk costume – his promoters announced him as 'the little
shepherd' and such like – nauseated him. The role of the poet
could only be for him a condemnation, a crucifixion –

'I'll never shake off this torment
of knowing the voice of the earth,
I'm the lake that mirrors
the sudden comet in the heavens.'

Esénin eventually found his *point d'appui* in the Imaginist movement, introduced by Shershenévich in 1919 with his slogan: 'The image and the image alone.' The Imaginists' anarchistic view of art and of the separation of art from the social order did not interest Esénin greatly. The main attraction for him was the emphasis on the *image*, which in any case had already featured prominently in Esenin's work before that time. Indeed some of his best poetry belongs to the years which preceded Imaginism.

In 1921 Esénin met Isadora Duncan, who was at the time on a visit to Moscow. They married, and Esénin accompanied his celebrated wife on her travels in Europe and America. After a period of misery for both of them, they separated. Esénin's last two years were spent partly at his mother's village home, and partly in Leningrad. Alcohol was no longer of any avail, and Esénin cut his wrists, writing his last poem in his own blood. This poem ends with lines:

'In this life it's nothing new to die,
To go on living, that's nothing fresh either.'

In another poem, one of his last, an unwelcome wraithlike guest torments him with his ruined past, a dismal procession of ghostly fragments. The poet's real life was lived beyond the reach of the cultivated imagination. The art forms Esénin used only mocked him. He became acutely conscious of his own tragi-comic role. Another late poem *My Path* throws into relief the lack of congruity between his humble origins and the achievements for which he was famed, between the 'village dreamer' and the 'top-ranking poet'.

After an early period of enthusiasm Esénin soon became disillusioned with the Bolshevik Revolution. The Soviet social temper was a threat to the unspoiled Russia his poetry was only now beginning to bring to light –

'Their idiom sounds so alien.
I'm like a foreigner in my own land.'

To his dismay Esénin now finds the villagers debating 'life'
in their Sunday best 'in clumsy, unwashed speeches'. A 'band
of komsomol peasants comes over the brow of the hill bawl-
ing furiously to the accompaniment of an accordion and chant-
ing *agit*-verse' —

'My poetry's not needed here.
Good luck to you, my lads!
Your life's not mine, your tune neither.'

Esénin was convinced that he was the last poet of rural
Russia, and that soon all would be destroyed by the machine
and the urban barbarian —

'Modest wooden bridge in verse
Last of village poets
Mine is a simple requiem
Of birches wreathed in incense.'

The poet lives precariously in an Age of Gold, 'crazy and
drunk with poetry', resigned to his own disappearance, lament-
ing that his dreams will be echoed not in the winds and
gust-driven cornfields, but only in musty tomes. It would be a
mistake to think of Esénin as a poet born centuries too late.
A poet like Esénin could not have been produced by circumstances other than exactly those of his own life. The noble
savage has nothing to tell us about communion with nature;
only about heroes, gods and myths. Only a man torn apart,
with one half of his life steeped in nature's ways and the other
half in the conventions and fads of civilized life, could have
had the urge to express the life of the former,- accepting its
terms and rejecting it at the same time.

'I – Mayakóvsky – versus the Universe!
Theme: – I am a poet. That's what is interesting about me.'

'Unique' is no mere hyperbole when applied to Vladimir
Mayakóvsky (1893–1930). He reminds us rather of some cata-
clysmic natural phenomenon – a hurricane, or a tidal wave.

And true to form, Mayakóvsky took such comparisons seriously – 'I feel my ego is much too small for me. Stubbornly someone goes on pushing his way out of me.' An egotist not big enough for his own boots, Mayakóvsky succeeded in combining outrageous statements like 'Glorify me! For me the great are no match' with a Rabelaisian capacity for fun and laughter. How is it possible that an uncomfortable blend of egocentricity, humour, arrogance and preposterous excess could have produced such outstanding poetry? One wonders how it is that Mayakóvsky overwhelms us with what in a less remarkable person would be megalomania or idiocy. In a poem with the unpromising title *An Extraordinary Adventure which befell Vladimir Mayakovsky in a Summer Cottage* we find the typical tomfoolery –

> 'this very thing
> began
> to arouse in me
> great anger . . .
> I yelled at the sun point blank:
> 'Get down!
> And stop crawling into that hell-hole.'
> At the sun I yelled
> You shiftless lump you! . . .'

The tirade ends with the poet inviting the sun to tea; and of course, this being Mayakóvsky, the sun accepts. The result is something only Mayakóvsky could ever hope to bring off.

> 'Spreading his beaming steps
> the sun strode across the field
> I tried to hide my dread
> and beat it backwards
> His eyes were in the garden now . . .
> His sun's mass pressing
> through the windows,
> doors,
> and cracks,
> in he rolled.'

Mayakóvsky excels not so much in what he says, but in how he says it. It was Blok who had completed the circle in bringing together all the significant achievements of literary poetry and the verse rhythms of the oral tradition, and creating out of this fusion a modern poetic language. But Mayakóvsky went even further and was able to use this new instrument in such a way that even the stalest slogans came alive at his touch. Every word Mayakóvsky uses, even down to the preposition, sounds as if it had been newly forged, and there is something miraculous about the way in which he succeeds in breathing fresh life into the most everyday clichés and idioms.

Mayakóvsky moved among his fellow men like a locomotive. There was always too much of him in any one place. 'We each of us hold in our fists the driving belts of the world' was his way of seeing things. Mayakóvsky was well aware that he often overdid things, and knew that this failing had made him 'a prolonged dirty joke' among his contemporaries. Above all he was acutely aware of the distance in *time* between him and them. In *The City* the poet goes on to say –

'I'm fed up – I'd like to gaze in the face
of just one soul who's keeping up with me.
It's boring here, ahead of everyone on my own earth.'

People frequently mistook outward aggressiveness for lack of sensitivity, and rudeness for bullying. But none of it was put on for effect; rather it was his reaction against the strain of living in a world not geared to men like him. A somewhat romantic expression of this strain is to be found in an early poem *The Backbone Flute* –

'Over the abyss I've stretched my soul on a tightrope
and juggling with words totter above it.'

Mayakóvsky discovered normalcy only in his poetry:

'Whenever my voice rumbles bawdily
Jesus Christ may be sniffing the forget-me-nots of my soul.'

Born in a remote settlement in the Caucasus, Mayakóvsky took to politics early. At fifteen he joined the Bolshevik party (long before power was in sight) and 'graduated' as their propagandist. Twice arrested, he spent a year in the notorious Butyrki prison in Moscow. In 1912 Mayakóvsky ran into Burlyúk the eccentric founder of Russian Futurism. Their friendship began as they were sauntering out from the 'melodised boredom' of a Rachmáninov programme. The next morning Burlyúk introduced Mayakóvsky to someone as 'my genius friend, the famous poet Mayakóvsky'. Before Mayakóvsky could recover from astonishment, Burlyúk had taken him aside and bellowed – 'Now write, or you'll make a bloody fool of me!'

Mayakóvsky's earliest poems, even when outlandish, proliferate with hair-raising images, sometimes outrageously mixed: – 'crossroads crucify policemen'; 'In the reading-room of the streets I have often leaved through the volume of the coffin'; 'The Universe sleeps, its huge paw curled upon a star-infested ear'; 'The crazy cathedral galloped in drops of downpours on the cupola's bald pate'. The later poems are less contrived and often seem like improvisations. But improvisations they were not; Mayakóvsky regarded writing poetry as the equivalent of the heaviest industrial labour –

'For the sake of a single word
    you waste
a thousand tons
    of verbal ore.'

Composition took place not in any study but on the move. Mayakóvsky described himself as the 'barefoot cutter of diamond verse'. Society and party bosses were urged to pay as much attention to the poet's labour as they would to that of a worker – 'I want Stalin to deliver his politbureau reports on verse as it is actually made just as he would on pig-iron.'

Despite his popularity as the poet of Revolution, Mayakóvsky's acceptability was never complete, but always at one remove. His public recitations were more like riots, and most of the time was taken up with vicious heckling and equally virulent repartee from the platform. The audience never got the upper hand, and critics even complained that Mayakóvsky was a living affront to all the rules of literary decency. Even Lenin took exception to his 'shouting and distorted words', and personally gave his preference for a more bourgeois poet, Púshkin. Lunachársky was reprimanded by Lenin for printing 5,000 copies of one of Mayakóvsky's poems – 'I consider that ten copies of a thing like that is enough'. Stalin, a better judge of poetry had him virtually canonized. Posthumously, note; for it would have been surprising if Mayakóvsky, had he lived a few more years, had not gone with the rest of his generation to the concentration camps.

Mayakóvsky's suicide has been the subject of considerable debate. The real reason or reasons – an unhappy love affair, growing disillusionment with Lenin's State, or some other – may never be known. What *is* known is that Mayakóvsky often toyed with suicide, and played Russian roulette with himself as other people play patience. Probably it had something to do with the internal tensions and the fierce pressure under which he lived. Pasternák believed that Mayakóvsky's entire life was some kind of act; and that he went through the motions 'with such callous disdain that his performance was terrifying.' Suicide though was not something to be proud of, and Mayakóvsky condemned Esénin for taking the easy way out. In his suicide note – 'To Everybody' – Mayakóvsky wrote: 'Blame no one for my death, and whatever you do, don't gossip . . . Mama, sisters, comrades, forgive me – it isn't the right way out (I don't recommend it) – but there is no other way.' His last major poem *At the Top of My Voice* is a moving document, spelling out Mayakóvsky's belief in man and the future. The poem is addressed to those scholars of many generations hence who 'rummaging around in crap' will come across these words:

> 'My verse will reach you
>   across the peaks of ages
> over the heads of governments and poets.
> My verse
>   will reach you . . .
> not as a worn penny
>   reaches a numismatist
> not as the light of dead stars reaches you.

My verse
  by labour
    will break the mountain chain of years
and will present itself
  ponderous,
    crude,
      tangible
as an aqueduct
  by Roman slaves
constructed,
  enters our own days. . . .
Die then this voice of mine
  die like a common soldier.'

Marína Tsvetáeva (1894–1941) was a very lonely poet. The poetic means she chose did not endear her to the average reader. Her diction is peculiar to her, and her language is highly condensed as well as difficult. Like Joyce, Tsvetáeva stretched her linguistic resources to their furthest limit, and beyond this limit. She is not an esoteric poet like Vyacheslav Ivánov, but always at the level of ordinary humanity. All she needs is a thoughtful reader, one prepared to linger a while before reading on. Her poetry is so prolific however that it would take years to read it all at the rate it ought to be read. Seemingly bizarre assemblages of images, allusions, puns, rhythms, assonances, and many other devices belie her fastidious intentions. She hated anything contrived, and was able to point out false lines even in Púshkin. Her poems were written by God's hand, she believed, not hers. Hence her total lack of timidity in the face of the most forbidding ventures.

Like nearly all the writers of her day, Marína Tsvetáeva was born into the thick of the Russian intelligentsia. Her early work did attract attention, but reactions were condescending more often than not. Perhaps with justification, since it is only after the Civil War that she achieved any kind of greatness. In 1922 she decided to leave Russia, and with her baby daughter went to join her husband (who had been a White Guard) in Berlin. After Berlin they moved to Prague and later to Paris. She kept aloof from émigré circles and, as her writing brought her in a negligible income, she lived in extreme poverty. In 1933 she wrote in a letter: 'We are simply dying a slow death from starvation.' This was also meant figuratively because she found separation from her country too much to bear. Having been given assurances that no harm would come to her husband and son, they went back to the Soviet Union in 1939. Tsvetáeva's naive hope that she would be welcomed soon turned to dismay when she was refused employment as a humdrum translator. Eventually no one would take her on even as a charwoman. In the meantime her husband had been arrested, and her son had vanished at the Front. In August 1941 in some remote outback, Tsvetáeva put an end to her life

'I refuse – to go on existing
in a bedlam of inhumanity
I refuse – to go on living
with the wolves in public places.

I refuse – to wail . . .
To your insane world
there is but one answer – to renounce it.'

It may not be too soon before the English reader will be able to read Tsvetáeva in translation; if only because there is no poet more difficult to translate. Her language is beyond Russian almost, perhaps beyond any language –

'You'll never take the flush of life from me,
powerful as the rush of rivers in flood.
You are the hunter, but I'll not yield.
You are the chase, but I the one that eludes.
You'll never take the heart of me alive.'

Her poetic roots seem to lie outside existence, for they are our roots too. There is nothing remote or mystical about her work, and it never fails to convey the incommensurable beauty of life and her love of it – even though the world destroyed her:

'What is there for me, poet and first-born
in a world where the blackest is but dull grey!
where inspiration's stored in thermos flasks!
with this limitlessness of mine
in a world of limits.'

For the most experimental poet of the period we look not
to Esénin or Mayakóvsky or Tsvetáeva, but to Velimír
Khlébnikov (1885–1922). Mayakóvsky called Khlébnikov
'the Columbus of new poetic continents afterwards settled by
us'. Although a Futurist, Khlébnikov was interested in
primeval times, in the gods of pagan Russia, in Shamanism
and folk cults (The reader may be already familiar with this
trend in Stravinsky's *Firebird* and *The Rite of Spring*).
Khlébnikov's linguistic experiments resulted primarily from
his attempts to get back to the earliest stages of linguistic
evolution, to the moment at which language was born.
Convinced like those English writers – C. S. Lewis, J. R. R.
Tolkien and Owen Barfield – that the quest for origin of language is a quest for the origin of origins, Khlébnikov stated
his purpose thus: 'Without breaking the links between the
roots, I set out to find the philosopher's stone of the reciprocal
interrelationship between all Slavonic words, freely dissolving
them into one another. This is my own conception of the word
– the Word per se, outside and beyond human existence.' His
most famous experiment is *Incantation to Laughter*, a poem
created out of a single lexical root 'laugh' and its historical
antecedents. The Russian language, itself based transparently
on roots and affixes, provided the possibilities, and the poet
went on to invent new words and new derivations in a multi-
tude of variants. Even to a foreign reader of Russian the effect
of the poem is uncanny, and Russians have been affected by
it as if by a spell or charm. The best English translation I
have seen does not convey any of this, partly I suppose
because the English language is constructed so differently. The
root 'laugh' in English does not carry anything like the same
force, and in any case Khlébnikov's technique is not just a
matter of linguistic permutations. His experiments were far
more than experiments in linguistics, and those who came

under his influence – especially Pasternák – were well aware
of this.

It may seem that I have been devoting too much space
to the poets of this period. For this reason I am passing over
a number of poets some of whom it would be presumptuous to
classify as minor – Nikolái Klyúev (1887–1937), Vladisláv
Khodasévich (1886–1939), Georgy Ivánov (1894–1958), and
a number of others. That leaves only the poet whom many
consider the greatest of this stunning generation – Borís
Pasternák.

It is generally the fate of Russian writers these days that
they become famous abroad only when they make political
headlines. Such is the case with Borís Pasternák (1890–1960).
Very few people outside Russia would know of his existence
had his *Doctor Zhivago* not become a *cause célèbre*.
Pasternák for his part was deeply dismayed by the political
capital made both at home and in the West out of the publication abroad of his novel, and he was tormented at the
prospect of being exiled from his own country. He refused
a Nobel Award, and implored Khrushchev to spare him – 'to
be forced to leave my country would be tantamount to a death
sentence'. It is an indictment of the new managers of culture
that a poet who by the early nineteen twenties was one of
Russia's foremost had been almost entirely forgotten, except
by a discriminating few, at the time of his death. Not long
before his death Pasternák writes to his editor: 'Though I
am forgotten to the point of complete obscurity I did not think
I had been forgotten so completely that my book would not
go through at least ten editions . . . I realize, of course, that all
this does not depend on you, for people in high office keep
interfering with the future of literature.' Unlike Mayakóvsky
– who once declared that he and Pasternák lived in the same
house but in different rooms – Pasternák could never have
achieved mass popularity. Pasternák's manner of perceiving
the world and the relationships between things, his vast,
eclectic vocabulary, his imagery, make him largely unintellig-
ible to the ordinary reader. In this respect he had much in
common with Tsvetáeva whom he greatly admired. Their
quest though dissimilar was complementary, and the means

they employed sometimes went beyond the confines of
modern poetry. In the words of Mandelstám: 'After
Pasternák Russian poetry is once again moving out into the
open sea, and many of its regular passengers are having to
bid farewell to the vessel.'

The language of Pasternák's later poetry – after his return
to lyrical verse in the thirties – is more transparent and less
difficult than the earlier experiments of *My Sister Life* (1922)
and *Theme and Variations* (1923). This greater simplicity was
not an admission of defeat, but something Pasternák achieved
only after a long struggle. Actually the simplicity is deceptive
in that the language and imagery of the later work carries a
higher poetic charge; and the craft, though less obvious, attains
incredible heights. The later collections *On Early Trains* (1943)
and *When the Weather Clears* (1959), and the Zhivago poems,
made Pasternák one of the world's greatest poets.

The early poetry is a rediscovery of everyday life and
things. It is exuberant, always seeking out movement –

'My sister, life's in flood today, she's broken
her waves over us all in the spring rain . . .'

We are cut adrift, and everything is swept along in the up-
roar –

'The stars rushed headlong by. Sea washed the headlands.
The salt spray blinded and the tears were dried.
Bedrooms were dark and thoughts rushed headlong by.
The sphinx gave patient ear to the Sahara . . .'

'Pasternák himself I'd rather relate to the very first days of
creation,' writes Tsvetáeva, 'the first rivers, the first dawns,
the first storms. He is created *before* Adam.':

> So be it

Daybreak sets the candle swinging,
flames, on the swooping martin scores a bull.
Out of my memory I drag:
Thus, even thus will life be new.

Dawn like a volley in the dark.
Bang! Bang! the bullet wad's afire.

But on its flight the fire's blown out.
Thus, even thus will life be new ...'

As for poetry itself it is born amid living things – in the pools, crannies, shafts of light, the wildness of birdsong, our own mental stirrings:

'This way they start. At two years' old
They fly their wetnurse into murk of melodies.
They chirrup and they whistle – words appear
In their third year.
.... And so before them opens up, in flight
High over fences where a house should be,
Sudden like a sigh, the sea
This way iambs will begin to be.
.... This way they begin to live in verses.'

But poetry is not something pleasant or glamorous; it is a state of being – 'not a strutting of sweet singers' but 'summer on a third-class ticket':

'Poetry when once an empty truism
like a zinc bucket's at the tap,
then, only then it's sure to flow,
the copy book's spread open – spout!'

or like that image from some grim tale, when Pasternák compares poetry with 'the malevolent whirling of a dozen windmills at the edge of a bare plain in a bleak, hungry year.'

Too much weight should not be given to Pasternák's well-known dissatisfaction with all the poetry he wrote before the war. As Sinyávsky has reminded us, Pasternák was perpetually reevaluating his own literary past: 'Such judgments upon himself, though not always just, are part of his nature, for he preferred not to accumulate but to abandon.' Finally Pasternák abolished the nagging gap between ends and means. It had been Yúri Zhivágo's dream all his life, 'to write with an originality so covert, so discreet, as to be outwardly unrecognizable in its disguise of current, customary forms of speech. All his life he had struggled after a language so reserved, so unpretentious as to enable the reader or the hearer to master

the content without noticing the means by which it reached
him. All his life he had striven to achieve an unnoticeable
style, and he had been appalled to find how far he still
remained from his ideal.'
Sinyávsky thinks that the key to Pasternák is metaphor. It
is metaphor that draws together the separate parts of reality
into a single whole and 'thus embodies the great unity of the
world, the interaction and interpenetration of phenomena.
Pasternák proceeds from the idea that two objects, set side by
side, closely interact with and penetrate each other – so he
connects them.'

'The street makes friends
With the bleary window,
The white night and the sunset
Are inseparable by the river.

In the passage can be heard
What's going on outdoors
And April's casual gossip
With the dripping waters of the thaw.
April knows a thousand stories
Of human sorrow
And along the fence the twilight grows chill
Spinning out the tale.'

Unlike Khlébnikov, who had set up a theory about the
structural relationships between phonetic elements and
abstract meanings, Pasternák was more concerned with the
concrete living affinity between sounds and things. Doubtless,
as modern linguistics has demonstrated, there exists an
ordered correspondence between groups of sounds and semantic
content. The poet however is not a linguist, and the former's
task is to extend the reaches of the language he uses, to extend
its lease of life – 'Phonetic links are the expression of links
of meaning,' writes Sinyávsky 'neighbouring images are
fastened together by a similarity of sound which tells ultimately of the harmony existing between the different aspects of
existence, interconnected and interpenetrating.' Pasternák was
not concerned with incantation, verbal magic for its own

sake, and in his later work we do not notice at all the metaphoric-acoustic witchcraft. Quite unawares, we find him tuning a new assonance, a new meaning-sound identity, but without any straining for effect. Frequently, as in the Zhivago poems, this technique attains the incredible – the mad trilling of the nightingales (something the urban reader can scarcely imagine) quite beyond the capacity of the tape-recorder, because of the unity of setting, atmosphere, white night and mood, of which sounds are only one aspect; – or the timelessness of the encounter between George and the dragon, a time context which stretches from beyond the earliest moment of history, through the present, and aimed at the future on the swing of some hidden pendulum. Pasternák's feat is that he has brought the tangible and intangible, the five familiar and the transcendental senses together : he brings the forests, dripping rain clouds and streets of everyday along with Resurrection, other worlds and other times, into the very bones of our being.

There has been speculation as to how Pasternák managed to survive the Purges, when everyone else perished, including two of his closest friends, the Georgian poets Tabídze and Yáshvili (the latter having blown his brains out in anticipation of some worse fate). One theory is that, unknown to himself, Pasternák exerted some mysterious influence over Stalin, as a result of which Stalin had seen to it personally that no harm came to him during the mass arrests. Among the supporting evidence for this theory is Pasternák's reaction to the news of the death of Stalin's wife in 1932. A stereotyped letter already signed by many other writers was passed to him for his signature. Instead of signing it, Pasternák added an enigmatic postscript: 'I had been thinking, the evening before, deeply and persistently about Stalin; for the first time from the point of view of the artist. In the morning I read the news. I was shaken as if I had been present, as if I had lived and seen it.' These were of course dangerous words, and they would have cost Pasternák his life sooner or later, if Stalin had not interpreted them as clairvoyance (the incident is still cloaked in obscurity). We also know of Stalin's quasi-religious superstition. Whether the theory is true or not,

Pasternák came unscathed through the worst of the pre- and post-war Terrors (the secret police must surely have known about his work on Zhivágo) only to be reviled in the relatively liberal period of the late fifties.

'The noise is stilled. I come out on the stage.
Leaning against the door-post
I try to guess from the distant echo
What is to happen in my lifetime.

The darkness of night is aimed at me
Along the sights of a thousand opera-glasses.
Abba, father, if it be possible,
Let this cup pass from me . . .'

We have arrived at the present. A completely different generation – their fathers suppressed, driven abroad, killed in the war, incarcerated or liquidated – has been paying precious little heed to Party dictates and police intimidation, and has been busy clearing away the spiritual debris of Stalinism. Many of the voices are anonymous. A few of them get a hearing, but more often than not outside Russia. From time to time, on some pretext or other, they are · sentenced to exile or hard labour – like Josif Bródski, for instance, whose activities as a translator of literature were construed as 'work shyness'; or Yúri Galanskóv, given a seven year sentence which brought him near to death. Sometimes writers are committed to mental institutions. There was the well publicised case of Zhorés Medvédev a few years ago. Poets who are too popular are censored to the point of extinction: Voznesénsky or Akhmadúlina, and even in some degree the 'establishment disestablishment poet' Evtushénko.

Andréi Voznesénsky (b. 1933) must surely be the brightest star of the generation of young poets brought into being by the relatively liberal years of the Khrushchev era. It seems to me that there are few contemporary poets to equal him. Perhaps my own estimation has something to do with the gay stoicism shared by all the major Russian writers of the post-Stalin era, of a generation that fears absolutely nothing on this earth.

Voznesénsky's range is remarkable, and so is the range of his humour. He resembles Mayakóvsky, but also Auden and more recent poets like Lowell or Grass. Like them too Voznesénsky is thoroughly contemporary, with a firm grip on the modern world, with a mixture of dread and fascination for technology, and an awareness of what Mailer has diagnosed as the insanity at large in our world, to be found 'wherever fever, force and machines could come together'. In *Wall of Death* a young woman motorcyclist tyrannized by her trainer hurls herself maniacally into orbit –

'During intermission I make my way
To her . . . 'Instruct me in the horizontal!' I say
But she stands there like lead
The Amazon, and shakes her head;
Still shaking, dizzy from the wall,
Her eyes blurred with
          such longing
             for the horizontal!'

The post-atomic world is in such a pickle, the poet asks himself –

'What century is it? What era? I forget.
As in a nightmare, everything is crumbling;
     people have come unsoldered; nothing's intact.

He finds escape in 'Antiworlds' where 'the rat race and the rut' can be overcome. This antiworlds metaphor is one of Voznesénsky's favourites, as too is his Bloom-like man Bukáshkin (in English, Buggins). Bukáshkin dreams of bright antiworlds floating above his head 'like balloons of blue and red' –

'On them reposes, prestidigitous,
Ruling the cosmos, a demon-magician,
Anti-Bukáshkin the Academician
Lapped in the arms of Lollobrigidas.'

An even more absurd and comic version we find in *Oza*. The poet is at a formal dinner which takes place in inverted space – 'It is all too vaguely familiar. Under this world suspended on the ceiling there is a second world, an upside-down one, which also has its poet and its toastmaster. The napes of their necks almost touch – they are counterpoised like two halves of an hourglass ... What is this upside-down country? Lost in these thoughts, I absentmindedly started eating a red-caviar sandwich. Why is that provincial celebrity, who hangs opposite me like a smoked ham, looking at my stomach with such horror ... He whispers in his neighbour's ear and immediately heads are threaded together by rumour on beads of string. Red snakes of tongues dart into neighbouring ears. Everybody looks at my caviar sandwich – 'And all *we* get is sardines!' the celebrity hisses.'

Voznesénsky learnt his craft from Pasternák, whom he knew during his last years. But he has carried the technique far beyond anything attained by his master, especially in the direction of semantic rhyme and assonance. Translation of course can convey nothing of this; and Voznesénsky's dazzling feats are accessible only to the reader of Russian, and only then to one who is conversant with different classes of slang. Only the crazy swerving from leg-pull and parody into those Russian depths with which we are so familiar is preserved in translation. Suddenly we find ourselves in the middle of a prayer addressed to the Blessed Virgin of Vladímir, as beautiful as any of the Marian hymns of the European Middle Ages.

Behind everything is Vozesénsky's leitmotif; a vigorous campaign against the pollution of the human spirit by just about every ingredient of modern living: political manipulation and cynicism, bureaucracy, technocracy, automation, mass media, mass anything—

'The world is not junk up for auction
I am Andréi, not just anyone.
All progress is retrogression
If the process breaks man down.'

And farther in the same poem (*Oza*) –

'Only one thing on earth is constant
Like the light of a star that has gone;
It is the continuing radiance
They used to call "the human soul".
We shall melt away and again be there;
It matters little when or where.'

If – as Mayakóvsky said – Pasternák and he lived in the same house but in different rooms, then Voznesénsky has knocked these two rooms into one and added to them his own extension. Voznesénsky shares Mayakóvsky's immense popularity; like Mayakóvsky but unlike Pasternák he is a poet of the people. On one famous occasion late in 1962 Voznesénsky and Bela Akhmadúlina reciting their own poems managed to pack a Moscow Sports Stadium with an audience of 14,000. Like Mayakóvsky, Voznesénsky is fascinated in an apocalyptic way by modern technology – orbiting satellites, particle accelerators, robots, electronic brains, and the rest – and following the example of Mayakóvsky's *Brooklyn Bridge* he creates his own technoramic vision of *New York Airport at Night* in all its bizarre and overpowering extra-humanity. Unlike Mayakóvsky, but like Pasternák, Voznesénsky concerns himself with the living essence of the individual human being: 'When a man writes he feels his prophetic mission to the world. The task of the Russian poet is to look deep inside man. When I read my poetry to a great number of people, their emotional, almost sensual expression of feeling seems to me to reveal the soul of man – now no longer hidden behind closed shutters, but wide open like a woman who has just been kissed.' Like Zhivago, the poet is someone indestructible, miraculously preserved –

'Under the cold stars, I wander alive
With you Vera, Vega, I am myself
Among avalanches, like the Abominable
Snowman, absolutely elusive.'

It should not surprise us that the cosily entrenched toe-the-liners of the Stalin period and since should feel menaced by striplings like Voznesénsky. Criticism against him and his like had mounted by 1963, and Khrushchev gave his general support to attacks on these 'rotten, overrated, abstract, smelly writings'. But despite his having been officially relegated to the literary wilderness, and restricted and censored in every conceivable way, Voznesénsky continues to be a best-seller; not long ago a first printing of 100,000 copies of his latest poems was immediately sold out, with people queueing outside the bookshops.

As an epilogue to this hasty survey of Russian poetry none could be more fitting than these lines from Voznesénsky's *Master Craftsmen*:

'For an artist true-born
revolt is second nature:
he is tribune
and troublemaker.

They've bricked you up in walls
and burned you at the stake
and the priests like swarms
of ants have danced at your wake.

But art survives . . .'

3 Prose

The ageing countess in Púshkin's *Queen of Spades* – a story set in the early years of the nineteenth century – asks Tomsky her grandson to send her something to read. 'Wouldn't you like a Russian novel?' he asks. 'I wasn't aware there were such things as Russian novels', is the countess's reply. 'Please send me some, dear boy. I'd like to see them.'

The only Russian prose works that had been available in the countess's youth were either translations, or pale and stiff imitations of the more fashionable European writers of the day. The man to change all this was Nikolái Karamzín (1766–1826). Novelist, historian, journalist, the first important writer of Russian prose, Karamzín developed a style which was comfortable, flexible and elegant, if over-elaborate. Taking as his model the language of the Russian aristocracy, Karamzín did not eschew innovation, deriving new words and expressions at will from other European languages. At the same time he borrowed and shaped the early Romanticism of Rousseau's *Nouvelle Héloïse*. Karamzín's stories, even if their subject-matter is outmoded, can be read without indulgence and quite often with pleasure by the modern reader. All the prose writers of the generation that followed admired him greatly, and were always influenced by him even when they could not resist a few good-humoured gibes at his expense. Karamzín's knowledge of Europe is impressive; and this cosmopolitan and inside knowledge is reflected in his journalism, which puts him on a par with Cobbett. Under Alexander I Karamzín became Russia's official historian, and he devoted the remainder of his life to his *History of the Russian State*. This work was based on years of painstaking research, but it reads more like Scott than a historical chronicle.

Dostoévsky's Alyósha Karamázov relates how a German living in Russia once said: 'Show a Russian schoolboy a map of the stars, which he knows nothing at all about, and the next day he will give you back the map with corrections on it.' Russian prose was barely in existence when a whole new generation was busy experimenting with and producing masterpieces in prose genres that were far from familiar even to European writers. The first wave came in the 1830s; first with the brilliant novellas and short stories of Púshkin, and slightly later with Gógol, Lérmontov, and a number of minor writers including Vladímir Odóevsky and Vladímir Sollogúb.

Púshkin's popularity was already in decline at the time when he took to writing prose. The prose works belong in fact to the last seven crowded years of his life. Putting aside his verse novel *Evgény Onégin* Púshkin writes: 'Though I love my hero still ... I'm in no mood for him ... The years to austere prose incline ... to other chill dreams, other stern cares.' Not all the prose works are finished – tantalizingly so *Dubróvsky*, a powerfully written romantic adventure story, which peters out before we discover what becomes of the squire turned bandit and his lover; and the three strange extant chapters of *Egyptian Nights* with its awe-inspiring invocation of Cleopatra, more Surrealist than Gothic (it is understandable that a poet like Bryúsov should have attempted to finish what Púshkin had begun).

The five 'tales' with a preface *The Tales of Bélkin* are virtuosity itself. The device of the author hiding behind a fictitious character who in turn has heard his stories from someone else was not particularly new. Scott had made use of it, and it was a favourite device of Goethe. It only remained for Púshkin to give the device an extra twist. Bélkin, the fictitious narrator, is much more than a technical pretext; he is a living character with his own foibles, prejudices, snobberies and ways, and there is enough internal evidence that if we wanted to we could bring Bélkin out of these stories whole. The most important thing is that it is Bélkin who tells the stories in his way, not Púshkin's. In the Preface we are shown Bélkin through the eyes of a doddering editor, whose formal reportage produces one of the best pieces of farce in Russian literature. *The Shot*, probably the best known of the tales as far as the English reader is concerned, is a superbly told suspense story, which in the same breath manages to parody the Manfreds and Hernanis then in fashion. *The Snowstorm* telescopes events with the deftness of the cinema and is about a rude awakening of two lovers from their romantic trysting, a sharp intrusion of reality into the cosy neatness of a novelette. Karamzín comes in for some gentle parody in *The Stationmaster*. It was a cliché of the day that a girl of the lower classes when seduced, or abducted, or both, would end up a prostitute or pauper. But, whereas Karamzín's own 'poor Liza' drowns herself, Púshkin's Dúnya marries well and lives happily (on the whole) ever after, her affection for her lowly father undiminished, natural and without the least trace of either condescension or guilt. The last of the tales *Lady into Peasant* is pure fun, a romp like any of Mozart's rondo finales. The critics, strange to relate, failed to grasp the real point and essence of the *Tales*. The simplicity and slightness disconcerted them. The explanation is not hard to find. This kind of narrative composition was new to them, lacking in landmarks. The *Tales* were completely different in style from the ponderous, ornate stuff they had been brought up on. They could not have noticed that Púshkin had deliberately set out to create a Russian prose diction freed from all rhetoric and stylization. Púshkin's narrative is fast, clear, economical; and especially so when one considers the time at which these stories were written. *The Shot* has been described as a *War and Peace* in four pages. It took another great prose writer—Prosper Merimée—to realize what Púshkin had achieved.

One of the first short stories, in the modern sense of the term, is Púshkin's *Queen of Spades*. The narrative is elliptical, descriptions are kept to the minimum, and a great deal is conveyed by implication. There is plenty beneath the surface too, and the reader is left with ample opportunity for allegory detection. It has been suggested that the Countess and

Hermann represent the conflict between old but resourceful
Russia and the craftiness and clamour of European civilization.
But the contrast could equally be between life and the negation of life – the uncanny vitality of the now crotchety old
lady which vacillates between fierce emotion and passivity
('one would have thought the old woman's rocking to and
fro in her chair came not of her own volition, but by the action
of some hidden galvanism') and spills over like some narcotic
into Hermann's already twisted imagination. First he thinks
he sees her ghost, then extracts what he believes to be a secret
card trick from her, and finally sees her winking at him from
the very queen of spades that loses him a fortune, and leaves
him insane. Púshkin alludes to the Napoleon parallel more
than once, and it is Hermann's calculating cynicism and
diseased conscience that ultimately let him down.

The last of Púshkin's prose works originated in his historical
research into the Pugachév peasant uprising of 1773
(Nicholas I was trying to keep Púshkin out of mischief by paying him a salary to do this). The Captain's Daughter was the
result. The story is told by the hero Grinév. The unusual thing
about this novella is that the narrator grows visibly older and
more mature as the story progresses, for he is also its hero.
The way in which Púshkin achieves this, by a series of stylistic
devices, is an entire study in itself. The opening chapter is
pure Candide or Marriage of Figaro, but by the end of the
story Púshkin has pulled out every stop in his magnificent
repertory. The novella is also rich in satire, parody and
allusion. Grinév first meets Pugachév, in grisly guise, in a dream;
it is only later that he meets the real Pugachév. The dream is
prophetic, assuring Grinév that he need not fear for his own life,
and this serves like some charm to protect him. If Evgény
Onégin is a novel in verse, The Captain's Daughter is a poem
in prose. In truth The Captain's Daughter is so much like a
poem in the solidity of its construction that it cannot be
unravelled at all. Grinév represents the chivalric virtues
shared by Old Russia and civilized Europe – truth, honour,
duty, gallantry, law. Pugachév on the other hand embodies
all those human qualities which are boundless and dangerous;
yet feeble in that they can be easily manipulated and cowed.

Grinév risks this life rather than tell a lie, but Púshkin makes us see the churlishness of this virtue in the context of the whole. Pugachév is a vainglorious braggart, brave but soft, cruel but capricious, easily flattered, contemptuous of civilized ways. But paradoxically it is Pugachév who remains 'true' to Grinév, not the other way round. Pugachév commits the most horrible villainy but puts personal loyalty first. Grinév risks his life for the sake of his ideals; Pugachév because he cannot believe that Grinév will betray him. This technique of ambiguity became the basis of Dostoévsky's later and vaster explorations.

An important landmark in the development of the novel is Lérmontov's *A Hero of our Time*. In Russia it is the first of a long line of 'psychological' or 'analytical' novels, and is written in a prose style in advance of its time – exactly as if Russians had been writing novels for centuries. Lérmontov learnt his craft from Púshkin, but instead of trying to emulate his example set about solving a particularly formidable problem, forcing himself to come to terms with what Púshkin called the 'diabolical difference' between a novel in verse and a prose novel. For us it is difficult to conceive of a time when writing verse novels was easier than writing prose novels. In his *Princess Mimi* published two or three years before *A Hero of Our Time* Odóevsky had this to say: 'Do you realize, dear readers. . . . that the most demanding type of composition is the novel or short story; and that the most difficult novels are the ones that have to be written in Russian; and the most difficult Russian novels to write are those depicting contemporary moeurs.' Odóevsky apologizes to the reader for raising the curtain on him like some small-time stage-manager, who makes excuses about the difficulty of 'turning clouds into sea, a housekeeper into a princess, or a knave into a *premier ingénu*.'

Lérmontov is ahead of his own time in still another respect – his conscious lack of polish. That is not to say that Lérmontov's prose is awkward; rather it twists and turns with the situation, becoming as jagged as the mountains he at times describes. Lérmontov's *un*literary style anticipates Dostoévsky and later writers.

The 'hero' of Lérmontov's novel is Pechórin; like the author a young army officer. Romantic agony there may be, but there is more than a streak of the 'anti-hero' of our own century as well. In one place Pechórin describes himself as a moral cripple – 'My soul has been warped by the world, my mind is restless, my heart insatiable. Nothing suffices. I grow accustomed to sorrow as readily as to joy, and my life becomes emptier by the day.' Pechórin's boyhood quest for truth, for 'the sublime and beautiful' had long been abandoned – 'I had lost one half of my soul for it had shrivelled, dried up and died, and I had cut it out and cast it away, while the other half still stirred and went on living, adapted to serve everyone. No one had noticed this because nobody suspected there had been another half...' Bliss sometimes seemed to be in the offing, but whenever Pechórin gave way to his intimations he always came rudely up against stony reality. Like Baudelaire's 'le plus triste des alchimistes' Pechórin found himself turning gold into base-metal, and paradise into hell. The 'hero' kidnaps a young tatar girl, thinking she would satisfy his desires once and for all. But his mistake was a grave one – 'the love of a barbarian is little better than that of a well-bred lady. The ignorance and simplicity of the one is as boring as the coquetry of the other.' The girl dies in a long-drawn-out agony after being shot accidentally, but Pechórin seems unmoved. When his companion tries to console him, Pechórin laughs like some fiend – 'That laugh sent cold shivers down my spine... I went off to order the coffin.' A second incident, this time deliberately and ironically 'literary', appears in the self-contained section *Taman*, a story set in a cluster of hovels on the sea coast. An enchanting mermaid-like creature who seems to be luring Pechórin towards unknown delights, turns out to be an accomplice in some squalid smuggling racket. *Taman* is famed for its blend of the romantic and the real; with Pechórin straddling both modes. The episode leaves him saddened by his own futility: 'Like a stone hurled into the placid waters of a well, I had disturbed their tranquillity, and like a stone had nearly gone to the bottom myself!' *Taman* is also Pechórin's inner life in allegory, one part of his being holding up a cracked mirror to the other – 'I weigh and analyse my own feelings and actions with a stern curiosity, but without sympathy. There are two men in me: one of them lives in the full sense of the word; the other reasons and passes judgment on the first.'

Lérmontov's novel was not well received. In the opinion of Nicholas I it was no more than 'an exaggerated account of the kind of despicable characters found in foreign novels.' The critics got their reply in the form of a Preface in which Lérmontov exposed their half-baked sensibilities: 'The *Hero of our Time*, gentlemen, is indeed a portrait, but not of one man in isolation. It is a portrait built up of all our generation's vices in full bloom ... You say morals will go by the board. I don't agree. People have been fed dainties enough to turn their stomachs. What we need now are bitter remedies, acid truths. But don't get it into your heads that the author was out to reform his fellow creatures. God preserve him from such boorishness! He simply wanted to describe modern man as he sees him, and as he so often, to his own misfortune as well as yours, has found him to be. Suffice it that the disease has been diagnosed. How to cure it, heaven alone knows!'

Pechórin eventually kills someone in a duel. The setting, a Caucasian mountain slope, was a portent of Lérmontov's own last duel in which he was killed.

Perhaps the least penetrable of all Russian novelists is Nikolái Gógol (1809–1852). A century or more of critical and scholarly endeavour has taken us no spectacular distance beyond the insights of Gógol's own contemporary, Belínsky. Nor do we know a great deal about Gógol the man. Those who counted as his more or less regular acquaintances in Petersburg, Moscow and Rome probably knew as much or even more. We have to make do with inspired guesswork.

My readers will at some time or other have read *The Over-coat*, and many will have read *Dead Souls* too. For this reason I shall not be giving a systematic outline of Gógol's work. Instead I shall be singling out those features that hold a particular interest for me. And in any case there would be no point in my trying to compete in a few pages with the many excellent studies of Gógol.

One of the biggest puzzles is Gógol's personality. Not a few of those who came in contact with him have remarked upon his strange and often madly infuriating behaviour. Sergéi Aksákov's view is typical: 'I can't think of a single person who loved Gógol as a friend, irrespectively of his merits as a writer. People used to laugh at me when I said that Gógol did not exist for me as a personality so far as I was concerned.' And again, many years after Gógol's death: 'To such an extent was Gógol not a human being in my eyes that I, who in my youth had been terribly afraid of corpses, could not arouse in myself the feeling of natural dread in the presence of his dead body.' The alleged 'defects' in his nature were well understood by Gógol, even though he could make no sense of them either – 'I am considered an enigma by everyone. No one has figured me out completely . . . Would you believe it, that deep down inside I was laughing at myself along with the rest of you.' Perhaps it is only because Gógol has not fitted any of the fashionable hypotheses that he has so far eluded the psychoanalysts.

Part of the 'enigma', it seems to me, is Gógol's inability to separate himself from the world of his characters and their situations. It is of course not unusual for novelists to project themselves, especially whilst actually writing, into a dream. But in Gógol's case the boundary between his personal life and the lives he projected in his books was literally unclear, and in places perhaps totally absent. It is as if Gógol moved freely between his own personal world and other fictitious worlds without any conscious awareness of his 'transgression'. It should not surprise us that Gógol lived fiction in his daily life. As an actor he possessed an uncanny talent, although a talent not always entirely under control. As a schoolboy he could feign madness so convincingly that his mentors were terror-stricken; yet he failed abysmally at an audition years later for the Bolshoi Theatre. One hardly need mention Gógol's apparently 'totemic' need to dress up in the most outlandish rigouts when at work. The poet Zhukóvsky on one occasion found Gógol absorbed in composition dressed in a fantastic array of Russian woollen stockings, decorative velvet jacket, capacious multicoloured scarf, and gold-embroidered peasant headdress. Even Gógol was alarmed at himself, and invariably put himself out of bounds on such occasions. As a comedian Gógol was never other than completely serious even when his readings reduced his audience to stitches. The effect could also be eerie. Once he began reading in the middle of what seemed to be an ordinary conversation; it was some moments before his listeners realized the performance had already begun. The seriousness extended to practical jokes. At the time he was writing *The Government Inspector* Gógol thought of putting his plot to the test. He was on his way to Moscow with a couple of friends, when he asked one of them to go on ahead giving him explicit instructions to mention in passing at all the coaching stations en route that a government inspector was travelling incognito. Gógol acted the part of the latter with such brilliance that his prank promised to be even more illustrious than Khlestakóv's.*

A complete picture of Gógol is lacking (unless we count Ivánov's famous portrait) partly because those who knew him had little idea of his true nature, dismissing all they failed to understand as eccentricity, obtuseness, and – eventually – insanity. Even as a young man Gógol viewed his writing as a kind of psychic safety mechanism: 'The reason behind the gaiety of my earliest pieces is to be sought in my own inner need. I became prey to fits of melancholy which were beyond my comprehension. To get rid of them I imagined the most comic things – funny characters in the funniest situations I could think of.' In later life we find Gógol glumly sheltering behind his own creations: 'My characters have not yet become entirely separate from myself . . . But I don't love my own nastiness as my own characters do theirs. I have managed to extricate myself from my own worst vices only by giving them to my characters.'

Too much has sometimes been made of the derivative elements in Gógol, and this can conceal his uniqueness as a writer. It is true that he culled his plots from others (the ideas for *The Government Inspector* and *Dead Souls* were freely given to him by Púshkin), but many other writers have done this, Shakespeare not excluded. The influence of

* The principal character in *The Government Inspector*.

E. T. A. Hoffmann is beyond doubt; but Gógol's technique of blending reality and fantasy is original. In Hoffmann reality is merely a foil for fantasy; in Gógol the two are integrally interwoven. Gógol's stories are not so much uncanny as bizarre, precisely because the author is unwilling to divide the spectrum. In Gógol fantasy and reality are equally natural and matter-of-fact, equally far-fetched and 'fantastic'.

Gógol was a great admirer of Scott and closely acquainted with the latters views on the historical novel. For all that, Gógol's *Tarás Búlba* based on the history of the Dnieper Cossacks is totally unlike Scott. This applies equally to another historical work where Scott's influence might be expected most: the surviving fragment of a play based on the life of the English king, Alfred. To quote a recent critic: 'Gógol's literary models are numerous, but they serve only as material on which to imprint his own unmistakable stamp.'

Gógol's Russian too is entirely his own. But, for all its quirks, Gógol's language possesses an immediate appeal, as if it were the natural language of ordinary people. As one of his editor friends said: 'You get carried away by his stories; you swallow everything eagerly from start to finish; you read him a second time and you still don't notice what a queer, unnatural language he uses. The moment you begin to scrutinize it from an expert's point of view, you realize that no one would ever talk or write like that. But try to correct it and you ruin it — not one word of it can be altered. What would happen if he were to write real Russian!'

Another striking . feature is Gógol's naturalness, almost complete except for a sprinkling of purple passages. Gógol seldom overplays, and even his caricatures seem drawn from life. About *Dead Souls* Belinsky wrote: 'We can see nothing farcical or funny about it . . . Everything is serious, sober, true, and profound.' *The Diary of a Madman*, which would have induced a lesser writer of his time to commit every kind of extravagance, is compiled as objectively as if it had been the work of a psychiatrist; yet it contains some of Gógol's funniest passages. It is never a question of dead-pan humour but always of humour inherent in the mundane. The imagined exchange of letters between the two dogs ranks among the

least plausible episodes in Gógol, but the reader has no difficulty in suspending disbelief. And the ending is recorded with
equal and harrowing accuracy. The 'madman's' delusion that
he is Ferdinand VIII of Spain is superbly handled, and the
collapse of the clock-time dimension is as weird as anything
in science fiction.

In Gógol reality is illusion, and illusion reality. Gógol was
a minute, meticulous observer, but he always sifted and selected, and then came up with a fresh synthesis – 'I never *painted*
a portrait by simply copying it. I *created* portraits, but I did
so on the basis of reflection rather than imagination.' Just as
the expert conjurer remains apparently calm in face of the
increasing complexity of his tricks, so Gógol gets Kovalyóv's
nose jauntily out of its (his) carriage, and dresses it (him)
in a uniform of gold braid with a large stand-up collar, leads
it (him) through an entire escapade, and eventually returns
the nose (him/it!) to its owner. As with the conjurer, we are
not persuaded to believe, we are convinced from the outset.
But that is not all. Gógol's is a special kind of illusionism,
a template against which to compare one's own picture of
reality, one's own world. According to him we are all artists
more or less, and this means we are all illusionists too.

This brings us to the deeper meaning of Gógol's art. In
Part One of *Dead Souls* Gógol created out of the nondescript
flotsam of life a series of characters – some would say caricatures – who on the face of it deserve only our contempt or
ridicule; but Gógol forces us to recognize them as people in
their own right. After reading the novel a second time we
begin to love these characters; and not as amiable or feckless
or misguided or cantankerous or downtrodden people, in an
idealistic or sentimental way – but as we love ourselves. This is
not applied Christianity, but Gógol's own discovery of what
happens to be a Christian precept, through his own art. Art
is akin to love. And Gógol achieves his effects often with
caricature and dissection of the most merciless kind.

The title *Dead Souls* of course suggests allegory. And we
are not disappointed; a vast web of interesting levels ranges
from social and political satire to the least explored realms
of the human spirit. In delving into what Gógol termed 'all

the terrible, shocking morass of trivial things in which life is entangled, the whole depth of frigid, split-up, everyday characters with which our often dreary and bitter earthly path swarms' the artist is capable of 'redeeming' the 'dead souls' he finds there. It is not out of curiosity, idle or scientific, nor for satirical or humorous purposes merely, that Gógol has dredged these people out of the 'morass', but for them themselves as they actually are and must be. Their mediocrity and spiritual poverty in the hands of the artist generates its own joy. It is, Gógol seems to be saying, those of us who have remained blind or become blind to the breadth of the world, whose souls are 'dead'. That is perhaps the rump of the allegory. And Gógol was sure that we should find a bit of Chíchikov* in each one of us.

The humdrum chaos of life, swarming with fragments of living souls, can be redeemed by comic art, which is also love. But the residual chaos is neither inert nor indifferent. According to Gógol it is animated by evil powers, which can be polarized and held at bay again only by the artist, the artist that is each one of us. Gógol's most original, if strange, idea is that a man's life must be converted into art for him to be saved. *The Overcoat*, at one level a social satire, is also a kind of miracle play in the folk tradition (probably that of the Ukrainian puppet theatre). Akáky Akakyevich represents life at its diminished and diminutive – symbolized by many details in the story. The tailor and his new overcoat are the personifications of evil. Akáky is destroyed through his own increasing insignificance in the face of this evil. According to one authority the key figure in the piece is the folk-devil of Russian popular tradition. Even the robbers who snatched Akáky's new overcoat from his back are more like diabolical phantoms and there is no lack of tempting reasons for supposing that they belong to the same company as that lone ghost who appears at the end of the story. The reader may have noted that they all wore mustachios and were all larger than life. But an even more intriguing exposition of Gógol's theory occurs in his macabre story *The Portrait*. A portrait recently acquired by a young artist named Chartkóv seems to be

* The principal character in *Dead Souls*.

gazing at him with living human eyes. Chartkóv is not so
much terrified as affronted. This to him was life in the raw,
untransformed by art, and therefore unbearable, even horrific
– 'This was no longer art; it destroyed the harmony of the
portrait itself!... The eyes seemed to be cut out of a living
man and put there. There was no longer any of that sublime
feeling of joy that encompasses the soul at the sight of the
work of an artist, however terrible the subject might be.
The sensation he received was rather one of joylessness, pain-
fulness, and anxiety ... Why on earth should it give me this
strangely unpleasant feeling? Or is a faithful, slavish imitation
of nature such an offence that it must effect you like a loud,
discordant scream? Or if you paint a thing objectively and
coolly, without feeling any particular sympathy for it, must it
necessarily confront you in all its terrible reality, unillumined
by the light of some deep, hidden, unfathomable idea? Must it
appear to you with the reality which reveals itself to a person
who, searching for beauty in man, picks up a scalpel and
begins to dissect a man's inside, only to find what is disgusting
in man.'

Gógols' creative life was packed into ten short years and
for the last seven of them he antagonized everyone with manic
pronouncements. Today the term 'insanity' oversimplifies and
frequently misleads. And there is no substantial clinical evidence of mental disturbance in Gógol's case. We know only
that he was desperately unhappy, and spiritually tormented.
Twice Gógol burned the completed sections of *Dead Souls*;
the second time along with the rest of his unpublished manuscripts, shortly before his death. His death is a mystery, but
Turgénev was convinced that Gógol deliberately killed himself by starvation. It is ironical that a writer who rescued so
many of his own characters, could not save himself. His
dying words were: 'Give me a ladder!'

Turgénev for me is one of those writers who on re-reading
always transcend expectations. The reason is not far to seek.
Regrettably or unregrettably, Turgénev's world is not ours;
and his people are guided by sets of values which have long
since been reduced to smithereens. But even if we do not

always share their refinement, evenness, moral fastidiousness and magnanimity, we also generally lack their myopic smugness, their worship of property and propriety, their caste consciousness. Also, the style is too near nineteenth century realism for our taste. We can easily overlook the wood for the trees, the fine penetration beneath what occasionally seems to us a fussy surface texture.

Born into the better off Russian landed gentry, Iván Turgénev (1818–83) received a fairly standard upbringing for his time. The only exception in the vast household was his tyrannical mother. The reader will recognize her in Turgénev's story *Mumu*. Her cat-and-mouse play with her two sons was a relatively minor fault compared with the cruel floggings of her serfs, her having them arbitrarily shipped off to Siberia, and reports that domestic staff were forced to throw babies into a pond because she refused to have children around the house. After short periods at Moscow and St. Petersburg Universities, Turgénev immersed himself for the time being in the 'German sea'; he went to Berlin and not only soaked up Schelling, Hegel, Feuerbach, and much else, but came into direct contact with other Russian rising stars, like Hérzen and Bakúnin. Turgénev then returned to Russia, and had almost abandoned all hope of becoming a writer, when his first story *Khor and Kalínich* received sudden acclaim. This was the first of his *Sportman's Sketches* which were published serially over a period of years, and which were cumulatively to become the *Uncle Tom's Cabin* of Russian literature. These 'sketches', modelled in turn upon Maria Edgeworth's studies of the Irish peasantry, were recognized as an oblique but powerful criticism of serfdom in Russia. Alexander II (not yet on the throne) later told Turgénev personally that it was his book which in part had brought him round to emancipation. Shortly after the *Sketches* had been published, Turgénev was exiled to the family estate for writing an allegedly controversial obituary on Gógol. This period of exile was a blessing in disguise for it not only gave Turgénev the accolade of martyrdom, but more important, gave him time to work out the framework for a novel, always the bugbear of the Russian writer, who had always been weak on plots and the

larger canvas. On his release from exile in 1856 Turgénev
went abroad, and stayed abroad for practically the entire
remainder of his life, moving from place to place in the wake
of that idol of his, the celebrity primadonna Pauline Viardot,
whom he worshipped in a fetishistic kind of way. He did not
marry. By 1861, in the short space of six years, he had written
four of his six major novels: *Rúdin*, *A Nest of Gentlefolk*, *On
the Eve*, and *Fathers and Children*. As early as *Rúdin* and with
another twenty-five years of life ahead of him, Turgénev
considered himself played out; forty-four he considered the
'peaceful haven of old age'. This seems especially incongruous
when one considers that Turgénev was only three years
younger than Dostoévsky, and at that time Dostoévsky was
still in Siberia, not even having published any of his major
works.

All the more surprising this attitude of 'renunciation' and
pessimism in view of Turgénev's immense popularity, first
at home, and later abroad. In effect Turgénev was the first
Russian to be accepted as a European writer of eminence. By
the 1870s his work had been translated into all the major
European languages. French writers – it was in France where
he mostly lived – particularly admired him. Flaubert and
Mérimée rated him very highly. Georges Sand sat at his feet.
In Paris Turgénev along with Flaubert, Zola, Daudet, and
Edmond Goncourt became known as the Five. But Turgénev
was the opposite of vain, and instead of glorifying himself,
was busy propagating Púshkin. His pains were wasted on
Thackeray for one, who roared with laughter at the outlandish sound of Turgénev reading one of Púshkin's finest
lyrics. In general, and despite reciprocal admiration, Turgénev
could not make much sense of the English with their
guffaw-ridden humour. To his friend Fet he described the
English as 'marvellous, queer, grandiose, stupid, all in one, but
chiefly something wholly alien to us'. Yet, of all the Russian
novelists, Turgénev is nearest to the Anglo-Saxon tradition.
As Henry James wrote: 'There is perhaps no novelist of alien
race who more naturally than Iván Turgénev inherits a
niche in a library for English readers'. Conversely, it has been

said* that 'Europe can understand Russia much better through a reading of Turgénev than through a reading of any other Russian writer'.

Reading Turgénev is rather like observing some fast-working painter at his canvas. Stroke by stroke, line by line, excitingly the picture takes shape. Looked at in another way, since of course narrative requires a time dimension, Turgénev's scenes, situations, and characterizations seem to unroll before our eyes: a strand here, a glimmering there, grows, is filled out, and flows into the mainstream. This is especially so in the novels, but we sometimes have this impression even in the short stories. For this reason Turgénev is never meretricious, but always delights the mental eye as well as the senses. Nothing is ever flat; everything is in constant flux. There is no writer better at nature. Even when his scenes are overdone, as they are occasionally in his earlier work, we can still be fascinated. The sunset, for example, in *Yermolai and the Miller's Wife*, with its meticulous account of the order in which the various species of birds fall silent, verges on the ludicrous; but even here we have the compensation of Turgénev's fine perception of growing darkness. In the later work the essential is given in a few swift strokes, with breathtaking verbal photography: 'I watched how the church, built close by, above the lake, at each flash of lightning stood out, at one moment black against a background of white, at the next white against a background of black, and then was swallowed up in darkness again . . .' (*Faust*). It is the same with people. Turgénev was a great observer of people's behaviour. Take for instance the pampered valet in *The Tryst* where we learn far more from gestures than from the words spoken by this otherwise inarticulate oaf; or Rúdin's unnatural, disjointed character reflected in his equally unnatural and disjointed gait. Rúdin is playing at loving, and his victim falls for his blandishments – ' "I am happy," he declared, in a whisper, "Yes, I am happy," he repeated, as if anxious to convince himself. He drew himself erect, tossed his curly head, and strode swiftly out into the park, waving his arms to and fro.' With a life-

* R. Freeborn : *Turgenev: A Study*, London, 1960.

time's experience behind him, Turgénev attains such ease that, even from an otherwise tired novel like *Virgin Soil* we may take at random a portrait like this: 'Valentina Sipyágina was full of special charm which is peculiar to attractive egoists; in that charm there is no poetry nor true sensibility, but there is softness, there is sympathy, there is tenderness. Only, these charming egoists must not be thwarted; they are fond of power, and will not tolerate independence in others. Women like Sipyágina excite and work upon inexperienced and passionate natures; for themselves they like regularity and a peaceful life. Virtue comes easy to them, they are inwardly unmoved, but the constant desire to sway, attracts and, to please, lends them mobility and brilliance . . . Hard it is for a man to hold his ground when for an instant gleams of secret softness pass unconsciously, as it seems, over a bright, pure creature like this; he waits, expecting the time is coming, and now the ice will melt; but the clear ice only reflects the play of light, it does not melt . . .'

Henry James was right in suspecting that Turgénev possessed a language of his own, 'an individual accent' which does not come through in translation. Turgénev's Russian, working within the easy limits of the language of the Western-ized aristocracy, achieves a perfection which is unsurpassed. It is also, with certain exceptions, the easiest Russian for those learning to read Russian. There is nothing literary about it, like Gógol's Russian for instance, but it is always crystal clear and beautiful. We know that Turgénev worshipped the Russian language in a way unlike any writer before him.

Like every Russian novelist of the last century, and many of the present century, Turgénev drew his sustinence directly from Púshkin. In doing so, he perfected a style worlds apart from that of either Lérmontov or Gógol, and a form which became the blueprint for many a later writer: Tolstóy, Chékhov, Górky to mention only three, and indirectly for some non-Russian writers as well. James described Turgénev as the 'novelist's novelist', not because only novelists would fully appreciate him, but because his method and presentation are always transparent, 'an artistic influence extraordinarily valuable and ineradicably established'.

Turgénev's style, it has been said, is a continuation of Púshkin's classicism, in turn a late transplantation from eighteenth century France. It is thus that Turgénev managed to carry the classical tradition through into the age of realist prose fiction. Classicism deals with man as a whole, or types; realism deals with actual people. The gap was effectively bridged by Turgénev. And this was his most important achievement. Turgénev's characters combine all the universality of classical drama with the particularity to be found in Balzac or Dickens. A good illustration of this is Rúdin, the chief character of the novel of that name. Rúdin is clearly modelled in part of Molière's Tartuffe. But Tartuffe is any man who finds himself in the particular situation set for him in Molières's comedy. Turgénev's Rúdin is a special 'case'. He is only Tartuffe if you misjudge him. To do him complete justice we have to admit that he is for himself a complete enigma. Lezhnév, who is Rúdin's only important antagonist, realizes that Rúdin is not even a Tartuffe, because Molière's Tartuffe at least knew what he was after, whereas Rúdin had no idea at all. Without this and other technical advances on Turgénev's part, it is doubtful if Tolstóy would have been able to create his epic novels. Writers like James and Maupassant recognized Turgénev's achievement for what it was, and they learnt from it.

But Turgénev is of course far more than a mere stepping stone. His work may not have any of the draconian agony of Dostoévsky, or the splendour of Tolstóy, but it stands easily up to theirs. Many readers surely come to Turgénev for relief, for a breath of sanity, for his good sense and 'finer consciousness'. It is with a light touch that Turgénev achieves his depths, his passion, grief, suffering, love, his gloom or his ecstasy, more by implication than directly. I don't agree with Edmund Wilson that Turgénev is an expert detached observer rather than a searching psychologist. I think he is both. I don't dispute though that 'his characters come out best when they are presenting themselves to other people.' Turgénev was never any good at analysis, and he knew it. His early attempts at the kind of thing Lémontov or Dostoévsky excelled at are sorry specimens. So *un*successful is the narrator in the *Diary of a Superfluous Man*, a monologue of the analytic type, that in sheer desperation he tries to 'prove' to the reader that the term 'superfluous' really does apply to him!

It is a mistake to suppose that, because his manner is easy, light and gracious, Turgénev's work is shallow. It is simply that one can so easily fail to notice or skim over the depths, whereas in a novelist like Tolstóy or Dostoévsky everything is reiterated double forte. True, the novels at their worst resemble tracts, and even at their best they appear as one recent critic has put it, 'monolithic'. But the short stories never cease to amaze with their range. Were it not for their unmistakable diction, they might well have been written by different authors. At one extreme a story like *The Unhappy Girl* contains quite as much 'laceration' as anything in Dostoévsky; a short story like *Babúrin and Púnin*, although it runs through all the social and political implications of *Virgin Soil* and much else besides, seems as inexplicit and as reduced to bare bones as anything in Chékhov; *Múmu*, the story about the deaf-mute life of a deaf-mute servant, or *The Lear of the Steppes* approaches Hardy; whereas *Ásya*, a Russian Mignon, or *First Love* could not have been tackled, let alone written by anyone but Turgénev. As Henry James so well said, Turgénev understands so much we almost wonder he can express anything.

Turgénev early acquired the reputation of a 'political' writer. In fact Turgénev's attitude to Russia was ambivalent. Like Hérzen, another great prose writer, Turgénev was a political and social thinker of extraordinary insight and subtlety. And like Hérzen too, Turgénev managed to transcend the Westernist-Slavophile controversy (very fairly presented by Pánshin and Lavrétsky in *A Nest of Gentlefolk*). Turgénev could understand the Russian, the ordinary Russian as well as the intellectual, in a way that few ostensibly more committed writers could. He never doubted the importance of his own roots: 'Everyday I see more clearly that torn away from one's native soil one cannot keep on writing'. In Russian villages 'the air was thick with ideas'; and no one knew better than Turgénev that 'without national sense, there is no art, no truth, nothing'. Yet he found the Russian atmosphere especially that of Moscow, 'poisonous'; and regretted that Tolstóy could not be persuaded 'to extricate himself from the Moscow bog' into which he had got himself : 'In this chaos a man must perish. That's the way it always is in Russia.' Whereas Lezhnév (*Rúdin*) argues that 'Russia can get along without any one of us, but not one of us can get along without Russia' and that 'cosmopolitanism is all rubbish'. Potúgin (*Smoke*) insists that Russians are 'impoverished barbaric fools' and that 'our mother, Orthodox Russia, could disappear into the bowels of the earth and everything would remain quietly in its place, because the samovar, the bast shoe, the shaft-bow, and the knout – those famous products of ours – even they were not invented by us'.The important thing in Turgénev's view is not theories and generalizations – 'systems are only dear to those who cannot take the whole truth in their hands' he told Tolstóy – but the reality itself. 'You have a decidedly poor opinion of Russians', Bazárov (*Fathers and Children*) is told. 'As if it mattered!' he replies. 'The best thing about a Russian is the poor opinion he has of himself.' Pàklin, the buffoon-like character in *Virgin Soil*, has some curiously prophetic things to say about Russia: 'We Russians are a queer lot, you know, we expect everything; someone or something is to come along one day and cure us all at once, heal all our wounds, extract everything like an aching tooth. Who or what this panacea will be – Darwinism, the Village Commune, a foreign war, anything you please! Only, we must have our teeth pulled for us !'

Ideologically, Turgénev could be described as a liberal stoic. Life he regarded as 'substantially a disease', even when 'interesting'. Lavrétsky heedless of his own personal happiness, sets to work 'with teeth clenched' to till the soil, to improve by a single atom the lot of his peasants. Bazárov dies through others' negligence, of an infected wound, but he dies like the true stoic: 'And now this giant's task is to die a decent death, and that is no one else's business ... All the same, I'm not going to put my tail between my legs now.' Nature is truly monstrous, and its only counter-force is art: 'Nature is inexorable; she has no need to hurry, and sooner

or later she takes her own. Unconsciously and inflexibly
obedient to laws, she knows not art, knows not freedom,
knows not good; from all ages moving, from all ages changing,
she suffers nothing immortal, nothing unchanging ... Man is
her child; but man's work – art – is hostile to her, just because
it strives to be unchanging and immortal'. (*Enough*). A nightingale may be sending us into ecstasies when at the same
moment an insect is dying in the grass. At times Turgénev
comes very close to Tolstóy's renunciation, but with none
of the thunder, and more simplicity. A man leaves only seeds
behind him, which are destined to come up only after his death
(*Faust*). The faint fragrance of an insignificant plant outlives
all man's joys and sorrows – outlives man himself' (*Asya*).

One of the most widely read of Russian classics is *Oblómov*.
Outside Russia the fame of its author Iván Goncharóv (1812–
1891) rests solely upon this one novel. Not many are aware
that *Oblómov* is only the second novel of what Goncharóv
himself regarded as a trilogy – 'I see not three novels, but one.
They are all connected by a single thread, a single, consistent
idea.' For all its claim to authenticity though, Goncharóv's
opinion should not blind us to the obvious differences, especially between the first of his novels *The Same Old Story* (or
An Ordinary Story) and the second and third. With its almost
Shavian devil's advocacy *The Same Old Story* is in many ways
more likely to appeal to the modern reader. Its wit is sharp,
its descriptions concise, and its characterizations brief and
telling; the dialogue is among the best every written by any
Russian writer. It is so different from *Oblómov* and *The
Precipice* that, were it not for the proneness to the Oblómov
way of life developed by its romantically disposed Alexander
Aduyev, this novel might have been written by a different
author. The third of his novels *The Precipice* (otherwise known
as *The Ravine* or *The Abyss*) is Goncharóv's longest, and it
took him a good twenty years to write. It fails to reach the
standard of its predecessors; it rambles, and is frequently
marred by didactic outbursts and an excessive load of unnecessary detail. In one of his less charitable moments Turgénev
described it as 'a novel written by an official for officials and
their wives'.

Goncharóv grew up in a household not unlike that depicted in Oblómov's dream recollections of his childhood. After graduating from Moscow University, Goncharóv became bent upon combining writing with a career in the civil service. He proved none too successful at the latter, and after a good many years of boredom he eventually got himself taken on as secretary to a Russian expedition which was about to make its way round the world on a frigate. Goncharóv's impressions were subsequently written up at considerable length, but with typical no-nonsense, in his *The Frigate Pallas*. On returning home Goncharóv entered the censor's department, thereby incurring the wrath and contempt of many of his contemporaries. Actually Goncharóv in his new post managed to steer many an important work of Turgénev, Dostoévsky, Pisémsky and others past the worst bureaucratic hazards. Needless to say, he never relished this work; but not so much because it was ignominious, rather because it was far too tedious. Before very long he resigned and tried his hand, not too successfully, at journalism. A year later he was back in censorship, this time with the notorious Press Council. His final resignation came in 1867, at about the time when he had become maniacally embroiled with Turgénev, whom Goncharóv accused of plagiarizing from *The Precipice*, and even of passing on his ideas to various European writers. Goncharóv spent his last twenty years as a recluse, virtually or actually insane.

Goncharóv in common with every other major Russian novelist is a law unto himself. Moreover, there is much about his work, especially *Oblómov*, that was improperly understood by his contemporaries, and even today leaves room for thought. There is a double strain in Goncharóv, a conflict between the settled carefree world of the nearly feudal past and the active, tidy, efficient life led by the modern urban European. Goncharóv's contemporaries made too much of what they believed to be an all-out attack on the evils of Oblómovka, and endemic Oblomovitis. The radicals of the sixties saw only political and social criticism in this novel, and Oblomovism (Oblómovshchina) became their watchword. Dobrolyúbov in a famous essay supposed that Goncharóv

in writing *Oblómov* was concerned with burying Oblomovism
once and for all, and pronouncing its 'funeral oration'. The
cliché became so well established that even Lenin drew
upon it more than once. Today we are more likely to
see Oblómov as a nineteenth-century drop-out. Although
Goncharóv had, as we know, on the surface at least a good
deal in common with the practical, cynical Adúyev uncle
(*The Same Old Story*) and with the more idealistic but
equally practical Stolz (*Oblomov*), inwardly he was much
nearer to Oblómov—'What struck me most of all was the
image of Oblómov in myself and others'. In *The Precipice*
the patriarchal mores of the grandmother are made to seem
more significant than the hollow, destructive nihilism of
Vólokhov; and even Túshin, a man of both worlds, intended
by the author as a synthesis of the opposites, is not a successful
amalgam. Nowhere had Goncharóv been more struck by
the negative side of modern life than on his visit to London
(while waiting for repairs to be completed on the frigate at
Portsmouth). He was dismayed by the machine-like motivation
of the people there, the lack of warmth and charm – 'it seemed
that honesty, justice, compassion were obtained like coal'. As
for *Oblómov*, he never showed any interest in a career, for
he knew how little the *real* man is needed for a career.
Oblómov never doubts that his own mind and heart are 'peace-
fully asleep', but he does regret that society people fail to
realize that they too are dead: 'They are asleep, they are
worse than I! . . . Aren't they all dead men? Aren't they
asleep all their life sitting there like that? Why am I more to
blame,' he asks his friend Stolz, 'because I happen to lie about
at home and do not infect the minds of others with my
talk of aces and knaves . . . They infect each other by a sort
of tormenting anxiety and melancholy; they are all painfully
searching for something.' Oblómov had long since diagnosed
his own illness – Oblomovitis – a disease which began with
'your inability to put on your own socks and ended with your
inability to live'. Anyone in whom the light has been shut up
for too long, whether brought up in Oblómovka or not, will
develop like symptoms. The socks may then be mental ones,
but that makes very little difference. He asks Stolz a very

reasonable question: 'Doesn't everyone strive to achieve the very thing I dream of? Why, isn't the whole purpose of your rushing about, all your passions, wars, trade, and politics to attain rest – to reach this ideal of a lost paradise?'

That brings us to the most controversial of all Russian writers – Fyodor Dostoévsky (1821–1881). I have argued elsewhere* that Dostoévsky is a writer who does not date. His novels have something to say for every generation. As our outlook changes, constant reinterpretation and re-examination of almost everything in Dostoévsky is called for, even of fundamentals. The views of many of Dostoévsky's earlier critics, valid for their own time, have quickly receded into the past, leaving Dostoévsky high and dry in the present, demanding new and ever more compelling reinterpretation. It is only since Kafka and Nietzsche, since depth psychology, since the phenomenologists and existentialists that Dostoévsky has been at all rightly understood. Dostoévsky was certainly well in advance of his own time. And it will be interesting to see how far he is ahead of our own.

To attempt to say anything significant about a writer like Dostoévsky in a few paragraphs could not be more absurd. His novels – Crime and Punishment, The Idiot, The Devils, The Brothers Karamázov, to mention only the most daunting—are still largely unexplored territories. The Brothers Karamázov in particular is such that any number of critical surveys would be swallowed up by its vastness. And the sternest deterrent to those undertaking a study of Dostoévsky is the knowledge that scrutiny of this author is rather like peering into a queer kind of mirror, the suspicion that after protracted labour nothing more will emerge than one's own distorted image. Any thesis one cares to put forward can be refuted by arguments based on exactly those points which appeared to support one's own. The temptation to decipher messages in Dostoévsky has produced a curious and recurrent phenomenon. Traditions of interpretation have sprung up which perpetuate themselves regardless of their source, so that it is almost impossible for the modern reader to come for the first

* Lord, R.: *Dostoevsky: Essays and Perspectives*, London, 1970.

time uninitiated to Dostoévsky, for he somehow picks up
this tradition. Readers find an understandable need for frames
of reference, and there are a number of relatively facile inter-
pretations that satisfy this need.

The situation has even been worsened by those who could
not resist the temptation to seek out the real Dostoévsky in
his characters, and in what they have to say. A difficult enough
temptation to resist. For in what other writer do the characters
make such astonishing, profound and intriguing statements for
such a great proportion of the time? Even Dostoévsky was
never absolutely certain of his own convictions, suspecting
that all the while he might be actually or at least on the verge
of humbugging himself as well as his readers. Dostoévsky is
not unlike his own creation, the Man from Underground (in
Notes from Underground) who warns the indecently inquisi-
tive reader: 'It would be better if I myself believed in anything
I had just written. I assure you most solemnly, gentlemen,
there is not a word I've just written that I believe in! What
I mean is that perhaps I do believe, but at the same time I
cannot help feeling and suspecting that for some unknown
reason I'm telling a pack of lies...' Even the relationship
between Dostoévsky and his characters is a highly peculiar
one, as though they were on the same footing with him.
Dostoévsky frequently gets lost in the interstices between
his characters. The characters seem to carry about with them
their own worlds; they could not be more unlike mouthpieces
of their author. They have as little relationship with each
other as they have with Dostoévsky; they have no access to
each other's lives, but seem to clash blindly. This state of
affairs is particularly trying for the critics since, just at the
point of coming to grips with a problem, they tend to lose
themselves in the same dilemmas as the characters.

Dostoévsky's life falls into two parts abruptly divided by
more than a decade of imprisonment, hard labour and exile.
This meant that the literary activity of these two divisions
of his life belongs almost to different ages, for a dozen years
in the middle of the last century represented in Russia a very
long time indeed. The first years of his literary activity, cut
short by his arrest in 1849 for his part in an alleged political

conspiracy, consisted of short stories, novellas, and Gogolesque
fantasies, some of which are important only in retrospect,
and few are of high intrinsic worth. His first published work
Poor Folk earned him the praise of Belínsky, and thereafter
success seemed assured. Two further important works of
this period are *White Nights, The Double*, and *Nétochka
Nezvánova*. All his major works were either conceived during
his exile, as for example *Notes from the House of the Dead*
based on his experiences as a convict, and subsequently. All
the major novels were written after his return from Siberia.
It seems likely that it was in the labour camp that he developed epilepsy of the *grand mal* type. Not long after gaining
his freedom he began to run seriously into debt, and this was
worsened by a recurrent gambling mania to which he became
prone on his trips to Europe. He was saved from ruin by his
second wife whom he met as his stenographer and who
proved to be a competent business woman. It is doubtful if
without her stabilizing influence we would have had
Dostoévsky's three last monumental novels: *The Devils, The
Raw Youth* and *The Brothers Karamazov*, which spread themselves over a period of some ten years. Dostoévsky was
seen by many as a reactionary after his return from Siberia,
and especially during the seventies when he seemed to lend
his voice to various strains of nationalist and Panslavist jingo-
ism.

Of the many facets of Dostoévsky I shall restrict myself to
three. The first is a device he took from Gógol and developed
in his own characteristic way. We have already seen that
Gógol blended fantasy and reality in a usually uncontrolled
manner. Dostoévsky perfected a *conscious* control, and by
the time of *Crime and Punishment* had learnt to produce
spectrum shifts from hallucination to reality; without, that
is, either pole – definitely real and definitely hallucinatory –
becoming entirely obliterated. This accounts for the dream-
like atmosphere which often prevails in his later novels.
Thus, for example, a character like Svidrigáylov in *Crime and
Punishment* seems to emerge—although Raskólnikov is never
quite sure about this—from Raskólnikov's dreams; so that
when Svidrigáylov eventually takes on an unmistakable flesh-

and-blood character and eventually shoots himself, we are made to sense, however obscurely, that the whole world of our perceptions is as unreal as the dreams we dream. Similar features recur in the novels which followed: *The Eternal Husband* and *The Idiot*; and the technique reaches sublime perfection in Ivan Karamázov's nightmare.

My second point has to do with the stylistics of Dostoévsky. It was a Russian critic* writing in the nineteen twenties who showed that Dostoévsky's originality lay in his ability to form 'an artistically objective conception of his characters and to project them as entirely independent entities, without having to resort to lyricism or to insert his own voice among theirs, and at the same time managing to avoid constricting them in a circumscribed psychological reality'. In other words, each character in Dostoévsky's novels inhabits his own particular world, not the author's. The interplay of these characters and their separate worlds is of a 'polyphonic' kind, more like an interweaving of independent voices than a harmonious blend; an interweaving, one might add, of an entirely unpredictable kind. Dostoévsky's novels literally generated themselves. His own contribution was to develop the range of techniques (one of which I have already discussed) which would allow his characters and situations to develop in the way they needed to develop. It is here that stylistics comes into the picture. There seem to be three interacting levels which might be termed 'levels of discourse'. The first and most immediately available of these levels is the prose surface itself, which is an amazing patchwork of ill-assorted styles. Everything on which Dostoévsky draws on the pages of his novels and which imparts various tones in different places are here combined, in the manner peculiar to him, along with newspaper journalese, anecdotes, parody, documentary, grotesquery and farce: 'He daringly tosses into his melting pot more and more new elements, knowing full well that the raw scraps of everyday reality, sensational material from cheap thrillers, and the pages of the Bible would blend and become fused into a new amalgam, bearing the unmistakable imprint of his own personal style and tone.' The second

* M. M. Bákhtin.

and even more important level has been called the workings
of 'contrapuntal inner dialogue'. Briefly, what happens is that
whenever characters in Dostoévsky meet and talk to one
another they set up a 'sympathetic response' in each other.
This response is covert, and it is for this reason that the term
'inner' dialogue has been used. It is from the mechanism of
this level of discourse that all action, all the contingency, all
the switching from reality to dream is achieved. The third and
deepest level of discourse remains unexplored. There is not a
single thought, idea, view or sentiment of Dostoévsky which
is not embedded in and intimately bound up with discourse.
The same thought in two different settings becomes two
different thoughts. In this way we are brought to a kind of
ethical and metaphysical relativity, not far different from
that preached by various thinkers in our own time. Truth
depends not upon what is said, but on who says it, how it is
said, and in what circumstances. Thus, for instance in *Crime
and Punishment* there is never any question of Raskólnikov's
powerful denial of Christian love cancelling out its validity
for Sónya, because Christian love is here two entirely different
concepts. The interesting part is not their contradiction but
their interplay at a level so deep that it escapes our notice,
but as surely as could be, in conjunction with the second
level of discourse, produces the required resolution, having
allowed Raskólnikov and Sónya to impinge upon one another.
Dostoévsky's métier was writing; it is natural then that
he should have chosen discourse – and not logic, or psychological analysis, or ethics, or some other – as his medium. In
Dostoévsky discourse maps the entire metaphysic of morals.
Ethic and aesthetic, human conduct and stylistics merge in a
layered mosaic of discourse.

My final point concerns freedom. Many theories have been
squeezed out of the pages of Dostoévsky. The temptation is
admittedly great, sometimes overwhelming. But it must be
resisted. In Dostoévsky all theories, all philosophical and
religious ideas are traps. Yet the traps are set not only for the
reader, but even for the characters themselves. Not a few have
fallen into these traps, on occasions with dire consequences. I
am not suggesting that Dostoévsky was playing practical

jokes for the fun of it; only that he wished in a sense to make his novels the *measure* both of his readers and his characters. If the reader surrenders to a particular solution of a parodox, that is no longer the author's responsibility, for we had been given enough hints that solutions were to be resisted at all costs. They are mere temptations; like the temptations of Christ in the wilderness so aptly dramatised in Ivan Karamázov's poem 'The Grand Inquisitor'. Solutions are traps. They are limiting, enslaving, and accordingly evil. This 'living with the paradox' we find best of all represented by Dimitri Karamazov. His discovery is that Beauty is so terrible because it cannot be fathomed: 'Here the boundaries meet side by side ... I can't endure the thought that a man of lofty mind and heart begins with the ideal of the Madonna and ends with the ideal of Sodom ... Yes, man is broad, too broad. Indeed, I'd have him narrower'. For Dimitri beauty embodies the ultimate paradox, for man is not capable of dividing good from evil. The choice is not given. Freedom and unfreedom are identical. Dmitri lives with his either/or.

What to say about Tolstóy? The relationship between Russian literature and Leo Tolstóy is rather like the relationship between a planet and its satellite, between Earth and Moon. The question as to whether the one could go on existing without the other is of course purely hypothetical; and it is anyone's guess what Russian literature – not to mention *world* literature – would have been like without this colossal living myth. Either one has to write a whole book about Tolstóy, or nothing. So I shall take advantage of this opinion and write nothing.

The writer most frequently paired with Dostoévsky is Leo Tolstóy (1828–1910). 'Tolstoyevskyism' came of age with Merezhkóvsky's monumental study in contrast, and the tradition is by now long established. Tolstóy and Dostoévsky were contempóraries; though in fact they never met. They both wrote very long, complex, and disconcertingly original novels, teeming with characters, sometimes preoccupied to an abnormal degree with 'the ultimate questions'. And yet, it is difficult to find two major writers so *un*-alike.

In the first place, Tolstóy was much more than a man of

letters. He was an author who had outgrown his métier; and not just any author, but universally regarded, well within his own lifetime, as the greatest of classical novelists. Tolstóy's disparagement of his own superb creations is well-known, and is not necessarily to be taken at its face value; though it did sometimes amount to self-deprecatory disgust. To his friend Stásov, an art and music critic, he described *Anna Karenina* as an 'abomination' which 'no longer exists for me, and I am only annoyed that there are people who consider this sort of thing necessary.' Gibes about the notorious 'Gospel according to Leo' can be ignored, for it has to be admitted that Tolstóy is among the great religious figures of modern times. Theological radicals like Strauss and Renan, despite their contemporary fame, seem puny by contrast; and Tolstóy surely belongs in stature rather with Newman or Kierkegaard. Long before he came to reject novel writing as an 'idle occupation depraving to the soul' Tolstóy was readily distracted by what he considered equally important preoccupations. One of his life-long consuming passions was education, especially popular education. The kernel of his conception of the school as a kind of pedagogical laboratory he derived from Rousseau. Considered cranky and wrongheaded in his own day, Tolstóy's theory and practice has in more recent times gained surprisingly wide acclaim.

Politically Dostoévsky has been generally looked upon as a reactionary. But Tolstóy could neither be described as radical nor reactionary: 'I'm not for the government and not for the revolutionists – I'm for the people!' Tolstóy rejected all government, and considered all governments equally good and equally bad. Ironically this stance made of him a formidable political force. Towards the end of his life it was said that Russia had two Tsars: Nicholas II and Leo Tolstóy. 'To protest in Russia is impossible' Tolstóy knew this from bitter experience. Like Solzhenítsyn today, Tolstóy had become a living protest, too well-known and too much admired in every part of the world to be silenced by any official means. The Holy Synod the secular governing authority of the Russian Orthodox Church only made of itself a laughing-stock by having Tolstóy excommunicated. Even the rumours deliberately spread around among the peasantry that Tolstóy was the latest incarnation of Antichrist did little to counteract the affection and respect of countryfolk who actually came in any sort of contact with him credulous though they were. Police surveillance was the rule, and nothing new. Armed guards were placed on his estate at Yásnaya Polyána at the slightest pretext.

Despite the great significance that had accrued to him – and not only as a novelist – he never rated himself too highly. Indeed he considered there was no justification of any kind for 'great men' as institutionalised targets of reverence. Running right the way through *War and Peace* is the view that even Napoleon was of no greater significance than the ordinary soldier. Throughout his campaigns Napoleon had merely 'acted like a child who, holding a couple of strings inside a carriage, thinks he is driving it.' In the Second Epilogue to *War and Peace* – which so many readers skip – Tolstóy argues: 'So long as histories are written of separate individuals, whether Caesars, Alexanders, Luthers, or Voltaires, and not the histories of *all*, absolutely *all*, those who take part in an event, it is quite impossible to describe the movement of humanity without the conception of a force compelling men to direct their activity towards a certain end.' But power is a word the meaning of which we do not understand; and to associate it with great men and military leaders is simply the historian's easy way out: 'The movement of nations is caused not by power, nor by intellectual activity, nor even by a combination of the two as historians have supposed, but by the activity of *all* the people who participate in the events, and who always combined in such a way that those taking the largest direct share in the event take on themselves the least responsibility and vice versa.' This latter point is worth noting, in that it relates to Tolstóy's overall social philosophy, which is concerned with the *real*, *true* order of society, as opposed to the superstition and prejudices of the economically developed world, the world of 'progress', which has got everything the wrong way round, and where so-called order is unnatural and immoral. Tolstóy's philosophy of history has sometimes been compared to that of Marx; but, as Tolstóy could see, Marx and the rest of the theologians, sociologists, philosophers and historians were merely cloaking themselves as scientists in order to prove that the existing order of things is

the one that ought to exist (*Modern Science*). Tolstóy's theory
of history, if it is to be properly understood, must be placed
within the context of his unending search for real moral truth,
as opposed to the lesser truths of positivist science and sociology. In his essay on Tolstóy's view of history* Sir Isaiah
Berlin has reminded us that 'Tolstóy's philosophy of history has,
on the whole, not obtained the attention which it deserves . . .
Those who have treated Tolstóy primarily as a novelist have at
times looked upon the historical and philosophical passages
scattered through *War and Peace* as so much perverse interruption of the narrative, as a regrettable liability to irrelevant
digression characteristic of this great, but extremely opinion-
ated, writer . . .'

Tolstóy was opposed to almost everything that the Western
world of progress had to offer. He was anti-culture ('that most
terrible of words'), and anti-science ('in a few centuries hence
the scientific activity of our own time will furnish an inextin-
guishable fund of mirth and pity to future generations'). Indeed
there was very little Tolstóy was not 'anti'. His views on
art are widely known. The art of nearly all his contemporaries
he dismissed as counterfeit art. And with no less aplomb than
Voltaire's Pococurante he scathingly dismisses venerated figures
of the past. He considered that Shakespeare especially was rated
in inverse proportion to his worth. Art had become either a
means of trying to meet the insatiable needs of the moneyed
consumer, or else had gained a strange mass-hypnotic sway over
a herd-like public unable to discriminate between the genuine
and the false. Whereas real artistic activity is that which brings
dimly-perceived feelings or thoughts to such great awareness
that these feelings are transmitted to other people (*On Art*).
Thus, to become an artist one need not, according to Tolstóy,
be highly cultivated, highly skilled, or unusually sensitive and
refined; one need not be a 'genius'. Art is a communal affair,
arising at all times and all places in many different forms. It is
the means of achieving union among men, joining them
together in the same feelings: 'We are accustomed to understand art to be only what we hear and see in theatres, concerts,

* Berlin, Sir Isaiah, *The Hedgehog and the Fox*, London, 1953.

and exhibitions; together with buildings, statues, poems, and novels . . . But all this is but the smallest part of the art by which we communicate with one another in life. All human life is filled with works of art of every kind – from cradle song, jest, mimicry, the ornamentation of houses, dress and utensils, to church services, buildings, monuments, and triumphal processions. It is all artistic activity.' (*What is Art?*)

Tolstóy was undeniably a supporter of cranky lost causes; not least of which was Henry George. But he was no less deadly a devil's advocate than either Voltaire or Shaw. The difference was only that his 'advocacy' usually seemed to be in dead earnest. Above all he was a practical man, and whatever he set out to do he usually accomplished exceedingly well. His experimental village school at Yásnaya Polyána, started in 1859, was both well-run and a success. Three years later there were as many as thirteen such schools in the vicinity. As a landowner he was hard-headed, down-to-earth, and more than averagely successful. We get many a glimpse of the embattled but thriving gentleman-farmer through his early piece *The Landlord's Morning*, as well as much later in *Anna Karenina*. In later life he abandoned established political economy. His views, which give pride of place to the labourer, are well in advance of his own time. Among his most outstanding achievements in the practical realm are the virtually single-handed relief campaign which he himself organised and directed on the spot in the worst stricken areas during the great famine of 1891–2. The famine was being kept a kind of state secret, and the public was slow in responding to appeals from Tolstóy. The government complained that he was exaggerating the seriousness of the situation. As it happens, Tolstóy's fund-raising campaign was barely in the nick of time to prevent a calamity which might have been without precedent even in Russia. His other successful campaign was that waged on behalf of the Doukhobórs*, a religious community and sect holding views not unlike his own. As a result of Tolstóy's and his Quaker fellow-campaigners' efforts treatment of the Doukhobórs became less harsh; and eventually

* See the recently published *The Doukhobors* by G. Woodcock and I. Avakumovich, London, 1968.

permission was secured to allow them to emigrate en masse, first
to Cyprus, and then to Canada. What Tolstóy wrote about John
Ruskin (in 1892) applies with equal justification to himself : 'He
is one of the most remarkable men not only in [Russia] and of
our generation, but all countries and times. He is one of those
rare men who think with their hearts; and so he thinks and says
what he has himself seen and felt, and what everyone will think
and say in the future' (An Introduction to Ruskin's Works).

In Russia Tolstóy became the exception to every norm, the
towering alarming misfit. He was too unorthodox to be accept-
able to the intelligentsia, radical and critical though they were.
Conformity was not in Tolstoy's line, and the ideological sym-
metry of the intelligentsia could not accommodate him. But his
influence was felt all right; massive and amorphous like the
Russian peasant folk whose advocate he believed he was. How
could the respectable radicals do otherwise than shun anyone
capable even of thinking, let alone. writing in this vein : 'I
myself belong to the highest order of society and like it. I am
not a bourgeois ... And I say boldly that I am an aristocrat by
birth, by habits and position ... I am an aristocrat because I
cannot believe in the loftiness of intellect, refined taste or in the
absolute honesty of a man who is capable of picking his nose
and at the same time holding converse with God.'* And yet,
Tolstóy held such radical and farseeing views on many issues
that there was hardly a Russian thinker to compare with him.
Lenin's land policy – summed up in the slogan 'All land to the
people' – adopted only late in his career, was not more-radical
than Tolstóy's. If private land had been abolished and land
nationalisation introduced when according to Tolstóy it should
have been, the unrest of 1905 and the later Revolution and Civil
War might have been avoided. The last thing the peasants
needed was 'radicalising'; what they needed was land. For the
rest they could fend for themselves, and far more successfully,
in Tolstóy's opinion and experience, than their city-dwelling
champions.

Whenever writers or publicists referred to Tolstóy they

---

* Appearing in the early drafts of War and Peace, Soviet Jubilee
Edition, Polnoye Sobranie Sochinenii, 1925–1958, Vol. xiii, p. 238.

generally adopted an awkward tone and manner. Even
Turgénev, who had come to know Tolstóy intimately during
their long and turbulent relationship, sounds slightly ridiculous
when in a letter to Tolstóy from his death-bed he writes: 'I am
writing to you particularly to tell how glad I am to have been
your contemporary.'
In the very next sentence Turgénev pleads with him to
'return to literary activity.' We know very well what Turgénev
meant, but it is a very odd thing to say when Tolstóy went on
being the most prolific of Russian writers by a long chalk. The
Soviet Jubilee Edition of his writings runs to fifty volumes. And
we have to look abroad for comparisons: Carlyle, Emerson,
Ruskin, and so forth. The spectrum of what Turgénev meant by
'literary activity' Tolstóy considered too narrow. He did not
draw the normal boundary between literature as belles lettres
and the other sorts of writing he produced. He devoted as much
care to his children's ABC as he did to many a novel of his. The
period during which he was thought to have (and Turgénev
supposed he had) given up 'literary activity' – the period following upon his crisis, an account of which occurs in his *Confession*
– produced some of his best writing. *The Death of Ivan Ilych*
(1886) is as perfect as anything in *Anna Karenina*, and *The
Kreutzer Sonata* (1889), even if it moralizes too much for everyone's taste, remains a work of crushing power. Even lesser
known pieces like *Master and Man* (1893) reveal an even
greater degree of technical accomplishment in dealing with
descriptions similar to ones occurring in his early story *The
Snow Storm*. His last full-length novel *Resurrection* completed
in 1899 – and one of the works of Tolstóy the critics sometimes
make apologies for – contains some of his best writing. The
truth of the matter is that Tolstóy had long outgrown the
literary conventions of the novel. He had never really sub-
scribed to them even, and it is this that men like Turgénev failed
to grasp. Tolstóy had not wanted *War and Peace* to be labelled a
novel, and he once declared that 'every great artist is bound to
create his own form.' 'From Gógol's *Dead Souls* to Dostoévsky's
House of the Dead there is not a single prose work rising at all
above mediocrity in the recent period of Russian literature
which quite fits into the form of a novel, a poem, or a story.'

But if *War and Peace* is not a novel, then what is it? Here is one answer: 'If there are any rules to which an author must conform if his work is to be assigned to a recognisable genre, Tolstóy did not know them and did not care. We can only say that *War and Peace* marks a new stage in the history of the Western European novel because of its concern with historical, social, ethical and religious problems on a scale never attempted in any previous novel.'* In spite of his admiration for Dickens, Thackeray, or Stendhal, Tolstóy did not dare to emulate them. And the territory he was marking out in *War and Peace* was going to be developed not only by Tolstóy but by many a later European novelist.

It makes no difference how determined we are to categorise, to bring within manageable limits this Russian phenomenon Tolstóy, our efforts will never bring more than the most meagre reward. Nevertheless, it has not gone unnoticed that, in outlook at any rate, Tolstóy is very much a man of the eighteenth century. In his attitude to art, science, morals, and life in general, reason plays a very great part. Reason, Tolstóy was convinced, is the one thing we are sure of; it is the law by which life is accomplished. This is the Reason of Descartes, Hume, or Kant, a specifically *human* law for *human* beings, with its own limits which in themselves prescribe and define human goals and purpose. This is Levin's conclusion (*Anna Karenina*); it is better, he decides, not to try to probe into the beyond. The snow-storm is a recurring metaphor in Tolstóy, as in Russian literature as a whole. In his later writings Tolstóy turns metaphor into parable: 'We are lost in a snow-storm. A man assures us, and he believes, that there are lights over there and a village, but it only seems so to him and to us because we wish it were so. We have walked towards those lights, and found none. Another man has walked through the snow, he has reached the road and he shouts to us: "You will get nowhere, the lights are in your own eyes, you will go astray and perish. But here is the hard road; I am on it, it will keep us right." That is very little . . . But if we listen to the first man we shall certainly perish, and if we listen to the second we shall certainly reach our destination.'

* Christian, R. F., *Tolstoy's War and Peace*, London, 1962, p. 121.

(*What I Believe*).

But then comes the twist in the tale, because Tolstóy then goes on to claim that reason is preserved intact only by the working man; whereas an individual who has all his life occupied his mind not merely with insignificant and futile matters but also with things such as it is not natural for man to think about – a positivistic scientist, or a consumer-created artist, for example – has not a free mind, and is a slave to un-reason. Even Tolstóy's Christ, as he appears in the *Gospel in Brief*, is a Christ of Reason. He is no miracle-performer or Redeemer, but a man with 'a clear, profound and simple ex-planation of life, which corresponds to the highest need of the human soul.' Tolstóy does not deny the divinity of Christ, as some might suppose. On the contrary, Christ is the 'Son of the Father', the significance of this relation being that he is the bearer of truth, showing men how they must live, and how they must die – and in particular showing Tolstóy the way out of his own suicidal impasse – how to choose and find immortal life, though never beyond the bounds of what is dictated by reason. Like men of the eighteenth century Tolstóy had no room for 'the madness of the Cross'*. Tolstóy was ready to accept any religious faith so long as it did not demand of him a direct denial of reason. For him everything inexplicable had to be *necessarily* inexplicable, and not something that he was under an arbitrary obligation to believe.

Even Tolstóy's literary style is reminiscent of the eighteenth century. His prose is always firm as well as limpid, like that of Gibbon or Voltaire. It has no fat on it. Púshkin was the model, and not those contemporaries he otherwise admired far more. One special characteristic of Tolstóy is his method of satire, which has also been compared to that of Swift**. Tolstóy's particular method is that of 'making things strange' (*ostra-néniye*). By this device he manages to avoid calling things by name, and instead describes them as if they were being seen for the very first time. Sometimes this satire does not go beyond mischievous caricature, as when Natásha (*War and Peace*)

---

* See Foucault, Michel, *Madness and Civilisation*, London, 1967.
** Bayley, J., *Tolstoy and the Novel*, London, 1966, pp. 103–4.

observes what is taking place on the stage during an operatic performance: 'The floor of the stage consisted of smooth boards, at the sides of which were some painted cardboard representing trees, and at the back was a cloth stretched over the boards. In the centre of the stage sat some girls in red bodices and white skirts. One very fat girl in a white silk dress sat apart on a low bench, to the back of which a piece of green cardboard was glued. They all sang something. When they had finished their song the girl in white went up to the prompter's box, and a man with tight silk trousers over his stout legs, and holding a plume and a dagger, went up to her and began singing, waving his arms about . . .' Young Natásha has lived all her life in the country, and the spectacle is genuinely strange to her. The pastiche then does not infringe plausibility. But when the same device is used to show up *King Lear* as a bad play, we may not take kindly to the deception. The opera parody Tolstóy does yet again, with Wagner this time, (in *What is Art?*) and once more we can enter the spirit of the caricature or reject it as vulgarity, depending on whether or not we are fervent admirers of the Ring cycle. The Russian critic Viktor Shklóvsky has pointed out that all the battle scenes in *War and Peace* are presented by this method of making things seem strange. It must be admitted that the use of this device to present the battle of Borodinó through the uncomprehending and distracted eyes of Pierre Bezúkhov is a supreme vindication of it. Pierre wanders aimlessly about the battlefield looking for a battle which he never quite seems able to find; just as Natásha could see the boards, the backcloth, and people, but no opera. Instead of finding what he was looking for – the event historians have named the battle of Borodinó – Bezúkhov finds only the ordinary confusion of individual humdrum human beings.

But when we turn to Tolstóy the man we no longer find the poise and self-assurance of the eighteenth century. There is as much confusion as in Pierre's battle of Borodinó, but now it is within the soul of a tormented and anguished human being. Tolstóy made no secret of it. In his *Confession* though there is none of the humbug we find in Rousseau's. Tolstóy is as alienated a figure as any in his own nineteenth century, and he lays himself bare with unremitting honesty. The solipsism of youth has not dispersed with maturity. After his 'crisis' it merely assumes more obstinate and perverse forms. In his early quasi-autobiographical *Boyhood* Tolstóy writes: 'I imagined that, besides myself, no one and nothing exists anywhere, that objects are not objects, and images appear only when I turn my attention towards them, and that as soon as I stop thinking about them they vanish completely ... Asking myself about what I am thinking, I replied: I am thinking about what I am thinking. And what am I thinking about right now? I am thinking that I am thinking about what I am thinking, and so on ...' Very many years later we find the following remark in his diary (January 3 1890): 'I read that they told Emerson that the world would soon end. Emerson answered: "Well, I can get along without it". Very important!' Tolstóy in his old age has long outgrown the skin-deep solipsism of his youth, and he is now taken up with his real self, the one that has been 'dead' in the Christian sense, and is now alive and ready to merge with the Whole; but it is the very self that, despite his genuine concern for his wife's despair, he cannot and will not put back into the chrysalis from which it has emerged. The definition of religion Tolstóy gives in *Religion and Morality* (1894) is tailor-made to his own situation: 'Religion is a relation man sets up between himself and the endless and infinite universe, or its source and first cause.' Pascal's 'wager' is as if translated into Schopenhauerian renunciation: 'I know that my life, aiming at personal solitary happiness, is the greatest absurdity, and that at the end of this stupid life there is inevitably nothing but a stupid death. Therefore things cannot be at all terrible for me. I shall die like everyone else, like those who do not fulfil the teaching [of Christ]; but both for me and for all, my life and death will have a meaning. My life and death will serve the salvation and life of all, and that is what Christ taught' (*What I believe*).

But resignation did not go with Tolstóy's temperament. More than any of the Russians perhaps, he was restless, cross-grained, seldom in equilibrium. Even as he lay dying in the station-master's house at Astapóvo, he was heard to say: 'To seek, always to seek.' In his earlier days he could poke fun at himself in the person of Levin. He stands in sharp contrast to his boy-hood friend Stiva, who is always predictably the same, and who accepts that Levin is everlastingly in and out of one 'phase' after another, and teases him about it. But Levin is too baffled by his own changeability to be really amused. His nature constantly throws up to the surface the unexpected, volcano-like. In the closing pages of *Anna Karenina*, the sensation becomes over-powering: 'Obscure, but significant thoughts as in a swarm burst out from somewhere, from behind locked doors and, all heading towards one single goal, whirled inside his head, blind-ing him with their light.' In the *Confession*, written not long afterwards, we find Tolstóy frantically throwing up his own barricades against doubt and inner contradiction, against which all art, philosophy, established religion, and faith in ideals had been powerless. His determination, renewed time and time again during the last thirty years of his long life, to 'live the real living life' sounds more like a challenge than a resolution. Perhaps there was more than a shade of Anna's 'Vengeance is mine: I will repay' in Tolstóy himself, even in his most serene and saintly moments.

In important ways nevertheless, Tolstóy belongs to our own time. He anticipates mid-twentieth century thinking in a number of respects. Many a modern investigator would approve of his tenet that it is expedient to use in different situations or contexts the methods that fit it best. 'We are what we are, and live in a given situation which has the characteristics – physical, psychological, social, etc. – that it has; what we think, feel, do, is conditioned by it, including our capacity for conceiving pos-sible alternatives, whether in the present or future or past.'* Though the peasant speech of Platón Karatáev (*War and Peace*) is culled largely from the Russian lexicographer and folklorist Dal, Tolstóy's way of conceiving Karatáev's speech and action anticipates modern anthropology: 'Every word and action of his was the manifestation of an activity unknown to him, which was his life. But his life, as he regarded it, had no meaning as a separate thing. It had meaning only as part of a whole of which he was always conscious. His words and actions flowed from him as evenly, inevitably, and spontaneously as fragrance exhales from a flower. He could not understand the value or

* Berlin, Sir Isaiah, *The Hedgehog and the Fox*, p. 73.

significance of any word or deed taken separately.'

Yet these are mere incidentals compared with Tolstóy's major 'modern' discovery: the Third World. By this I do not of course mean that Tolstóy was the first to grasp the real essence and evils of colonialism, for this awareness antedates even Marx. But, before Tolstóy, it had been too easy to point the finger at greedy plantation owners, slave traders or bungling administrators; or, failing that, to the abstract workings of the laws of economics. But in his article on the Russian Famine in 1891–2 Tolstóy writes: 'We Russians are especially well situated for seeing our position clearly. I remember, long before these famine years, how a young and morally sensitive savant from Prague who visited me in the country in winter – on coming out of the hut of a comparatively well-to-do peasant . . . in which, as everywhere, there was an overworked, prematurely aged woman in rags, a sick child who had ruptured itself screaming, and, as everywhere in spring, a tethered calf and a ewe that had just lambed, and dirt and damp, and foul air, and a dejected, careworn peasant – I remember how, on coming out of the hut, my young acquaintance began to say something to me, when suddenly his voice broke and he wept. For the first time, after some months spent in Moscow and Petersburg – where he had walked along asphalted pavements, past luxurious shops, from one rich house to another, and from one rich museum, library, or palace to other similarly grand buildings – he saw for the first time those whose labour supplies all that luxury, and he was amazed and horrified. To him, in rich and educated Bohemia . . . it might seem (though incorrectly) that where comparative liberty exists – where education is general, where everyone has the chance of entering the ranks of the educated – luxury is a legitimate reward of labour and does not destroy human life. He might manage to forget the successive generations of men who mine the coal by the use of which most of the articles of our luxury are produced, he might forget – since they are out of sight – the men of other races in the colonies, who die off working to satisfy our whims; but we Russians cannot share such thoughts: the connexion between our luxury and the sufferings and deprivations of men of the same race as ourselves is too evident. We cannot avoid seeing the price paid in human lives for our comfort and our luxury.' (*Afterword to an Account of Relief to the Famine-stricken in the Government of Tula in 1891 and 1892*). The Third World is on Russia's doorstep. The 'developed' world, to which Tolstóy, his Prague friend, and many people today, particularly in the West, belong, is a parasitic world, living off the backs of numberless wretched peasants and urban slum-dwellers in every part of Asia, Africa and Latin America. Only in the past couple of decades have 'comfortable Europeans' been weaned from the 'pastoral' of quaint, colourful colonial peoples, and instead become grimly familiar with what Tolstóy had long known: 'If this year we do not hear of want, cold, and hunger ... this is not because these things will not occur, but only because we shall not see them – shall forget about them, shall assure ourselves that they do not exist, or that if they do they are inevitable and cannot be helped.' It was this side of Tolstóy which appealed so directly to figures like Gandhi, who found that they shared so many of his views and so much of his experience.

But Tolstóy is not of any particular epoch. He is a man for all time. His search for a moral, social and religious set of truths which are beyond the reach of modern science and 'men of culture' – and only to a limited extent within Tolstóy's own reach – is a search that is both timelessly ancient and disturbingly 'advanced', and yet these truths lie within easy grasp of the simplest and least sophisticated of ordinary men. But, like a tree, mankind needs room for its spreading roots and branches, and Tolstóy believed that the time has come for men to realise that they have once and for all outgrown the social and governmental stages of history, and are ready for true creative anarchy. State, class, money, laws, and social mores are the last superstitions to be overcome by mankind.

To sketch in the closing decades of the nineteenth century in two or three pages is no easy matter; minor writers proliferate, and there are several major ones. My selection of three – Leskóv, Chékhov, and Górky – is based partly on there being none greater than them, but also partly on the availability of good translations. There are two writers nevertheless who should be mentioned in passing: Mikhaíl Saltykóv-Shchedrín (1826–89) a biting satirist, a 'Russian Swift', and one of the few important writers to emerge from the hard core of the radical intelligentsia; and secondly Vsévolod Gárshin (1855–88) a psychologist and highly-strung writer with a subtlety equal in many respects to that of Dostoévsky. It is to be hoped that more and better translations of both these writers, especially Gárshin, will become available before long.

Little appreciated and little known in his own lifetime Nikolái Leskóv (1831–95) has since become one of Russia's classics. Not only that, his influence on generation upon generation of Russian writers has been enormous, and shows no signs of diminishing.

Leskóv is different from all the other foremost writers of his time. In the first place, he was the first important prose writer of lower class origin. He grew up amongst traders, minor officials, priests, business people; and until well on in life these were the only people he knew. His schooling had been cut short by a sudden set-back in the family fortunes, and for many years Leskóv earned his living variously as a civil servant, salesman, business agent, and later, working for his English uncle (a man named Scott, who exerted a powerful influence on Leskóv as a young man), as estate-manager, and supervisor oñ a stud farm, during which time he travelled the length and breadth of Russia, mixing with people of every conceivable walk of life. 'I know Russia like the back of my hand,' he used to say. 'I didn't have to study the ordinary people from conversations with Petersburg cab-drivers; I grew up *in their midst*.' Leskóv knew the mentality and way of life of the Russian man-in-the-street from the inside. Returning to Tolstóy or Turgénev after reading Leskóv is I think a salutory experience, for it makes one realize that the intelligentsia, however highly perspicacious and however deep their understanding, were little better than tourists in a foreign country.

In many ways Leskóv resembles the new-style American writer of that time. But, whilst Leskóv's material is closer to that of Bret Harte or Jack London, his manner and style remind

me most of all of Mark Twain. There are several curious
parallels. Leskóv and Mark Twain had not only knocked about
a great deal, but they had both actually worked on river boats;
both started out as writers from journalism; both were adepts
at the tall story; and both were fine *recorders*, and not just
acute observers, of the inflections and individual variations in
ordinary speech. Because of this, Leskóv is so difficult to translate: his language teems with colloquialisms, puns, slang, his
own coinages and he has his own special narrative diction
in the bargain – 'This popular, vulgar speech in which many
of my pages is written is not of my invention; I heard it from
peasants, from semi-illiterate people, from windbags, from
half-wits and half-saints. For many years I collected words, expressions, sayings, picking them up in the street, in recruiting
offices, in monasteries.' But none of his craft is haphazard.
On the contrary, Leskóv worked over every phrase and snatch
of dialogue with the minutest care; and he would have agreed
with Mark Twain: 'The difference between the *right* word
and *almost* the right word is the difference between the lightning and the lightning bug.' But Leskóv, who only became a
writer 'by chance' (although with not a little encouragement
from uncle Scott), was opposed to literature as belles lettres;
for him literature was something 'from which we all suffer
directly or indirectly'. Letting pass the many opportunities to
associate himself with the various literary coteries, Leskóv
resolved to remain a lone wolf, and to get on obscurely, if
passionately, with what he thought himself best cut out for
– 'I am merely a crossings sweeper, and I am going to stick
to my broom.'

Leskóv's lack of success in his own time is mainly due
to his falling foul of the critics quite early on. Belínsky was
long since dead, Hérzen was too far away in London,
and literature was now under the dictatorship of the day led
by Písarev, too blind and too philistine to comprehend that
Leskóv's early novels, just because they were not committed to
any particular political view, were not for that reason simply
all-out attacks on the radicals. Leskóv paid the due penalty
however, and for the rest of his life was branded a reactionary

and forced to publish in all kinds of obscure corners, in children's and religious magazines, even in naval supplements.

A prolific writer, Leskóv's works run to a thirty-five volume edition. His earliest work *The Musk Ox* (1862) is also one of his best. The 'Musk Ox' is an outsider in a specially impenetrable Russian kind of way who had drifted by chance in and out of the author's life over a period: 'He never showed any of us that he was fond of anyone; but we were all perfectly aware that there was no limit to what he would do for the sake of every one of his friends and acquaintances. His readiness to sacrifice himself in the cause of his chosen ideal no one ever thought of doubting, but it was not easy to discover this ideal beneath the skull of the Musk-Ox.' 'What will you have me do?' he complains, 'My heart cannot stand this civilization, this nobilization, this scoundrelization!' Another time he tells them: 'No, it's you who get everything involved. With me, brother, everything is straightforward, peasant-like . . . You can't see beyond your aristocratic noses and you never will.' The 'Musk Ox' ends up by hanging himself. Leskóv's second major story *Lady Macbeth of Mtsensk* (1865), one of his best known in the west, partly because it became the libretto for a Shostakovich opera, is powerful and gruesome enough, perhaps a little overdone, and not typical of Leskóv's later work. The greater part of the first ten years of Leskóv's literary activity though was taken up by novels, the only important one of which is *Cathedral Folk* (1872) which contains some of Leskóv's most outstanding as well as least translatable prose, as well as some vivid characterizations of an archpriest Tuberósov and his deacon Akhilla. The Russian Orthodox Church was little more than a Department of State, and Leskóv set out to depict a clash between a truly saintly man, with all the human weaknesses, much loved by his people, and officialdom with all its machinery of agents provocateurs and intrigue. Tuberósov is a grass-roots, saint, a latter day Avvakum, who reads Bunyan, and is prepared to forego all rather than the fundamental Christian principles and laws. Finding as he grows older that 'the saddest side of life is its increasing shallowness', he writes in his diary: 'I have become shallower and shallower in every way until I have reached such a degree of shallowness that I am not even able to confide my vanity to dumb paper. He discovers however not long before his end that only then was he beginning to live the true life. *Cathedral Folk* is packed with humour and with striking characters, including an opportunist and ex-nihilist official who is remarkably like Pyotr Verkhovénsky in Dostoévsky's *The Devils*, a novel which appeared about the same time.

One of Leskóv's favourite genres was what he called 'drama-comedy of everyday life'. Some of his pieces in this vein are more comic than tragic, others more tragic than comic, and others leave us completely non-plussed. To the first group belongs *Iron Will*, in my opinion one of the funniest stories ever written. This is the story of an acute case of German pig-headedness. An engineer who has been brought to Russia to instal some plant, finally settles there and builds up a thriving business, but ruins first his reputation and then himself by his inflexible determination to carry out the dictates of his own will at all costs. There is little point in my trying to convey Leskóv's perfect grasp of character and situation, German and Russian, and can only recommend my reader to read it for himself. The third group includes *The Stinger*, which is about an efficient, understanding, liberal Englishman, called Dane, an estate-manager who has become the 'big noise' of the neighbourhood – 'he'd found employment even for the out-and-out thieves . . . and that wasn't all: he'd made supervisors of the most prominent ne'er-do-wells; while as for thieves who had several prison sentences behind them – why, he made them stewards and shopkeepers and accountants, and everything seemed to go like clockwork . . .' The trouble was that Dane's ways were far too different from the harsh repression to which the peasants had been hitherto accustomed. It wasn't simply that he treated them too well, but his punishments were so much like games that the peasants felt humiliated – 'the peasants somehow couldn't digest him'. Finally there was a mutiny during which the premises were burnt down. Even though the peasants were offered an amnesty if they asked Dane's forgiveness – a remarkably generous gesture in those times – the peasants decided to take the full and brutal consequences instead. 'Think: Half of you will be deported' says the narrator mediating on their behalf. 'No – no! We can't live with him,' they reply. 'We've nowhere to put the hell-hound.' 'But why is he hell-hound?' 'Well, what else is he? Tying a man to a thread, as though he were a sparrow ... We're prepared to beg his pardon.' 'And will you take back the manager?' 'No – we can't do that.' 'But why can't you?' 'He's a stinger.' With episodes like this Leskóv was able to throw into relief the alien and opaque nature of the Russian peasant, a creature that the 'going-to-the-people' Populists were worlds away from understanding.

Sometimes Leskóv's tales are of a legendary kind, again often brimming with humour. His *Left-handed Craftsman* is among the highlights of apocryphal literature. The story starts with the visit of Alexander I to England, when he is presented with a microscopic metal clockwork flea as a mark of British craftsmanship. Alexander's successor Nicholas I being more nationalistically inclined, was anxious to find out if his subjects could go one better. So, some craftsmen from Tula are commissioned to investigate this technical wonder. After much concerted labour the Tula craftsmen announce that their task is completed, and the Tsar eventually discovers that they have managed – although, mind, the flea can no longer dance – to shoe the flea. The left-handed craftsman who brought the modified flea to the Tsar is promptly sent to England, amazes everyone ('Our studies are really quite a simple matter,' says the craftsman, 'we know our psalm book and the *Book of Half-Dreams*, but we don't know much arithmetic'.) and is offered rewards to tempt him to stay. But the pull of Mother Russia is too great. The left-handed craftsman returns home only to be beaten up by the police on arrival for not having a passport, and is after much ill-treatment and pushing around left half dead in the corridor of a Poor House. He is rescued by his companion, an English sailor, who luckily finds him in time. Apart from the humour, there is a powerful charge of satire which is not only right on the mark but in its own way is curiously prophetic of Russia's future.

The genre which is virtually Leskóv's own creation is known as the *skaz*. The *skaz* is a narrative told by a fictitious

narrator rather than the author directly. It is essential that
the narrator is a very ordinary person, for in this way
speech forms can be used which are more original and vivid
than the style of ordinary creative narrative, told from the
author's point of view. One of Leskóv's masterpieces in this
genre is The Enchanted Wanderer which is a semi-tall story,
blending realism and fantasy in a manner peculiar to its
author. The narrator is also a larger than life picaresque figure,
a latter-day Ilyá Murométs. With no political or moral axes
to grind, but with the comic irony of Candide, and rather
far more subtlety, Leskóv manages to upset batteries of pre-
conceptions. Far-fetched as the wanderer's exploits are, they
never lose the ring of truth, and it is this that gives them
their legendary, human, and comic value rolled into one.

I am concluding this sketch with the oft quoted remark of
Górky's: 'Each of Leskóv's heroes is but a link in the chain of
men, in the chain of generations. One feels that in each of
his tales he was mainly preoccupied with the destiny of the
whole of Russia rather than with that of any one individual
... He is one of the foremost Russian writers – and his work
took in the whole of Russia.' If the reader is already familiar
with Leskóv, my own remarks will have been superfluous.
If not, I can only recommend that he read the tales (some of
them excellently translated) without more ado.

The critics have sometimes been hard put to it to isolate
precisely those features which actually make Anton Chékhov
(1860–1904) such a great writer. Perhaps this is to be ascribed
above all to Chékhov's style, which seems so exactly to fit
the subject-matter that it eludes analysis. Chékhov himself
believed that the only important thing about writing is that it
should be clear, such that that its meaning can be grasped at
once. He was convinced too that his knowledge of the natural
sciences, medicine in particular, had saved him from the
pretentiousness many writers sometimes fall victim to: 'I have
no doubt at all that the study of medicine has had an important influence on my literary work; it has considerably en-
larged my own powers of observation, has enriched me with
knowledge whose true value for me as a writer can only be
understood by one who is himself a doctor. It has also been

my guiding influence. It is probably due to my close association with medicine that I have succeeded in avoiding many
mistakes. Familiarity with the natural sciences has always
kept me on my guard, and I have always tried, where it was
possible, to be consistent with the facts of science, and where
it was impossible I have preferred not to write at all ... To
the category of those who rush into everything with only
their imagination to go on I would not like to belong.'

It has sometimes been observed that, although Chékhov's
people and situations seem real enough and as unique as
anything in life, we are left with an impression of sameness
after reading several stories in succession. To my mind this is
due in the main to Chékhov's dominant concern with what
I would call an 'increase in entropy' in human affairs and
relationships; in other words, the latter's increasing disorgan-
ization and irreversibility with the passage of time. This
quality has sometimes been labelled gloom and despair; at
other times sardonic irony. Chékhov thought of it simply as
comedy. 'Increase of entropy' may not be a magic key to an
understanding of Chékhov as a whole, but it does account
for more than a little. I propose to take two motifs and
to examine them in the light of it.

The first of these motifs is *love.* Above all else Chékhov
was the interpreter of love in its many different manifestations, and particularly of its disintegration and hopelessness.
So important was this ingredient that Chékhov confessed himself bored when writing a story with no female character in
it. Chékhov's own peculair insight into its hazardousness might
have had something to do with his putting off his marriage
till late in life, until he could be as near as certain that the
relationship was the right one—'To marry is interesting only
when one is in love; to marry a girl simply because she attracts
you is like buying something unnecessary at a bazaar merely
because it happens to be nice. The most important thing in
marriage is love, sexual attraction, being of one flesh—all the
rest is unreliable and dreary, no matter how cleverly one may
have calculated.'

The short stories are nearly all 'comedies' of human love,
all touched in a different way by pathos. In none of them

is there any real hope for human love which like every other mortal phenomenon is doomed to change and decay. In *The Darling* we find love at its most contingent. Olga, a quiet, good-natured girl, with gentle, soft eyes, whom everyone calls the 'darling', lives only for the one she loves. Life has no meaning for her beyond the lives of her husbands. Her first husband had been an entertainer, so all she could think about then was show business. Her second husband was a timber merchant; 'if he thought the room was too hot or business slack, she thought so too.' Without someone to love she had no opinions of any kind. Her mind and spirit became a vacuum. When sharing the life of a man 'Olga could have explained everything and would have expressed an opinion about anything you like, but there was the same emptiness now in her thoughts and in her heart as in her backyard'. Her affections finally found an outlet in a typically self-centred schoolboy. Even though this was to be the last, pitiful and least promising of her loves it did something to restore her love-bound sense of identity.

A different kind of contingent loving is feigned love. A type for whom this kind of loving has meaning is to be found in *Ariadne*. Ariadne is a sensualist, and like all sensualists she is frigid. The prognosis in this particular instance is none too good as her lover happens to be an idealist. He regards sensuality as ridiculous and revolting, as he believes most Russians do, and regards women as creatures of poetic beauty. Ariadne has all the refined sensuality of a whore, but her allurements are transparent, and her lover finds her cold: 'When she spoke to me of love I seemed to be listening to the singing of a nightingale made of metal.' The only man who could find happiness with her is one who would accept her as she is. The blame for the unhappiness in this case lies with neither party, but with the futility of human relationships, their being doomed to failure from the start. The enticing missed opportunity is yet another variation on the same theme. In a story *On Love* the narrator had been friends for years with the attractive young wife of an official, and they were often seen in public together. They are both afraid of love, the man more than the woman. Love spells danger, unknown possibilities. The man is sure that in this instance it has to be fought against at all costs – 'It would have been a different matter if I had had a splendid, interesting life, if I had fought for the liberation of my country, for example, or been a famous scholar, actor or artist, but this would have meant luring her away from one set of ordinary, everyday surroundings to another set just as commonplace, and perhaps even more so. And how long could our happiness have lasted?...' Chékhov lets us feel that this decision was the right one. Their pent-up love can find its moment only when Anna is safely aboard a train bound for the coast where she is to start treatment for tuberculosis, in those days the symbol of an inevitable rapid end. He is being insincere when he protests that the obstacles had been illusory and admits to having been a coward before; otherwise he would now have gone with her.

The one love relationship in Chékhov of any permanence is one that begins with a casual flirtation and turns as if by some relentless chance into real indestructible love. This is in one of Chékhov's best stories *The Lady with a Lapdog*. An uneventful holiday flirtation passes without any mutual regret, when one day Gúrov sets off on a mere whim to the provincial town where Anna lives quietly with her husband and children. Gúrov, an accomplished rake, is amazed when he begins to realize that this was an emotion he had ridiculed before – love. 'It was now quite clear to him that their affair would not come to an end for a very long time, if ever.... They could not help feeling that fate itself had intended them for one another, and were unable to understand why he should already have a wife and she a husband.' The problem is not their love, but the increasing complications introduced into their lives by it; the really difficult part of their lives has hardly begun when the story ends.

A second motif is *indifference*, the most final kind of irreversibility. One of the most remarkable portrayals of indifference in the whole of literature is Chékhov's *A Boring Story*. The 'story' takes the form of a diary – 'an old man's notebook' is its subtitle. This particular old man happens to be a world-famous medical scientist who on learning that he has hardly six months left to live discovers the emptiness of his

own existence. His own growing indifference frightens him
stiff: 'Philosophers and sages are said to be indifferent. That
isn't true. Indifference is paralysis of the soul, premature
death.' Once a lively teacher, a scholar of originality and a
considerable personality, now his whole attitude towards other
people and things around him has become quite disorientated
For a long time he has cared for no one and nothing, and
even finds his own outbursts of irritation directed along
entirely futile channels, and taking irrational forms. What
seems to be missing from his life is a 'ruling idea' – 'I think
and think, but cannot really think of anything. And however
much I were to think and however far I were to scatter my
thoughts, it is clear to me that the main thing, something very
important, is lacking in me. In my partiality for science, in
my desire to go on living, in all my thoughts, feelings and
ideas about everything, there is no common link, there is
nothing that might bind it together in one whole ... I am
beaten.' The professor's autobiography is so convincing that
it is difficult to imagine that it is not the autobiography of a
real person. With uncanny skill Chékhov has us see with
the same lustreless indifference and impatience. Even more
incredibly, we become involved in others' lives *only* to the
extent that the old professor does. Indifference is a word
of frequent occurrence in Chékhov's later work. His wife,
the actress Olga Knipper, once told him: 'Sometimes I feel
you do not want me ... You look upon everyday life with
total indifference'; and again: 'It isn't because you are cold
and indifferent by nature but because there is something in
you that prevents you from regarding everyday events as
of any significance.' We don't know what Chékhov's replies
were, but we do have a remark in his diary: 'One has to
respect even one's own indifference, and not exchange it for
anything, since indifference in a decent man is also a religion.'

    In a moment of typical self-mockery Chékhov produced
an anti-autobiography – 'I have a disease – Autobiographophobia.'
'Do you want my autobiography? Well here it is. I was born
in Taganrog in 1860 ... In 1884 I took my degree in medicine
at Moscow University. In 1888 I received the Pushkin Prize.
In 1890 I made a journey to Sakhalin across Siberia and back

by sea . . . I began writing in 1879 . . . The mysteries of sex
I fathomed at the age of thirteen. With my colleagues, doctors
and literary men I'm on the best of terms. I am a bachelor.
I should like to get a pension. I practise medicine, so much so
that in the summer I carry out postmortems . . . But, go on,
write whatever you like. If you haven't enough facts, substi-
tute lyricism.'

'Medicine is my lawful wife, and literature my mistress.'
Chékhov's 'illicit love' began early with a successful series
of potboiler stories and comic sketches, as well as various
attempts at writing for the theatre. In these years Chékhov
did not think of himself as a writer, and in later life he
referred to the work of this period as 'literary excrement'.
He was still convinced that his real calling was medicine.
There seems considerable plausibility in the suggestion that
it was not literature but medicine which aroused Chékhov's
social sense and laid up for us the great humanity of his later
writing. Medicine was something Chékhov lived with, like a
friend, with all its gratifications, drawbacks and compensa-
tions. It was Chékhov who diagnosed his own terminal illness, including the onset of death, which he accepted with
the clarity and inevitability that only a physician is capable
of.

Chékhov is the creator of the modern short story. He
wrote literally hundreds of them in the course of his life,
but it was only during the last fifteen years, when his rate of
production had fallen sharply, that the unmistakable Chékov-
ian genre took shape. All the stories of these last fifteen years
were in a sense experiments. They were not always successful,
even the ones he allowed to be published. But each of them is
an attempt to 'measure', to bring a particular real-life situation within artistic bounds. In some cases the stories contain
enough substance for several novels, whereas in other cases
there is no more than the evanescence of a single moment of
time. Among the former are *The Peasants* and *In the Ravine*.
Both are almost naturalistic in technique, despite their highly
condensed form. Also belonging to this category are *The Black
Monk* and *Ward 6*, in their different ways attempts to penetrate mental disorder. In *Ward 6* the author works entirely

through symptoms, and wastes little time on analysis. His approach to insanity is 'phenomenalist', and in line with much present-day thinking in psychiatry Chékhov manages to convey just how much misunderstanding, fear, and misdirected 'good intentions' lie behind many authenticated mental cases. It is a terrifying document in which we witness the dissection of a situation wherein a so-called normal person is transformed mostly by other people into a case of so-called abnormality.

The short-story technique developed by Chékhov has long exercised the critics. In an early letter to his brother Chékhov wrote: 'You will get the full effect of a moonlight night if you indicate that on the mill-dam a little glowing star-point flashed from the neck of a broken bottle, and the round, black shadow of a dog, or a wolf, emerged and ran, etc.' Too much has been made of this description which occurs in almost identical form in a contemporaneous story *The Wolf*. But Chékhov was only twenty-six at the time. And even though a similar remark occurs in *The Seagull*, they are the words of the played-out Trigórin. Closer to Chékhov's mature view is the one put forward by Tréplev in the same play: 'I'm more and more convinced that old and new techniques are neither here nor there. The thing is to write without thinking of technique – to write from the heart . . .'

Writing to Suvórin, who had been accusing Chékhov of stooping to mere journalism in his *A Boring Story*, Chékhov says: 'When someone serves you coffee, don't expect to find beer in it. When I offer you a professor's ideas, take them as such, and do not search in them for Chékhov's own ideas.' For Chékhov people were individuals with their own totally different lives, their own ways of thinking, speaking and acting. To recognize and bring forth the language and thought of each of his characters was Chékhov's sole preoccupation; the rest followed willy-nilly.

Science was infinitely more interesting to Chékhov than philosophy. Science meant for him two things: objectivity and humanity – 'A man of letters must be as objective as a chemist; he has to abandon worldly subjectivity and realize that dung heaps play a very respectable role in the landscape

and that evil passions are as inherent in life as good ones.'
He once took one of his female understudies to task for
condemning syphilis – 'Syphilis,' he told her, 'is not a vice
but an illness, and those afflicted with it need sympathetic
and understanding treatment. It is not a good thing if your
wife deserts her sick husband because he has an infection or
loathesome disease. She of course, may take whatever attitude
she likes, but the author must be humane to the tips of his
fingers.' In defence of gynaecologists whom popular legend
supposed to be perverts and cynics, Chékhov said: 'Gynaecologists have to do with deadly prose the like of which you
never dreamt . . . One who is forever plunged into prose
passionately long for poetry. All gynaecologists are idealists!'

'Our day is in need of the heroic' Górky once wrote to
Chékhov. What Górky appears to have meant was that
Russia could no longer get by without a renewed stock of
inimitably Russian heroes. Russia had become so feeble and
diminutive that it could not contain those disruptive,
mischievous, erratic and indigestible characters. The Russian
hero Górky had in mind was a combination of Don Quixote,
Robin Hood, Till Eulenspiegel, Schweik and many others, but
at the same time someone different from any of them – in two
important respects. As well as being the victim of such intoler-
able boredom that he becomes a riot of impulses indiscriminately towards good or bad, he is all the while experimenting,
trying himself out, measuring his strength. His prototype is
Váska Busláev, the hero of Russian legend, one of the great
knights of old, but an inveterate practical joker too. Górky
saw Busláev in himself, as in many a Russian, even Tolstóy:
awkward, irresponsible, even petulant, especially in the
fastidiously furnished house that was Europe and European-
ized Russia. Górky's prolific output is as unwieldly and hard-
boiled as himself: tumbling from genial to banal, intensely
real to artificial, from genuine to trumped up, from laughably
naive to high Dostoévsky. The novels and stories, were it
not for unmistakeable mannerisms, could have been written
by a whole series of writers.

The early part of Górky's life (1868–1936) is sufficiently well-known. Even those who have not already read his autobiographical trilogy *Childhood, My Apprenticeship* and *My Universities*, will very likely have seen some or all of the great early films based on these works. Although it just happens that these are among his best works, it would have taken a very bad writer not to have succeeded with such a wealth of personal experiences. Tolstóy told Górky that he was better than any of the books he had written. So all fiction pales by comparison with the reality of Górky's own life: his harsh, disturbed childhood in an old style merchant's family in the town that now bears Górky's name; later as a down-and-out in many different corners and outbacks of Russia; and later still as the formidable opponent and friend of Lenin and the uncrowned laureate of the Bolsheviks. Almost everything we know about Górky's life is incredible as make-believe, even down to incidental details, as for instance the occasion when he beat Shalyápin in an audition for a church choir.

Maxím Górky is a pen-name, derived from the Russian word 'bitter, misery'; his real name was Alexéi Péshkov. Górky used his assumed name right from the time of the appearance of his first story *Makár Chudrá* (1892), a tale of romance. As a youth Górky was much nearer his perplexed Fomá Gordéyev than his straightforwardly idealistic Pável (*The Mother*), and it is doubtful if he would ever have started out as a writer had it not been for encouragement from *naródnik* (populist) acquaintances. The call of the open road was very great, and even at the height of his success Górky was never happy amongst intellectuals, writers, or political activists. This call was never more demanding than when he spent any length of time amongst the intelligentsia. Petersburg, and even Moscow held no attraction for him. Chékhov insisted that he was overdoing his attachment to his home town: 'It is high time Alexéy Maxímovitch donned a frock-coat'.

It is a pity that Górky became the literary darling of the proponents of socialist realism. True enough, his *The Mother*, if we leave aside the enigmatic opaqueness of the peasant

Rýbin, is the very model of a socialist realist novel, but *Fomá Gordéyev* is the very opposite. Some of his best characters are positive like Chelkásh (*Chelkash*) or Vlásova (*The Mother*), but most of them are fundamentally out of gear, incomprehensible to themselves and to others alike – Orlóv (in *The Orlov Couple*), or Fomá Gordéyev, or that immensely loveable but hopeless misfit Konoválov (in the story of that name), who claims that he was 'born wrong' and insists that he is a 'special case'. When Górky tries to convince him he is the 'victim of circumstances and the environment' Konoválov insists all the more vigorously that he alone can be blamed for the state he is in. Konoválov is restless to the point of melancholia, and is so miserable that he feels he cannot go on living. Meeting the writer after a long interval Konoválov is still stumped by the problem of finding somewhere to settle – 'When you think of it, there's really no place fit for a man to live in – not the town nor the steppe nor anywhere else. But it's better not to think about such things – can't do anything about it, just put yourself in a bad mood'.

In common with almost any writer of any worth, Górky learned nothing from the critics. He did nevertheless give way to unnecessary self-disparagement on occasion. Works that even he admitted as failures contain some of the most interesting studies of personality ever recorded. Definitive biographical studies of Górky have been made. We may have to wait some time yet for a searching appraisal, and this might well upset many of our preconceived notions about a writer who has been too easily aligned in black and white with Soviet ideology.

At a time of radical literary change the new writer perforce associates himself, however loosely, with the trends of the day; or, better still, sets the trend himself. Alternatively he can ignore or even set his face against fashion and deliberately set out to cultivate well-trodden ground. Iván Búnin (1870–1953) chose the latter course. Yet, in doing so, he produced literature as 'modern' as any written in his own time.

Without being a decadent as such – he denied affiliation with any of the various schools – Búnin is probably the most truly 'decadent' if we adhere to the strict meaning of the term. Búnin himself came of an impoverished but formerly distinguished family, which had produced more than one literary figure, including the poet Zhukóvsky; he had been born in Oryól that most poetically fertile of all regions, which had produced greater writers than ever he was likely to become. In Búnin's eyes Russian literature had not progressed since the days of Púshkin and Lérmontov, nor was it likely to – the Futurists he denounced as an empty, vulgar 'literary army'. Búnin set himself to become not only one of the greatest Russian prose stylists, but also did not fight shy of themes that were by now hackneyed. The most important part of his early work is about rural life, with which he had become acquainted through journalism and local government. Undaunted by the achievements of Turgénev, Saltykóv, Leskóv, and later his own contemporaries Chékhov and Górky, he went on to an even deeper and intense portrayal. His *Village* which describes post-emancipation peasant life and portrays the new *kulák*, or peasant proprietor, dazzled his contemporaries, even Górky, who had lived at closer quarters; but some of his short stories surpass even this, especially his *Night Conversation* written at about the same time (1911). Búnin took an even more pessimistic view of the peasant than Górky, and this gruesome story expresses the disillusionment of a boy with a group of people whose lives he had wanted to share. They seemed human enough until one night in the barn when he hears their naive accounts of their own cruelty, from killing defenceless prisoners to wanton torture of farm beasts. The boy's horror and repulsion was symbolized by 'what he had seen so many times before with perfect calmness: a peasant's bare foot, dead-white, enormous, flat, with a monstrously grown great toe lying crookedly on top of the others, and the thin, hairy skin, which Theodot, having unwound and dropped the footcloth, began to scratch hard in a delectable fury . . . That is the foot of a real murderer!'

The stories that brought Búnin world fame were his cosmopolitan ones, especially his *Gentleman from San Francisco* (1915). This is one of the gems of Búnin's most fertile period, conpressed into the few years preceding the Revolution, a period during which Búnin travelled extensively, in Europe, the Middle East, and as far as Ceylon. The last thirty-three years were spent in exile, as the leading writer of the Russian emigration. In 1933 he became the first Russian writer to be awarded the Nobel Prize for Literature. After the Second World War he published a series of mostly very short stories entitled *Dark Avenues*, written for the most part during the war and not unreminiscent of Somerset Maugham. But the most important work of his later years is the *Life of Arsényev* (1930) (translated as *The Well of Days*). Despite Búnin's several denials to the contrary, much of this novel is clearly autobiographical, ranking among the best of Russian auto-biographical literature.

It has sometimes been said that Búnin's weakness is that he lacks a core, a philosophy. This judgement seems to me false. A philosophy there is, but a deep and very dark one. Perhaps the nearest writer to him in spirit is E. M. Forster. And it is interesting that they come most close in their exotica; Búnin in his *Brothers*, set in Ceylon. All the ingredients are brought together here: a something that goes beyond wonder in the sky at night, the unthinkable awesomeness of the sea, and the equally fearful image of a modern liner relentlessly confronting the 'moiling black mountains on the other side of the wall'; the fearful All-oneness resurgent in all life forms ('In India, in Ceylon, where history is so immeasurable, where at times one glimpses life veritably primitive, and where on dark, sultry nights, in the fevered gloom, one feels man melt-ing, dissolving in all this blackness, in these sounds, scents ...'); death which human beings of the civilized kind can no longer grasp – 'Our reason is as feeble as that of a mole ... We do not even fear death properly, neither life, nor sacred mysteries, nor the depths that surround us, nor death – neither our death nor that of others.' This thing called life is merely light breathing scattered time and again upon the universe. This is not Schopenhauer nor some belated Hinduism; it is a humanism which has seemed to many of Búnin's otherwise admirers like cold inhumanity but which surpasses any ordinary humanism. The starry universe and everything in it is us and we are it.

According to one of his contemporaries, Fyódor Tetérnikov-

Sologúb (1863–1927) 'had fallen from the skies as a Decadent'.
His philosophy was a mixture of Schopenhauer, Manichaean-
ism, and plain black magic; and his chief contention was that
existence, as far as modern man was concerned, amounted to
non-existence. Man had fallen so far, and had become so disin-
tegrated spiritually, that God had totally rejected him. There
was no longer any sense to be made of life, and all that
remained was to wallow in its aftermath. Though not unim-
portant as a poet, and a writer of general novels, and numerous
tales and sketches, Sologúb's main claim on posterity is *A
Shabby Demon*, a novel which he published late in life (1905)
and which earned him wide and immediate fame.

A *Shabby Demon* lies in that disturbingly uncharted region,
that 'no-man's land of the spirit' between Henry James's *The
Turn of the Screw* and Musil's *The Young Törless* (it lies
chronologically between them also). The main character of
A Shabby Dream is Peredónov, a perverse and uncouth
provincial schoolmaster, who enjoys seeing little boys flogged,
mixing this with sex, committing all manner of meaningless
petty abominations, including torture, generally poisoning the
air about him, and treating others as if they were as subhuman
as himself. Peredónov has since lent his name to a brand of
sado-masochism known in Russia as Peredonovism, a spectrum
of perversion perhaps better known to British readers from
the recent documentation of the 'Moors Murder' case. Two
other important characters are a girl called Ludmíla and
Sásha, a mere boy whose otherwise guileless play relationship
has an ambiguously sinister shadow cast over it by Peredonovism which prevails, as Sologúb believed, not only in his book,
but universally. A fourth character is regarded as one of the
supreme achievements of literature: the sickening grey, squalid,
stinking, pixie-like she-devil Nedotýkomka ('the Untouchable')
who flits in and out of Peredónov's diseased perceptions. The
precedent for Nedotýkomka could be the oppressive 'shabby
demon' in Stavrogin's Confession (Dostoévsky), but likely as
not goes back to Lérmontov's lines: 'Whether he was great
Satan himself or one of those shabby non-established demons,
I don't know . . .'

The present-day reader finds it puzzling that Sologúb's

contemporaries regarded *A Shabby Demon* as self-evidently autobiographical. Sologúb, it is true, had been like Peredónov, first a low-grade schoolmaster, and then a school inspector (this was Peredónov's dream in life). But Sologúb explicitly rejected the assumption that he was writing only about himself: 'No, my dear contemporaries,' he writes in one of his prefaces, 'it was about you that I wrote my novel ... about you.' The absence of autobiographical connection becomes obvious when we look at the novel as a technical accomplishment. The difficulties are stupendous. To create truly shabby people, devoid of moral or metaphysical overtones *in themselves*, is a different thing from naturalism, which even at its best hardly rises above sociology. *A Shabby Demon* is among the first, perhaps *the* first successful attempt to create shabby characters in terms of their own limited worlds. It stands at the beginning of that frayed line reaching down to recent works like Fowles' *The Collector*. Even more than Musil, Sologúb has taken us behind the bureaucratic mask of the mass, new-class society and helps us to understand the essential ingredient of Nazism, Stalinism, or any similar ism.

The great 'stylistic revolution' in Russian prose was mainly the work of Andréi Bély (1880–1934), discussed earlier as one of the symbolist poets. Bély had already composed his verse 'symphonies' as well as much of his best poetry by the time he turned his hand to his first novel *The Silver Dove* (1910). It was this novel that 'jerked Russian prose up on its hind legs, turned syntax topsy turvy, and flooded the dictionary with a mass of invented words'. Like Sologúb, Bély also introduced a new note into Russian literature. *The Silver Dove*, unfortunately still not available in translation, is the Russian equivalent of Lawrence's *The Plumed Serpent*. The 'silver dove' happens to be the totem of a Russian local sex cult, into which a young Russian poet-intellectual allows himself to be drawn, with not altogether edifying consequences. The village totem prefigures the terrible Fire Bird of mythology, and becomes a portent of the tide of Asiatic 'scythianity' about to engulf not only Russia but the whole world.

Bély's best novel is generally thought to be *Petersburg*. This novel first appeared in 1912, but it went on being revised

for more than a decade. It has sometimes been pointed out
that the nearest counterpart to Bély's 'Petersburg' is Joyce's
'Dublin'; but for all their similarity in prose alchemics and
impressionism, these writers remain essentially different in
form and intention. But readers, in case they are tempted into
unfair comparisons, should realize that Bély's novel is not
at its best in translation, and seems a paler than pale shadow
of the original. *Petersburg* derives from Gógol's 'Petersburg'
stories, from Púshkin (especially *The Bronze Horseman* and
The Queen of Spades) and from Dostoévsky. This capital
city of all the Russias was, according to one of Dostoévsky's
characters, the most abstract and premeditated city in the
world, and to Bély a city of geometrical configurations, 'a
sum to infinity of the prospect,* elevated to the 9th degree'.
In the novel the lord of this planners' paradise is Apollón
Apollónovich Ableúkhov; a blend of Bély's own father, a
distinguished mathematician, and Pobedonóstsev, the all-
powerful and reactionary Procurator of the Holy Synod and
the grey eminence behind the throne before 1905. Apollón
Apollónovich, like the rest of his breed, is the faceless
mandarin, overcome by panic when people recognize him in
the street, preferring the telephone to face-to-face confronta-
tions, and suffering neurotically from open spaces. He along
with all the other people in the novel is confined to a city of
shadows, a spectral miasma, perhaps from the graves of the
countless ones who died laying the foundations of this marsh-
bound city. Even the streets possess 'an indubitable quality:
they transform the figures of passers-by into shadows.' Petersburg belongs to the realm of spirits. Even the precise incisive
intellect of Apollón Apollónovich is a shadowy one. In this
city 'nearly everyone is sick' and their common desire at
bottom is for death.

The background is 1905, the onset of the Revolution. But
the tone of the novel is not so much political as apocalyptical.
Pagan myths, Satan, Christ, sorcerers, and Asiatic Hordes are
all involved. The ticking time-bomb set to kill Apollón
Apollónovich, and planted by his own son, is seen as a

* The name given to a number of main streets in St. Petersburg, the
most important of which is the Nevsky Prospect.

symbol of the violent explosion of consciousness from its
'four walls', and back into elemental chaos, which was to take
place not only in Russia but in the rest of the world too, in
Nazism, and in all the many forms of contemporary barbar-
ism, puny or catastrophic.

The two decades spanning the Russian Revolution were
lavish in prose as in poetry. The new prose writers were as
a rule powerful individualists, taking in their stride what half
a generation earlier had seemed the precariously stretched
limits of Russian prose. They include Rémizov, Zamyátin,
Pilnyák and Bábel. Many of the poets were prose writers too:
Gumilyóv, Mandelstám, Tsvetáeva, Pasternák. There were
satirists like Zóshchenko, and the rip-roaring partnership of Ilf
and Petróv. There were those who became important Soviet
novelists like Katáev, Fédin and Leónov; equally writers who
existed apart like Grin and Paustóvsky. To cover all of them
even in outline would take up half this book. So, once again,
I shall be guided in my choice by my own preference and
also by the availability of translations in English.

One of the outstanding figures of the period, Evgény
Zamyátin (1884–1937), was also a dominant influence upon
the first generation of Soviet writers. Ironically enough,
Zamyátin's most telling work, called simply *We*, has never
been published in the Soviet Union. It was its publication
abroad which whipped up the philistine frenzy of the Proletarian Writers' Association (R.A.P.P.) resulting in a general ban
on his books and plays, and a blocking of all his attempts to
earn a living. Like many writers since, Zamyátin did not
particularly relish the prospect of becoming an émigré;
only in despair did he write directly to Stalin requesting
permission to leave his country. He wrote: 'I have no wish
to make myself out to be a figure of injured innocence ...
I know that I have the very awkward habit of saying not
what is expedient at the given moment but what seems to me
the truth. In particular I have never concealed my attitude
towards servility, toadying and careerism in literature: I have
always thought – and still think – that this degrades both the
Writer and the Revolution.' This letter would have misfired

had it not been for Górky's intercession on Zamyátin's behalf. In 1931 Zamyátin was allowed to leave Russia, only to die in Paris a few years later of ill-health and nervous exhaustion. On the surface Zamyátin appeared reserved and punctilious. His nickname was 'the Englishman'. In one of his laconic autobiographies he writes: 'You will have to content yourself with a purely external view, with perhaps a fleeting glance into darkened windows. I rarely invite anyone inside, and from the outside you will not see much.' His work as a Naval architect never got in the way of his writing – 'I constructed several bulldozers and a few short stories' he remarked at one of his busiest periods. During the First World War he was assigned to England where he succeeded in combining the supervision of Russian ice-breakers with extensive travel and acute social observation. His English was near perfect and he once thought of becoming another Conrad. Zamyátin never lost his faith in the Revolution. He joined the Bolsheviks very early on and was active in the events of 1905. To be a Bolshevik in those times was to follow the line of greatest resistance, and this appealed to his inclinations. He was arrested, beaten up and gaoled, and saved from worse only by an administrative error. In 1911 he was barred from the Capital, and it was then that he began writing in earnest: 'If I have any place in Russian literature, I owe it entirely to the Petersburg Department of the Secret Police.' Disenchantment with the Bolsheviks came very much later. He was not in Russia when the October Revolution happened. On his return he said he 'felt like someone who, never having been in love, gets up one morning and finds he has been married for about ten years.'

Zamyátin's output, varied though it is, bears a single unmistakable stamp. Whether social satire, popular *skaz*, science fiction, or whatever, there is the same common factor, impossible to characterize and independent of style and genre. He considered himself a neo-realist; that is, one who had managed to surmount the two separate streams of Symbolism and Realism and to produce a synthesis of the two. His models were as diverse an assembly as Blok, Bély, Leskóv, Chékhov, and Rémizov. Especially the last. Alexis Rémizov

(1877–1957) had worked on Russian prose like Bryúsov had on poetry, alchemically, with a certain wizardry. Rémizov has been described* as 'a jester, forever inventing new quips and jibes, ridiculing his own heroes, and playing cat-and-mouse with his readers. He resembles a malicious sorcerer who delights in wonderful feats, yet can also cast weird spells and metamorphose men into beasts.'

Neo-realism was to dominate, or at any rate to influence, the best of Russian prose during the decade which followed the Revolution. As Zamyátin himself explained: 'The old Realist would inevitably have put it cautiously: "Semyon Semyonich seemed to be blinking with his whole body." The Neorealist submits completely to the impression; he fully believes that Semyon Semyonich blinked with his entire being. To the Neorealist this is no longer seeming; it is not "as though", it is reality' (*Contemporary Russian Literature*). This technique lent to the pieces he wrote in the *skaz* style an uncanny timelessness, for all their accurate wry observation of the lives of ordinary folk and their idiom.

The two satires he wrote during his stay in England are in a category apart. It is a pity neither is available in translation. They are among the best things to be written in the form, an-alien's-point-of-view genre, and also among the most penetrating satires on English life ever produced. The first of them, *Islanders* (1918), looks at a group of solid middle-class people in Newcastle (Jesmond). They are preponderantly people who live narrow, sheltered, hypocritical lives, who feel bound by rules and routine. A hot spell or the dawn chorus upsets the humdrum order of things. There is Kemble, a young fellow with a pigeon-hole mentality and clearly mapped tomorrow, whose raptures focus on a new electric iron. His conviction is that with every household gadget purchased for her his girl will become that bit more his wife. McIntosh, the parish secretary of the Honorable Society of Bell Ringers, with a head like a football and invariably clad in his kilt, is no better. The society to which they belong is ruled over by the Reverent Dewly with his time-table regularity and machine-like precision, for whom even salvation is determined

* Slonim, Marc: *From Chekhov to the Revolution*, London, 1962, p. 231.

by mathematical laws. Among these dead souls the ones with any life in them seem disreputable, dubious, capricious, and morally beyond the pale. Among them is an unpredictable Irishman, O'Kelly, and a professionally not very serious prostitute called Didi. The second story *A Fisher of Men* is mainly about the doings of a particularly unsavoury character. Mr. Craggs is 'something in the City' as well as an active philanthropist. In his off-duty moments we find him blackmailing a courting couple on Hampstead Heath. Craggs' symbol is metal: his iron eyelids, the blades of his eyes, the cast of his face. He stands and moves as if on a pedestal; and on his way to and from church he walks as if along a series of pedestals.

As far as literature in the West is concerned undoubtedly the most important work of Zamyátin's is *We*. This 'my most jesting and most serious work' is the precursor of *A Brave New World*, and more especially of Orwell's *1984*. In many ways *We* surpasses bóth these works. Written as long ago as 1920 it has dated scarcely at all. Zamyátin's 'The One State' is based on an 'ideal non-freedom' and on mathematically infallible happiness. People exist in a glass-cage world artificially sealed off from chaotic nature outside, and individuals feel themselves to be not individuals, but *one of*. The truly human past is preserved only in museums where the Utopians are permitted to savour in all its horror the 'savage condition of freedom'. Life here is not unlike an extrapolation of middle-class Jesmond; here too conversation is limited to the effects of barometrical changes in pressure – the weather. Pigeon-holing has led to control of intimacy between the sexes: 'Your case is subjected to thorough research in the laboratories of the Sexual Bureau, the content of sexual hormones is determined with the utmost exactitude, and a corresponding Table of Sexual Days is worked out for you. After obtaining this you fill out an application, stating that on your Sexual Days you desire to avail yourself of such and such a number and receive the appropriate book of coupons (it is pink). And that's all there is to it.' Zamyátin's Big Brother, otherwise known as the Benefactor, is reminiscent not only of Dostoévsky's Grand Inquisitor, but equally of the Reverent

Dewly. D-503, the Winston Smith of *We*, and a space research engineer, begins by discovering an alarming X-factor in the nature of things, breaks the Sexual rules, finds himself irrationally infatuated, and ends by being drawn into association with a group of rebels known as the Mephi, who alarm the One-Staters with their wild visions of freedom and nature. D-503 is saved from the common fate of the Mephi by a new invention, a painless surgical operation known as fantasiectomy, which the Benefactor persuades him to undergo at the last moment. Those who choose savagery (= freedom) are liquidated before D-503's very eyes. Unlike its successors *A Brave New World* and *1984 We* does not point to hopelessness. On the contrary hope springs from the presence of that nuisance X-factor in human beings—the irrational.

Zamyátin was no optimist about the future. The Revolution he had striven for was already dead. It had dissolved into 'entropy', and could only be revived by madmen and heretics who would all suffer an inevitable fate. Even the future of Russian literature seemed to be its past. If heretics did not exist they would have to be invented. 'Explosions are not very comfortable. And therefore the exploders, the heretics, are justly exterminated by fire, by the axe, by words. To every today, to every evolution, to the laborious, slow, useful, creative coral-building work, heretics are a threat. Stupidly, recklessly, they burst into today from tomorrow . . .'

Zamyátin is not the only writer to have raised storms of controversy in those days; not the only one to have become so truly an unperson that his name is virtually unknown to the Russian reader of today. There is another – Boris Pilnyák.

Pilnyák was likewise harassed by R.A.P.P. and for a similar traitorous reason – publishing abroad without official permission. Not so fortunate as Zamyátin, Pilnyák was not overlooked at the height of the Purges, despite not entirely unambivalent attempts to mend his ways. Formerly it was supposed that he was shot on the orders of Stalin shortly after his disappearance in 1937, but it is now believed that he died in a concentration camp five years later. Pilnyák's *The Naked Year* (1922) happens to be the first novel to have been written about the Revolution, and it is a panorama of chaos,

disintegration, and atavistic revelry that does little to flatter
the Bolsheviks and the New Era. Worse, Pilnyák dared to
cast dark hints. For instance, it was widely rumoured that
Stalin had arranged for Frunze, Trotsky's successor as War
Minister, to be put out of the way by ordering him to be
operated upon. In one of his most successful stories *The Tale of
the Unextinguished Moon* (1927) Pilnyák recreates the events
leading up to this incident. Stalin is not mentioned by name,
but the allusion to the 'man who never bends' who lives at
House No. 1 is unequivocal enough. We get a glimpse of this
man at the end of a telephone whom many had already begun
to fear – 'The house was wrapped in a silence which seemed
to have collected over the centuries. The man sat in a wooden
chair . . . Light fell from the ceiling and now the man's face
was visible. It was a very ordinary face, perhaps just a little
harsh, but certainly full of concentration and without a trace
of tiredness . . . The man spoke in a loud, firm voice and each
of his phrases was like a formula.'

For many of his contemporaries Boris Pilnyák (1894–1942?)
was all trees; rather impressive trees at that but which did
not form any kind of wood. Some saw him as a scion of
Bolshevism, others as an obscurantist. Few could grasp the
essential in this writer. His material seemed too hetero-
geneous, 'a literary junk yard' as someone put it. Many of his
ideas, for the reason that they have been interpreted simply
as ideas, seemed half-baked. His writing looked too uneven.
Those who picked on his newsreel style and lumped him
along with Dos Passos, failed to notice his Hemingway-like
economy, or a grandeur which rivals Faulkner. First and foremost Pilnyák is a Russian. His manner owes much to
Rémizov, to Bély and the Symbolists, to the mystical
sensualism of Rózanov and to Dostoévsky. Moreover he
stands as a link between these and many a later writer. It is
only from the vantage point of today that we can appreciate
Pilnyák's originality and literary genius.

Historians will quibble with his interpretation of the
Revolution. Pilnyák saw in it a break with Europe, the Europe
forcibly introduced by Peter the Great, and a reversion to the
Rus' of the seventeenth century. Western technology and alien

institutions like government were cast off at last. At one stage further removed was a return to the fierce freedom of the steppe, to the Mongol Horde, and even earlier than that to the Scythian past, when Russia was not a state but a way of life embracing many peoples reaching as far as China. The break up is symbolized in a variety of ways; the greater part of *The Naked Year* is taken up with it: a train expiring in the snowy fastness 'swamped by people, suffering and filth'; a return to stone-age metallurgical techniques, because steel needs salt and salt is unobtainable; the man-in-the-street failing to recognize a word like 'accumulator' but reshaping it into disconnected utterances in a residual language of his; people talking about Beethoven one minute and issuing death warrants the next. Shades of Pugachev are everywhere in Pilnyák. Slant-eyed Tartar horsemen appearing for a brief second above the brow of a distant hill, heralding some calamity. We see the new Mongol uprising from both ends of Asia. From the European end when, against the safe setting of the Cheshire Cheese in London, we read of atrocities by a gang of marauding Kirghiz once again plundering the settled farmlands of the Ukraine. At the Asiatic end we find a group of English colonialists making their way on some trade mission into the depths of Mongolia by a newly constructed railway (*The Big Heart*). There they meet a Hun chieftain only to be sickened by cruelty and barbarity such as they had never encountered even in China. Strangely the Hun's quarters are like any Russian merchant's house; Pilnyák even labours his point.

If there is a philosophy in Pilnyák it is a bitter one. A plant of special significance is wormwood; and it is wormwood which symbolizes the harsh domination of the 'packs of centuries', the empty finality of Scythian tombs excavated by archaeologists 'smelling of nothing, and every time they were entered one's thoughts became clear and calm, and sorrow entered the heart' (*Wormwood*). Russia's lack of history and futility of life among barbarians represent the essentiality of this borderless land mass. In *The Cheshire Cheese* a nest of erstwhile gentlefolk has been ransacked, the men slaughtered, and the women raped. One of the survivors Maria (the name is ironically significant) gives birth to a 'little, slant-eyed Kidghiz'. She cannot reject the child but cherishes it as if it had been her natural son. Another woman whose own child had died unborn 'used to come quietly, secretly to Maria to caress and fondle her baby. That's life, life – a terrible tragedy!' We learn that Maria had been to London as a girl and had admired there all the splendour of human culture. But recent happenings in Scythian Russia had revealed 'how far more ancient, more meaningful and terrifying is man's life' than any kind of culture. The life blood of history is destruction, a reality filling all those centuries of time buried away in those Scythian tumuli. Destruction is what makes history repeat itself ad nauseam, when now again 'at break of day soldiers came from the town and mounted machine guns on the tombs of that buried city.'

'I have been criticised for writing too concisely, but I find that Bábel's style is even more concise than mine, which is more wordy. It shows what can be done. When you've got all the water out of them, you can still clot the curds a little more.' This passing admission from Hemingway is one way of introducing perhaps the greatest short-story writer of modern times. Although he carried his art to the point of fanaticism, Bábel was not a prolific writer, and his best pieces are not more than a few hundred words in length. He once told his publisher point blank that he could have him thrashed for four hours a day, but would still refuse to hand over a manuscript until it was absolutely ready. With Bábel this was not merely a manner of speaking. He had realized better than anyone that 'a phrase is born into the world both good and bad at the same time. The secret lies in a slight, an almost invisible twist. The lever should rest in your hand, getting warm, and you can turn it only once, not twice.' Style and depth were one to him: 'there is no iron that can enter the human heart with such stupefying effect as a full-stop put exactly in the right place.'

Isaac Bábel (1894–1941) grew up in a Jewish quarter in Odessa. As a boy he witnessed the worst of the anti-Jewish pogroms, and incidents drawn from these are vividly recreated in stories like *First Love* and *The Story of my Dovecot*. Bábel's real rigours though were at home. In typically Jewish fashion, he was put through such an intensive academic regime that school by comparison was a holiday. Efforts to process him into a virtuoso violinist despite his being 'past the age limit set for infant prodigies' were thwarted by the boy's love of reading and story writing – 'In our family composition was a hereditary occupation. Grandfather Leivi-Itzkhok, who went cracked in his old age, spent his whole life writing a tale entitled "The Headless Man". I took after him' (*Awakening*).

In 1916 Bábel met Górky. Górky took an encouraging line and even published a handful of Bábel's stories. All the same Górky strongly advised him to go 'amongst the people'. The advice was taken, and during the seven years between 1917 and 1924 Bábel was 'a soldier on the Rumanian Front, an employee of the Cheka,* took part in foraging expeditions in 1918, fought in the Northern Army against Yudenich,** served in the First Cavalry, worked for the Odessa Regional Soviet, after that was a reporter in Petersburg and Tiflis, then a copy editor in the 7th Soviet printing plant in Odessa, and so on.' His collection of stories *Red Cavalry* (1926) were based on his experiences during the Civil War in Budyónny's army where he was a supply officer in a Cossack regiment. They brought him immediate fame, and not only at home. But a literary and political non-conformist was not a very safe thing to be in the years following the Revolution; under Stalin it was suicidal. Bábel was arrested in 1939 for alleged Trotskyism, and died in a concentration camp two years later. His 'rehabil-itation' could not be described as anything but lukewarm. The limited editions of his works published since 1957 have been immediately sold out, and to the mass of Soviet youngsters of today Bábel can be scarcely more than a name.

Although Bábel has been called a romantic he is anything but. His view of the Revolution and the Civil War unlike that of many of his contemporaries is neither epic nor apocalyptic. Instead, this man 'with spectacles on his nose and autumn in his heart' strips down his view until there is no view left. In

* Lenin's secret police.
** A general in the White Army.

Bábel there is only *byt*, that peculiarly Russian concept: life as it is lived by a given group of people at a definite time, in its individual as opposed to universal features. There are only people perpetrating kindnesses, more usually, bestialities, and the bare bones of the situations from which they emerge. In a wretched Jewish hovel in which he is billeted the story-teller finds himself in the same bed as a corpse whose throat has been cut (*Crossing into Poland*). Stopping at night by the roadside to urinate he stumbles upon the corpse of a Pole; urine 'was pouring out of his mouth, bubbling between his teeth, gathered in his empty eye sockets. A notebook and fragments of Pilsudski's proclamations lay on the corpse... With Commander-in-Chief Pilsudski's proclamations I wiped the skull of my unknown brother.' Compassion withers in this harshness; only nature now deserves it — 'I felt sorry for the bees. The fighting armies treated them most brutally. There were no bees left in Volhynia' (*The Road to Brody*). As for humans they are beyond comprehension, and make sense only in relation to *byt*. A woman with a bundle she says is her baby but turns out to be a bag of salt has hitched a ride in an overcrowded army train. She is eventually ditched and shot by one of the Cossacks who had at first taken pity on her: not so much for having deceived them but for trying to get off too lightly by comparison with the other girls: 'Look at them two girls,' the men tell her, 'they're crying now on account of what they went through from us this night. Look at our wives in the wheat plains of the Kuban that are spending their women's strength without their husbands, and the husbands, alone too, all through dire necessity violating the girls as come into their lives. And nobody touched you, you wicked woman...' (*Salt*). The narrator who like his author has specs on his nose and 'has been through a lot in the learning line' implores fate to grant him that simplest of proficiencies – the ability to kill. A Cossack comrade of his lies mortally wounded against a tree. His entrails are spilling out and he pleads with our hero to finish him off. But another Cossack has to do the job for him 'Get out of my sight,' the Cossack warns him, 'or I'll kill you. You guys in specs have about as much pity for us as a cat for a mouse' (*The Death of*

Dolgúshov). The cossacks were unrivalled in the spontaneity and grace of their cruelty. Bábel once defined the Cossack as 'layers of worthlessness, daring, professionalism, revolutionary spirit, bestial cruelty'. Rape and pillage in their wake, cattle-like slaughter of civilians, bútchery of prisoners, even a reluctance to shoot their victims – 'With shooting you only get rid of a chap. Shooting's letting him off, and too damn easy for yourself. With shooting you never get at the soul, to where it is in a fellow and how it shows itself. But I don't spare myself, and I've more than once trampled an enemy for over an hour. You see, I want to get to know what life really is, and what life's like down our way' (*The Life and Adventures of Matthew Pavlichénko*).

Not all Bábel is grim. The *Tales of Odessa* based on the exploits of a flamboyant Jewish gangster Benya Krik are in a totally different vein. They have been compared to Damon Runyan, and sometimes remind us of Joyce's Dublin characters. The miscellaneous stories contain plenty of humour, and *The Sin of Jesus* is among the world's funniest stories.

During the Stalin era Bábel became in his own words 'a master of the genre of silence'. What he wrote in the thirties he withheld as a rule from publication. Heaps of manuscripts were apparently confiscated at the time of his arrest. So far none of them has been located despite a willingness on the part of the authorities to cooperate in the search for them. Bábel's public appearances and interviews during these years of terror are masterpieces of irony and double entendre. Speaking at the First Writers' Congress in 1934, with typical black logic he recalled that everything is permitted by the Party and Government except one thing, the right to write badly. 'Comrades', he went on to say, 'let us not fool ourselves. This is a very important right, and to take it away from us is no small thing ... Let us then give up this right, and may God help us. But as there is no God, let us help ourselves.' Stalin was not amused.

In any literature humorists are rare. Russian literature has been no exception. Only the Soviet period stands out. For against the numerous weighty writers, few of them really good ones, can be set three of the greatest comic writers of all time: Mikhaíl Zóshchenko (1895–1958) and the unique partnership of Ilya Ilf (1897–1937) and Yevgény Petróv (1903–42).

Zóshchenko rose swiftly to fame in the early nineteen twenties with his hilarious skits on the new Soviet citizenry, on the easily detectable petty bourgeois beneath the Soviet ideological skin. These humorous anecdotes, in the *skaz* style and told as if by some typical man-in-the-street, ran into hundreds. Every aspect of the new scheme of things came in for its own special volley of ridicule: 'visitorphobia', induced by rampant cleptomania, in a once orientally hospitable country; a police dog provocatively sniffing around the ankles of a group of bystanders soon reduces one and all to confessions of all kinds of petty crimes; tragi-comic situations brought about by overcrowding, several families being obliged to share thinly partitioned flats; the spectacle of 'grand pianos in every cottage' at a time when townspeople were driven to sell their possessions to villagers in return for food; the conflict between the new ideal of emancipated womanhood and the average wife's natural inclination towards domestic indolence; a new-style police inspector annoyed at seeing a pig running loose in the street ends by arresting his wife; confusion among passengers on a Volga pleasure steamer when it changes its name rather too frequently en route; parodies of officialese, all the stray euphemisms long since come to stay. It is not surprising that the Russian public, sharing his sense of the ridiculous began saying to one another 'that's the kind of thing for Zóshchenko'.

Humorists are seldom gay; they are more often melancholy, sometimes even morbidly so. Zoshchenko was no exception. His autobiographical works are decidedly sombre. In his youth Zóshchenko had been everything from a shoemaker to an actor, and a policeman to a telephone operator. He was arrested six times, and once condemned to death. With this kind of luck and a depressive temperament to boot it is no wonder that he twice attempted suicide. What is original in Zóshchenko's case is that he tried systematically to get to the root of his condition, to find out the how and the why. Early on he had been an admirer of the psychologist Pavlov, and

Pavlov in turn had been attracted by one of his early stories
The Return of Youth. Freud was to become a much greater
influence. Zóshchenko's major autobiographical study *Before
the Sunrise,* published during the Second World War, consisting largely of a series of personal anecdotal sketches, strikes the
reader as a bizarre distillation of Pavlov and Freud, but a
dedicated attempt to probe the secrets of his earliest childhood.

The official line against Zóshchenko had hardened as long
ago as the early thirties. Adulation of Freud, and biting
satires like *Adventures of an Ape* did not endear him to
Zhdanov, who exhausted all his supplies of abuse in his
tirades against Zóshchenko. In 1946, in the company of Anna
Akhmátova, Zóshchenko was expelled from the Writers'
Union. Although readmitted in 1953 he was never again in
genuine official favour, perhaps because of his continuing
immense popularity. Quite early he had been pressed into
making concessions to party ideology; and this no doubt
spared him from the fate of many of his contemporaries. His
wartime stories about partisans operating in the rear of the
German front-line are vivid enough, and occasionally light
up with Zóshchenko humour, but they are seriously tainted
with the demands of doctrinaire socialist realism. His excom-
munication after the war left him hopelessly distressed, and he
virtually ceased to exist as a writer. His death passed without
mention in the Soviet press.

Successful partnerships in literature are so rare as to be
freakish. 'It is very difficult to write together. It was easier for
the Goncourts, we suppose. After all, they were brothers,
while we are not even related to one another. We are not
even of the same age. And even of different nationalities:
while one is a Russian (the enigmatic Russian soul), the other
is a Jew (the enigmatic Jewish soul).' But so successful were
this pair, Ilf and Petróv (their real names were Fáinzilberg and
Katáev), that they not only managed to amuse the Russian
public over a period of many years, but escaped unscathed in
the time of ideological troubles culminating in the Purges.
Ilf died a natural death in 1937, and Petróv by then a war

correspondent was killed during the defence of Sevastopol in 1942.

Ilf and Petróv first came together in 1927 and soon gained popularity with their 'letters to the editor', which started to appear regularly in *Pravda*. These often uproarious 'letters' got right at the core of Soviet bumbledom, red-tape and Parkinsonism. They wrote under various pseudonyms, including Tolstoyevsky, but their special brand of parody was always immediately recognizable. Many of these newspaper items have been published separately as 'feuilletons'. A typical incident is that of a young man who finds himself barred at every bureaucratic turn from marrying the girl he loves, or the setting up of a special committee to promote the taking of walks in areas of parks where in fact no one ever ventured. The ridicule poured upon officialese is such that one only wonders that it could have survived their onslaught. One story begins: 'Let us return to that summer. It was such a pleasant season in the current financial year ...' and keeps up this ludicrous mixture for pages on end.

Two superb picaresque novels *The Twelve Chairs* (1928) and *The Golden Calf* (1931) are the best things they wrote. The prime-mover in both these novels is a smooth operator, a Russian Felix Krull called Ostap Bender. Bender is of distinctly cosmopolitan origins and inclinations, and an opportunist of a type ideally adapted to the N.E.P. period which Stalin put a stop to. He is an oddly likeable cynic – 'Be cynical' is his philosophy 'people like it' – who always knows what he is going for, never asks too many questions, and avoids doing anything through third parties. He describes himself as 'a free artist and a chill philosopher'. Bender has an extremely good grasp of the mentality of Soviet man, especially the bureaucrat; and he exploits them with virtuoso-like ease. An updated version of Gógol's Chíchikov he shares the latter's fundamental innocence. It is perhaps because of this that his capers never seem reprehensible, only extremely funny. But there is nothing gloomy or earnest about him. Although a born profiteer Bender is not wedded to gain. His high spirits are the same whether he is regaling himself in a first-class dining-car or travelling hot and thirsty on a camel across Central Asia. In

The Twelve Chairs Bender, in league with a survivor from the *ancien régime*, sets out in search of diamonds which the latter's mother-in-law is supposed to have hidden in the upholstery of one of a set of twelve dining chairs. Their treasure-hunt takes them all over Russia, and in the course of their travels almost every section of the new society comes in for a drubbing. *The Golden Calf* is even more fantastic, introducing a motley assortment of other characters. Koréiko, for instance, a millionaire 'with an honest Soviet smile' who is 'saving himself for capitalism' trying to disguise his wealth by appearing to make do on his pittance of a salary; or Lokhánkin who gets flogged by his neighbours for always leaving the light on in the lavatory. We meet prohibition-crazed American tourists racing about the Russian countryside in search of recipes for home-made liquor; a group of responsibility-shy officials who have been turned out of a lunatic asylum where they had been shamming schizophrenia; someone who has devised the last word in bureaucratic automation, an all-purpose rubber stamp with standard replies to all conceivable correspondence. During the course of his wanderings Bender finds time to compile a 'comprehensive guidebook' for journalists consisting of 19 nouns, 7 adjectives, 10 verbs, 2 epithets and five miscellaneous parts of speech. Assembled in the appropriate order these items are all one needs for every kind of article, festive verse, humorous sketch, and other occasional composition. Ilf and Petróv must sometimes have found the ice very thin, especially after their scathing attacks on literary conformism. And there is one moment in *The Golden Calf* when they briefly sketch the fate of the Wandering Jew at the hands of a Cossack. This is as chilling as anything in Bábel. But somehow they managed to avoid overstepping the mark, for reasons probably they could not understand.

The first Five Year Plan, introduced in 1928 and largely Stalin's idea, brought Russian literature to the point of industrialization. Happily R.A.P.P.'s zeal was seen to be excessive, and the aim of subordinating art to economic planning was largely thwarted. But the relative freedom and experimentation of the early twenties was gone forever. Instead writers found themselves herded into the newly formed Union óf Soviet Writers, whose tyranny remains undiminished forty years later. The heyday of the hack writer had arrived at last. Shólokhov in 1954 in a vain bid to persuade this Union to mend its ways alleged that 'in twenty years a thousand authors' pens have produced about ten good books.'

Talented writers who emerged after the Revolution were forced to meet the ideological restrictions in their own way. Some came to terms with the new order and managed to retain some of their individuality and much of their quality. These include the major Soviet novelists: Mikhaíl Shólokhov (b. 1905), Konstantín Fédin (b. 1892), and 'the Dostoévsky of the Soviet Union' Leoníd Leónov (b. 1899). Without being significant innovators, and sometimes consciously perpetuating the tradition of the classical Russian novel, all three have managed to preserve their identity without falling irretrievably foul of official opinion, and have not been completely swamped by the dictates of socialist realism. Nevertheless it is significant that since the Second War none of them has produced anything to equal their earlier work. Shólokhov in particular emerged from the Stalin period with much credit, and might have retained it were it not for the bigotry he displayed in the Sinyávsky-Daniél affair and the suspicion of having published the work of someone else under his own name. There were other novelists like Vsévolod Ivánov (1895–1963) or Nikoláy Nikítin (1897–1963), vigorously original writers who, after the rise of Stalin, became shadows of their former selves. There were still others like Bábel and Pasternák who became virtually silent.

Now I shall deal briefly with only two of the many writers of this period: Boris Pasternák whose poetry we have already touched upon, and a writer who has in recent years undergone à resurrection – rather than a rehabilitation – Mikhaíl Bulgákov (1891–1940). Those who would like to know more about the Soviet novelists, Fédin, Leónov and Shólokhov in particular, are advised to read Ernest J. Simmons' *Russian Fiction and Soviet Ideology* (New York, 1958) with its extensive and unbiased account of their work.

Shortly after the end of the Civil War a group of young writers brought together by Zamyátin referred to themselves as the Serapion Brethren. Since their ranks included Fédin, Ivánov, Nikítin, Zóshchenko, and closely associated writers like Leónov it is superfluous to emphasize the part played by this 'Brethren' in early Soviet writing. The name had been borrowed from one of the characters in E. T. A. Hoffmann, the Hermit Serapion. Their policy was to oppose any kind of regimentation or sectarianism, and they proclaimed only the power of the imagination. None proclaimed this power more consistently and to greater effect than Mikhaíl Bulgákov.

Like Chékhov, Bulgákov had started out in medicine. He became a writer only after the War. His novel *The White Guard* (1925), and more especially the play based upon it *The Days of the Turbins*, produced the following year at the Moscow Arts Theatre, were an immediate success. But his subsequent plays, which incidentally were to have included *The Hooved Consultant* the model for his later novel *The Master and Margarita*, were too provocatively satirical and aroused wide criticism. In 1930 he was expelled from the Writers' Union. Bulgákov promptly wrote to Stalin asking to be allowed to leave the Soviet Union. With typical unpredictability Stalin phoned Bulgákov, offered him a post at the Moscow Arts Theatre, and ordered *The Days of the Turbins* to be put back on – a puzzling gesture when this play is mainly about the part played in the siege of Kiev by a group of young White Guards. It is true that they are not fighting the Bolsheviks but a peasant rebel and his Pugachevist army; none the less their view of the Bolsheviks is never less than disparaging. Even though they have been betrayed by their cowardly superiors, by the Germans, by the decadent bourgeoisie who have flocked to Kiev, these young White heroes believe they are the ones who are defending what is worth preserving in Russia from the barbarities of revolution and destruction. This did not prevent Stalin from seeing the play no less than fifteen times. After 1930 Bulgákov published nothing. The only new plays of his to be produced included one based on the life of Molière (*A Cabal of Hypocrites*) which was so garbled by the censors as to be unrecognizable. Bulgákov was brought back to life only in 1956, and early in the sixties a commission was set up to investigate Bulgákov's work. The complete list of manuscripts remains to be compiled, but of plays alone he is believed to have written some thirty-six.

The first of Bulgákov's novels *The White Guard* is a work of considerable polish and power. There was no new prose technique he had not mastered and the novel reads as if Russian had been written that way for centuries. We also can notice the way he has adapted and transformed Tolstóy's realist technique, even to the extent of being able to convey the gestures of his characters. Simultaneously Bulgákov was writing satires. The best of them belong to science fiction. *The Heart of a Dog* (1925) is a story about a transplant operation that goes wrong. A famous Moscow surgeon is carrying out experiments in rejuvenation by means of glandular transplantation. The pituitary gland and testicles are taken from someone who has just died and transplanted into a dog. Instead of being rejuvenated the dog starts to talk and assume human features until he is transformed into a particularly sombre specimen of Soviet proletarian man. Bulgákov brings everything off with such mastery that we readily suspend disbelief, and soon find ourselves becoming acquainted with an actual dog-man. We are reminded of Čapek's mass man in *The War with the Newts*, but in Bulgákov's story we are dealing with an irreducible, recalcitrant individual whom the professor and assistant become saddled with. In desperation they find a means of reversing the operation, and the story ends with the dog ruminating upon the advantages of a dog's life. Another story *The Fateful Eggs* again brings in a professor, this time experimenting with the effects of radiation upon primitive organisms. Things go wrong when he allows himself to be persuaded to loan his apparatus to a state farm which is planning to begin chicken farming following a nationwide epidemic of fowl pest. The eggs specially packed and imported from Germany are not hens' eggs at all but anaconda, ostrich and crocodile eggs. Irradiated they hatch out many times their normal size and wreak devastation all the way from

Smolensk to Moscow. Bulgákov is at his black humorous best in all his horrific descriptions laced with farce.

Bulgákov might well have remained a minor writer had it not been for the publication of *The Master and Margarita,* as recently as 1967. This novel is one of Bulgákov's last works, and one that had been maturing over many years. There is nothing to compare with *The Master and Margarita* in the whole of literature; it is in a category entirely apart. Despite this it is the summation and the bringing together of many different strands in Russian literature. His technique too owes much to his predecessors: Tolstóy's power of resuscitating history; Púshkin's mercurial line; Dostoévsky's technique of transposition of scenes. The demons derive more from the prank-playing Russian devil than from European folklore. Margarita though borrowed from Goethe is nearer Púshkin's Tatyána. *The Master and Margarita* can be read the first time as a piece of pure mystification, a second time as a parable, a third time as hilarious satire, and lastly as a piece of complicated metaphysics. At the centre of the novel is the master himself, the artist who through his historical recreation of Christ and the Crucifixion becomes unwittingly and by some decree of fate the saviour of Pilate. The novel is still too fresh for proper focus.

'What I have written is enough to give some idea of how, in my own case, life became converted into art, and art was born of life and of experience.' So writes Pasternák in his later autobiography. Those who have been disappointed with *Doctor Zhivágo* as a chronicle of the Revolution and Civil War have been disappointed for the wrong reasons. Those who have compared the novel with *War and Peace* have been on the wrong track too, because *Doctor Zhivágo* is not a historical novel. Pasternák is the very opposite of a chronicler. In Sinyávsky's words: 'Pasternák is more likely to tell us what the weather was like at a certain moment in history than to give a consistent exposition of the order and movement of events.' Even so, there are more searching reflections on revolution in general and the Bolshevik Revolution in particular than in almost any other writer. Yúri Zhivágo takes a sharply different view of the revolutionary ideals of 1905 which he and most writers shared and 'this new upheaval, born of the war, bloody, pitiless, elemental – a soldiers' revolution, led by its professionals, the Bolsheviks.'

The falsehood inherent in the bloody Revolution of October 1917 and the even more bloody Civil War was in Pasternák's eyes a disease of language 'the power of the glittering phrase'. The chorus of everybody else's opinions and catchwords become a social epidemic – 'Something went wrong. Instead of being natural and spontaneous as we had always been, we began to be idiotically pompous with each other. Something showy, artificial, forced, crept into our conversation . . .' The Party rhetoric was threatening to set humanity back to Biblical times of shepherd tribes and patriarchs: 'it's simply impossible to believe that this is meant to be taken seriously, it's such a comical remnant of the past.' But the *real* Revolution was happening all right, even if it was beyond the ken of the new commissars and party cadres. It was happening deep down in the social consciousness, and Pasternák was one of the few to realize that his own glimmerings did not match the elemental truth behind the bewildering chaos of events. 'The whole of Russia has had its roof torn off,' Yúri tells Lára, 'and you and I and everyone else are out in the open . . . Mother Russia is on the move, she can't stand still, she's restless and she can't find rest, she's talking and she can't stop. And it isn't as if only people were talking. Stars and trees meet and converse, flowers talk philosophy at night, stone houses hold meetings . . .' All that is left is 'the bare, shivering human soul, stripped to the last shred.'

The times through which Pasternák lived concentrated his sense of life. In an early prose work *The Childhood of Luvers* life was already more than just a metaphor: 'Life had ceased to be a poetic trifle and fermented like a stern black fairy tale, in proportion as it became prose and turned into fact.' Life the mystery lies at the centre of *The Childhood of Luvers* as it does of *Doctor Zhivágo*, written a quarter of a century later. To begin with, life seldom tells us what she has in store for people – 'She loves her purpose too well, and even when she speaks of her work, it is only to those who wish her success and admire her tools. No one can help her; anyone can throw her into confusion.' Our social habits, preoccupations and prejudices all prevent us from getting through to the real essence. This suits life very well, for she has no desire to work in the presence of man, and even tries various ruses to avoid him. The name *Zhivágo* itself derives from the Church Slavonic accusative form of the adjective 'living', and has been said to allude in particular to the text of the Russian Bible, when the women came to the grave of Christ and found the stone rolled away, and an Angel asked them: 'Why do you seek the living among the dead?' Life binds the destinies of Yúri and Lára. Yúri is the active vehicle of life, the subduer of death, George (Yúri) the slayer of dragons – 'There will be no death, because the past is over. Death is already done with, it's old and we are tired of it.' Lára is the passive *vehicle*, nearer to the elemental in life – 'My fate is to see everything and take it all so much to heart.' . . . 'This was exactly what Lára was. You could not communicate with life, but she was its representative, its expression, the gift of speech and hearing granted to inarticulate being.' They share an 'inward music' which for Yúri is 'irresistible power of unarmed truth' raising man above the beast; for Lára it is her indispensable accompaniment in bearing the burden of life, even when she was not always capable of composing this music for herself.

Doctor Zhivágo is without doubt one of the most complex novels ever written. Pasternák himself has said that the whole of his poetry, Russian poetry at its greatest, was to be regarded as a preparation for this novel. The symbolical features are intricate enough, but there is hardly anything that any character says or does which is not balanced or echoed or transformed in the speech or actions of some other character. Some have supposed the model is *Finnegan's Wake*; others have detected Rilke and Goethe. The closest specific model, to my mind, is *Evgény Onégin*. It will be recalled that Zhivágo reads this work over and over again in his Siberian retreat at Varykino. But the most important general influence is Shakespeare. Pasternák's glorious translations of Shakespeare

are by now a part of Russian literature. Remarkably free, yet perfectly imbued with the spirit of the original, these translations took Pasternák right to the heart of Shakespeare; and it is Shakespeare's diction which appears in the prose of Zhivago. Read in the original *Doctor Zhivago* produces the same intoxication; and as in Shakespeare every word is in perfect poetic resonance with every other word, an infinitude of interweaving ripples of sound and sense.

'Thaw' – the term used to denote the period from the death of Stalin to the time immediately following the Twentieth Party Congress in 1956 – is usually considered an apt enough way of describing the passing away of the worst of aesthetic official dogmatism. Laid bare was a dazzlingly fresh generation of Soviet writers emerging one after the other in rapid succession. These contemporaries of ours are not, or at least not primarily, experimenters or innovators like the post-revolutionary generation; their task has been to pick amongst the debris and to take up the threads of past and present; to say what they have to say directly, candidly, and courageously. It was not difficult for them to learn from the classical writers, and this they did: especially Púshkin, Gógol, Chékhov and Tolstóy. Not so easy was the rediscovery of what Rémizov, Zamyátin, Pilnyák, and the early years of the Serapion Brethren had done for Russian prose, if only because these writers were not readily available in print. They also had to turn their attention to what was going on in the West, since no literature today can exist in a vacuum. They found Salinger, Osborne, Sillitoe, Böll, Grass, Genet, and of course numerous others. Their most important influence at home was unquestionably Pasternák. A few of the present generation are established figures like Viktor Nekrásov and Ilya Ehrenbúrg. Although old in years these writers are close in spirit to the younger generation. Many of the new writers came into their own only after the thaw. And others were still hardly more than youths at the time of the Twentieth Party Congress. Difference in age is what matters least.

Until very recently the mainstay of this generation has been the short story. Two of its best exponents have been Yúri

Nagíbin (b. 1920) and Yúri Kazakóv (b. 1927). Nagíbin's approach to the short story is fairly traditional, though his preoccupation with slight motifs and chance encounters, particularly in his more recent stories, places him firmly in line with much younger writers. Kazakóv's are like Chekhov's in their irony and lyricism, but they take in the human damage left behind by totalitarianism, absence of social justice, and the devastation of the Second World War. The theme of the go-getting young fellow taking himself off to the city and leaving his wife or lover behind in the village is typical and recurrent. Kazakóv is something of an experimenter too. Perhaps following Pilnyak's example he has become an even greater master of the animal story. *Teddy* is the story of a bear seen convincingly through the eyes of a bear. Teddy began life performing boring tricks in a circus but, after his escape returns to the wild forests of the north and exercises his wits keeping clear of trappers. *The Outsider* (1959) is a mood story which puts Kazakóv in a class apart. A wayward, silent young drunkard of a buoy-keeper with an unusual gift for singing, summoned as if by an animal instinct ventures out onto the river with his lover, where they sing as a duet, the like of which could seldom have been heard since the bardic days of Russia.

Dudíntsev's *Not by Bread Alone* (1956) despite its impact at the time of its appearance now seems a comparatively dry, didactic novel. But it did clear the path for a thorough purging of the dishonesty and smug conformity that had reigned for over two decades. Among the most important landmarks in this direction was Viktor Nekrásov's *Kíra Geórgievna* (1961). Kíra, a successful artist, respectably new class, has her eyes, along with many like her, firmly fixed on the future. She is no longer young and was married once before. Her first husband Vadím had vanished along with tens of thousands of others in the Yezhov purges. She has all but forgotten about him. Vadím returns, but like many others of the camp survivors bears no one ill-will. He only refuses to blot out of his mind the bleak tragedy of those years. Kíra is now married to an academician, and even Vadim now has a second wife and a child. They try to take up what they remember of their earlier life together, but their attempt fails. Kíra is brought to realize that her art is worthless and that her relationships with people are a sham.

Another writer of like trend is Vladímir Tendryakóv (b. 1926). In his *An Extraordinary Event* (1961) a mathematics teacher and a high school girl discover about each other that they believe in God, and a critical situation develops. Both Nekrásov (b. 1911) and Tendryakóv have been attacked, the latter especially for his tale *Three, Seven, Ace* (1960) which tells how a discharged convict corrupts a team of honest-to-goodness lumberjacks. A third writer is Vasíly Aksyónov (b. 1932) one of the youngest of his generation, and the son of that remarkable lady, Evgénia Ginzbúrg, who published abroad her experiences of part of her twenty years in Soviet prisons and camps. Aksyónov's *A Ticket to the Stars* (1961) is about a group of teenagers who are disillusioned with the bourgeois ideals of their parents. Like their contemporaries in the West they are 'rebels without a cause'. These ideological drop-outs never read Soviet newspapers, their slang consists mainly of foreign expressions, and they concoct adventures to counteract the boring conformism and dullness of the older generation. Aksyónov has been particularly attracted by Sillitoe, whom he regards as a kindred spirit. Later pieces in a similar vein like *Halfway to the Moon* (1962) and *Oranges from Morocco* (1963) have come in for some fairly savage criticism.

Writers finding it impossible to get themselves published in the Soviet Union are faced with two alternatives: to have their work circulated in manuscript form underground by way of 'Samizdat' the Do-it-yourself Publishing House; or at much greater risk to arrange for their works to be smuggled out and published abroad. Abrám Tertz (b. 1925) the pen-name of the critic Andréi Sinyávsky, a writer directly in the line of Gógol, Rémizov and Bély, has published all his creative work abroad. He is known to the majority of his fellow countrymen as the renegade anti-Soviet propagandist who together with Yúli Daniél was sentenced to a long term of hard labour in 1966. It was especially Tertz's purely satirical tales like *Lyubímov* (1963) in which an eccentric dictator has a Russian provincial town declare its independence, and *Graphomaniacs* (1960) a cruel lampoon on the hack writer, that incensed the Establishment. Tertz is a writer of experimental inclination and remarkable individuality. Given a fair opportunity to publish in his own coutry he could well have become a major writer.

An important documentary novel making its appearance in 1966 was Anatóly Kuznetsóv's *Babi Yar*. Inspired by Evtushénko's poem of the same name, so powerful was this novel's impact that it brought the issue of anti-Semitism, which party leaders had been sedulously avoiding, out into the open. Although the novel is about Nazi atrocities against Jews and Ukrainians in Kiev, it is at the same time a paradigm of systematic genocide everywhere, and a clear if oblique indictment of Stalin's reign of terror. The horror of *Babi Yar* is that much greater for having been seen through the eyes of a boy of twelve.

Pasternák once said that 'prose seeks and finds man in the category of the spoken word'. The maxim applies nowhere better than to Bulát Okudzháva (b. 1924), mainly famed for the freshness and vigour of his poetry. Okudzháva is a Georgian by origin. His father was shot, and his mother spent some time in a concentration camp. Okudzháva describes his experiences as a mere boy at the front in 1941 in his autobiographical *Farewell Schoolboy* (1961). He has been in bad odour all along, and this book was removed from circulation not long after its appearance, no doubt because it runs directly counter to the version of the war put out by socialist realism. Okudzháva has virtually ceased to exist as a poet in recent years.

In 1945, towards the end of the war, a young artillery officer who had survived two major armoured conflicts and had been twice decorated, was unexpectedly summoned before his divisional commander. He was stripped of his insignia on the spot and bundled off to Moscow, to prison, where in due course he was informed that he had been sentenced without having been tried to eight years hard labour. His crime was a reference in a letter from the front to 'the man with the moustache'. His name is Alexander Solzhenítsyn.

Times have changed for the worse in Russia since the appearance (back in 1962) of *One Day in the Life of Ivan Denisovich*. This work marked the appearance of a major writer. Not only was the work a sensation, but it received official approval and was used by Khrushchev as a weapon against the conservative hard-liners. 'For a country to have a great writer is like having a change of government' says one of his characters. *One Day* was clearly recognized as a turning point and the end of an era of socialist realism. Yet, only seven years later, shortly after being awarded the Nobel Prize, Solzhenítsyn was like many before him expelled from the Writers' Union, called a 'colorado beetle' by his fellow Nobel laureate Shólokhov, and subjected to various forms of intimidations and provocations by the K.G.B. We can fear the worst, though the worst for Solzhenítsyn held no terrors. There was little he had not been through already. In *The First Circle* he sharply reminds his rulers that 'one can build the Empire State Building, discipline the Prussian army, make a State hierarchy mightier than God, yet fail to overcome the unaccountable spiritual superiority of certain human beings.'

Solzhenítsyn was born in 1918, and studied physics and mathematics at Rostov University, graduating in 1941. Even before being called up he had intentions of becoming a writer, though he was to have no opportunity for this until many years later. In prison he served part of his sentence in the concentration camp for scientific workers not far from Moscow, vividly re-created in *The First Circle*. Later he worked in a mining camp. Released from prison he found himself condemned to an indeterminate period of exile in Central Asia. It was at this time that he contracted cancer, from which he was eventually cured. *Cancer Ward* is based on his experiences among the inmates of a provincial hospital. Solzhenítsyn was rehabilitated by 1957 and was allowed to return to Russia where he worked as a teacher in a small town and began to concentrate on writing.

The 'tragic realism' of *One Day in the Life of Ivan Denisovich*, as of all subsequent works of Solzhenítsyn, is specific to our own time. But it is far more than just good documentary. Through being deliberately a laconic, undramatic expression of camp normality it becomes a prism in which much of the meaning of life and personal relationships is refracted. 'Descriptions of prison life tend to overdo the horrors of it. Surely it is more frightening when there are no actual horrors; what is frightening is the unchanging routine year after year. The horror is in forgetting that your life – the only one you have – is destroyed; in your willingness to forgive even some ugly swine of a warder, in being obsessed with grabbing a big hunk of bread in the prison mess . . . This is something that cannot be imagined; it has to be experienced. All the poems and ballads about prison are sheer romanticism.' (*The First Circle*). People in prison are decent on the whole; Iván Denísovich is gentle even; perhaps more gentle than he would have been as a carpenter back on the Kolkhoz. The camp has been a school for him and his fellow inmates. The prevailing savagery has served to bring out their more redeeming qualities – 'Prison gives you a chance to learn what life is about, what things are worth living for and what are not, and they reckoned that by the time a man is thirty-five, having done his ten years' hard, he can set about living on the right lines' (*The First Circle*). The inmates hate, but they hate impartially, only for a moment, and only that which is keeping them from getting back to camp out of the most severe cold. This can be anyone: the guards, more usually the person next to oneself. Read in the original, *One Day* takes on unexpected dimensions. The spoken language, largely narrative, has a completely new ring of truth about it. Solzhenítsyn has taken the *skaz* as his form, and he manages to combine ordinary first-person narrative with a peculiar kind of indirect speech in which the personality of the narrator intrudes, speaking of himself in the third person. As for the descriptive technique; if one looks closely at the text one finds no item of description which does not serve some complex purpose, exactly as in Chékhov.

Two further stories by Solzhenítsyn appeared in 1963: *Matryona's Home* and *For the Good of the Cause*. The latter is a long story, somewhat reminiscent of Chékhov. Matryóna, a neglected widowed peasant woman, is an outsider. She is generous at every point at which she comes into contact with others; generous to the point of assisting her relatives to pillage her own house, and to letting herself get killed on a railway crossing. She had not the qualities suited to the newly collectivized rural society. She was too warm-hearted and straightforward, not cunning enough; and people despised her for it. She is yet one more example of the anti-heroes with which Russian literature has teemed during the past decade, and is the antithesis of the Soviet socialist realist paragon. Moreover it is through her soul that the author himself really speaks. For all that, Nadézhda Mandelstám has insisted that Matryóna could never have existed in the Russia of today.

The late 1960s saw the appearance of Solzhenítsyn's two major novels *The First Circle* and *Cancer Ward*. At first sight *The First Circle* appears to be yet another story about life in Soviet labour camps, this time not in the arctic wilderness, but in the relative comfort of a 'special prison' for scientists and engineers working on 'top secret' projects. It is only as we read on that we begin to notice that the special prison, against the grimmer backcloth of the K.G.B. 'machine' and the death camps, is merely the setting for an exploration into the inner workings of man, and especially twentieth-century man. And we also notice that in this respect *The First Circle* is a continuation of the quest begun in *One Day in the Life of Ivan Denísovich*. What had been exceptional and aberrant in all previous times and places, imprisonment for political offences, had in Stalin's Russia became the normal thing. Prisoners had come to accept imprisonment as modern man's common lot. The only matter left to debate was at what period in one's life was it best to do one's stretch. Nérzhin, after his wife had asked him on one of her rare visits whether he liked prison, realised that his life in prison had acquired its own kind of validity. Where else but in prison, he reflected, could one get to know people so well, and where else could one reflect so well on oneself? Prison provided a man with a unique chance of learning to distinguish between what things are worth living for and what are not. A man of thirty-five after doing ten years' hard labour could set about living on the right lines.

At moments the prisoner could encounter real human greatness among his fellow inmates. Nérzhin even meets his Platón

Karatáev in the person of Spiridón, a red-haired peasant who
Mother-Courage-like had survived a train of adventures, each
one of which would have been sufficient to reduce to smithereens the life of an average mortal. Here was Nérzhin's man of
rough wisdom, the instinctive philosophical sceptic. Tormented
by the age-old dilemma of knowing right from wrong, now in
the context of the totalitarian state, where people bring about
other people's deaths believing themselves not to be doing harm,
where people continually harm others and destroy others yet
find ready justification, Nérzhin asks Sipiridón if he knows the
answer. Spiridón's life has bred its own truths: 'Wolf-hounds
are right,' he tells Nérzhin, 'and cannibals wrong.'

Not all is unrelieved greyness in *The First Circle*. Gloom
frequently gives way to comedy. One grimly risky comedy is
the prisoners' mock trial (in Chapter 50) of Prince Igor, 'born
1161, native of the town of Kiev, Russian, no Party affiliation,
no previous convictions, citizen of the USSR', charged under
the notorious Article 58 (the most common article under which
Soviet political prisoners were imprisoned, covering anything,
however trivial, that might conceivably be construed as trea-
sonous). Igor is accused of being a Polovtsian agent, after being
recruited by the Polovtsian intelligence service and sent back to
undermine the Kievan state. Even Bórodin, the main witness (it
was he after all who wrote the opera *Prince Igor*), is to be held
criminally responsible and placed in immediate custody. Both
Rímsky and Kórsakov (!) are also to be held responsible for
having completed this opera, which never should have reached
the stage. Solzhenítsyn's lampoon, no doubt based on an incident he recalled, is brilliantly worked out, and more telling than
a whole book of moral indictment.

The special prison with its scientist inmates is merely the first
circle of Hell. We have to wait for the *Gulag Archipelago* before
we can savour the rich array of tortures dispensed at random by
the security organs of a totalitarian state which put the deeds of
Nazi Germany in the shade. But from the first circle we suddenly leap straight into the ninth. At the pit of Dante's Inferno
lies the gigantic frozen body of Satan. Buried deep in his
'bunker' in Solzhenítsyn's totalitarian Hell is Stalin himself.
Even those with reservations about any part of Solzhenítsyn's

novel will be overcome by the truth, power and grim poetry of this portrayal. And it is no Judas Iscariot wriggling in his jaws, but a monster of his own making, Minister of State Security Abakúmov. Here, though, we find not a giant, but a little old man, locked away all alone, without friends or family, his only channel to the outside world a trusted lackey, his lust for power, with its cynical disregard for the millions it had consigned to unimaginably horrible deaths, now mean and manic.

In *Cancer Ward*, Solzhenítsyn's second full-scale novel, the metaphor of the human condition is no longer the prison camp, but the hospital. Its two focal characters are Rusánov, an establishment technocrat, an *apparatchik*, and Kostoglótov, who, like Solzhenítsyn himself, has developed a cancerous tumour while living in Central Asian exile. For Rusánov hospital is an abrupt descent. For him his new status as a cancer patient is like imprisonment : 'Having once undressed under the stairs, said goodbye to the family and come up to the ward, you felt the door to all your past life had been slammed behind you, and the life here was so vile that it frightened you more than the actual tumour ... In a matter of hours he had as good as lost all his personal status, reputation and plans for the future – and had turned into eleven stones of hot, white flesh that did not know what tomorrow would bring.' Be that as it may, Rusánov never gave any thought to the inconceivably worse situation of the labour camps into which he had once cast a friend through a routine denunciation. For him the confessed state criminal is hardly more than a blot on the general order that he and others like him spin in their respectable socialist heads. It escapes his notice, therefore, that the hospital, where he tries to get to sleep under the glaring ceiling lamps, or misses the privacy of an individual toilet, is a foreshadowing of the horror that people like Kostoglótov have spent many years at close quarters with. For Kostoglótov hospital is hope and freedom. He believes in his impending cure, and the women doctors and nurses become living symbols almost of his own resurrection.

Between Rusánov, Kostoglótov, and the rest of the patients move the hospital staff, the ministers of life and death. For all their dedication, skill and resourcefulness, they epitomize modern man's ultimate helplessness in the face of death. A

woman radiologist whose own terminal cancer has just been diagnosed, feels as she passes through the wards as though she has been 'deprived of her rights as a doctor, as if she has been disqualified because of some unforgivable act, fortunately not yet announced to the patients ... She no longer had the authority to pass verdicts of life and death upon others.'

Many readers of *Cancer Ward* will most remember the ending, when Kostoglótov, released from the hospital and about to leave for his exile place of residence, is offered the hospitality and affection both of a young ward nurse (with whom he has had a brief affair while still in hospital) and an older woman doctor. But after a few hours of 'freedom', in the neighbouring town, he makes for the railway station without having succeeded in calling on either. His life – cancer, the camp's, exile, a grey burden of knowing – has created an insurmountable boundary between him and the hospital doctor 'Vega' whom he might otherwise have been able truly to love. He leaves a letter for her in which he declares his love, and his refusal to destroy the rest of her life by coupling it with his – 'Something false and forced might have started between us ... You and I, and between us *this thing*: this sort of grey, decrepit yet ever-growing serpent.'

Sandwiched between a series of large-scale novels came Solzhenítsyn's essays in another favourite Russian genre – the prose poem. Lamentations of an intimate kind, they are also variations on the theme of the passing away of the harmony between nature and the human spirit. Here we find simple Russian christianity, invisible now, to all appearances extinct. Its most forlorn symbol the village church : 'When you travel the byroads of Central Russia you begin to understand the secret of the pacifying Russian countryside. It is in the churches. They trip up the slopes, ascend the high hills, come down to the broad rivers like princesses in white and red, they lift their bell-towers – graceful, shapely, all different – high over mundane timber and thatch, they nod to each other from afar, from villages that are cut off and invisible to each other they soar to the same heaven ...' Nowadays these churches are left to crumble. Slogans are slapped across their walls. They have been turned into tractor stations and workshops. 'People were always

selfish and unkind. But the evening chimes used to ring out, floating over villages, fields, and woods. These chimes, which only one old tune keeps alive for us, raised people up and prevented them from sinking down on all fours.' Meanwhile life goes on, the forms changing, and the loss of what seemed man's supreme glory already past. Yes, 'people were always selfish and unkind' but now selfishness and cruelty have become the norm, and the human spirit has to find new ways of flourishing in this present era of unfathomed inhumanity. Man must remain on the move even though his most precious institutions have crumbled in ruins or vanished. We can be no more than reflections in the water. 'If, try as we may, we never have and never shall be able to see, to reflect the truth in all its eternal fresh-minted clarity, is it not because we are still in motion, still living? . . .' Solzhenítsyn wonders what will be the fruit of all the senseless misery and suffering of millions in our own day: 'It is awesome to think that perhaps our own shapeless and wretched lives, our explosive disagreements, the groans of those executed and the tears of their wives, will all be clean forgotten. Will from this, too, come perfect and undying beauty?'

The repose of the prose poems is for a moment only. Upon us suddenly are three major works of Solzhenítsyn's recent years: *August 1914*, *Lenin in Zürich*, and the work that (like the Bible) defies all classification – *The Gulag Archipelago*.

Solzhenítsyn is at his best when his writing is related to his own experience. This is perhaps why *August 1914* appears so uneven. Its best pages only come when he is in the midst of the fighting on the East Prussian Front, much of it no doubt adapted from his own war experiences in the same East Prussia during the Second World War. *August 1914* promises to be merely the first of a long historical study. Its model is Tolstóy's *War and Peace*, though it soon becomes apparent to the reader that Solzhenítsyn's thesis runs in counterpoint, and contradiction even, to that of Tolstóy's. In *War and Peace* suprapersonal history is the shaper; in *August 1914* the mainspring is the wantonness, the fallibility, the eternal spark of the irreducible individual. *War and Peace* cast its impersonalism and irrationality upon the near-humane world of the late nineteenth century, in which not a single Dreyfus could be allowed to be

crushed unheeded. *August 1914* cherishes the rarity of the
individual in the darkness of mass terror and cynical, planned
destruction of the human heart. The First World War was, if we
read Solzhenítsyn rightly, the beginning of the descent. History
is like a river, 'break it off only an inch and it will not flow any
longer. And we are being told that the bed must forcibly be
diverted by several thousand yards. The bonds between generations, bonds of institution, tradition, custom, are what hold the
banks of the river bed together and keep the stream flowing.'
Gradually we discover that *August 1914* is the beginning of a
study, from the roots, of modern times. Its postscript reads:
'Untruth did not begin with us; nor will it end with us.'

Another study which stems from different roots of our time
is the short and highly concentrated *Lenin in Zürich*. Lenin is
unsympathetically depicted as almost an epitome of what
Russians used to call *meshchánstvo* (which could be translated
as a mixture of the quality of a *petit-bourgeois* and philistinism).
'All that Lenin lacked was breadth. The savage, intolerant
narrowness of the born schismatic harnessed his tremendous
energy to futilities.' But this 'schismatic narrowness' was
necessary to him. 'He found it easier to act if his surroundings
were simple and narrow.' Complementary to this was the
'whirlpool' of 'compelling power which manifested itself
through him, and of which he was only the infallible interpreter.' Power is the key word to Solzhenítsyn's study. In sharp
contrast to Lenin is another man of power, the Germanised
Russian Parvus. Shady Parvus, the 'little' man who was indis-
putably so big, was a socialist turned successful entrepreneur, a
man who had made millions, who was 'someone' at the court of
Kaiser Wilhelm, who even dared set the date for the Russian
Revolution (even if it proved to be the wrong date), and who
was instrumental in arranging for Lenin and his confrères to
pass through Germany during the First World War in a sealed
train. The struggle for dominance between these two contra-
dictory entities is deftly laid bare to its bones by the author.
Lenin sees of a sudden that he is bound to win: 'Though he had
made no revolution, though he was helpless and ineffectual, he
knew that he was right, he had not let himself be misled: ideas
are more durable than all your millions ... Under the crimson

flag of the International I can wait another thirty years if need be.'

Most of my readers will be familiar with at least the first volume of *Gulag Archipelago*, as a consequence of which they will need no introduction from me. The reader will already know that the *Gulag Archipelago* refers to the 'island prisons' scattered across the length and breadth of the Soviet Union. This world of arbitrary incarceration is such that it is 'all happening right next to you. You can almost touch it, but it's invisible.' This land of the Labour camp 'archipelago' is inhabited by a nation of 'zeks', 'politicals' by the million, who even speak a language of their own, quite different from Russian. So sensational, however, is the content, from beginning to end, that not everyone will have noticed that the initial documentary style serves as a foil for Solzhenítsyn's real purpose. For all that *Gulag* is by far the most horrifying condemnation of the Soviet regime yet, it is principally not about the camps, nor the K.G.B., nor even the totalitarian state, but – once more – about *man*. If *Gulag Archipelago* has a fundamental leitmotif it would be something like: 'how difficult it is to become a human being'. The chief point is not that for over half a century the ordinary innocent Russian citizen has been subjected to unremitting terror, demoralisation, arbitrary arrest and imprisonment, destruction of social ties and spiritual values, but that precisely these conditions have given modern man an opportunity of discerning a few truths, and of coming to terms with a problem that beset (mainly in theory) the Russian giants of the last century. 'The bounds of a human being! No matter how you are astounded by them, you can never comprehend . . .' 'A human being departs from life without even having learned into what kind of deep well of evil one can fall.' And our next quotation is in the spirit of the *Brothers Karamázov*: 'Gradually it was disclosed to me that the line separating good and evil passes not through states, nor between classes, nor between political parties either – but right through every human heart – and through all human hearts. This line shifts. Inside it oscillates with the years. And even within hearts overwhelmed by evil, one small bridgehead of good is retained. And even in the best of all hearts, there remains . . . an unuprooted small corner of

evil . . . A human being departs this life without even having
learned what kind of deep well of evil one can fall.'

The greatest art of *Gulag* is that Solzhenítsyn compels the
reader through his chilling and sickening documentary, through
his brilliant literary episodes, to reach his own realizations by
the very same road he once trod. It is this that truly puts it on a
level with the great masterpieces of all time. Like most other
great literature *Gulag* can be read by many different kinds of
people in many different ways, and at different depths. Some
will be satisfied with the sensational. Some with the shock and
horror ('It could never happen in my country!'). Others will
admire the cunning ways in which Solzhenítsyn dispels piece by
piece the state-promoted myth that the labour camps are an
aberration ascribable to the 'cult of personality'. Others will
shudder at the art Solzhenítsyn uses to transplant his reader,
more effectively than any movie screen, to an arctic wilderness
at 40° below zero. Still others will revel in Solzhenítsyn's
magnificent irony. Others will marvel at the way he transmutes
potential monotony (he has to keep reminding the reader it is
the same story over and over again) into a narrative that never
falters in over two and a half thousand pages. But only those
who have felt their inner beings cracking, a dread worse than
any depression, as they turn with trepidation from one chapter
to the next, submitting to the next impending blow, probably
only those readers will get to the heart of Solzhenítsyn's epic
text.

4   Theatre

Formally Russian theatre began only in 1672, with Tsar
Alexis' decree authorizing a Moscow pastor, a German by
the name of Gregori, to stage a 'comedy' in a special play-
house erected at the royal residence. But its origins are much
earlier, and, according to some, quite ancient. Even if certain
hypotheses about pagan ritual drama in ancient Russia leave
one sceptical, there can be no doubt whatever that Russian
folk customs could be not only ritualistic but peculiarly
histrionic as well. Marriages and funeral rites were so elabor-
ate and demanding that professional 'actors' were frequently
hired; especially as some of the episodes – the abduction or the
chase, for instance – usually bore no direct relation to the
situation in hand (Stravinsky's *Les Noces* gives us only an
inkling of the complexity occasionally to be found). The
Church was important too, and from the early sixteenth
century, a particular mystery play 'The Burning Fiery Furnace'
was regularly performed in the various provincial cities. The
strolling players, or mummers (*skomorókhi*) had become a
numerous and troublesome band by the sixteenth century
and even as early as the tenth century measures were already
being taken, repeatedly thereafter, to curb these unruly,
licentious no-respecters-of-persons.

From the time of Peter the Great, for whom the classical
theatre was yet another majestic symbol of the West, – even
if he personally preferred cannonades and firework displays
– development was rapid. A special theatre was built on the
Red Square, and foreign repertoire in translation, mainly

French and Spanish, was performed. Peter's main drawback was finding foreign players who could get by satisfactorily in Russian on the stage. Conditions of service were not ungenerous, the theatre was decently housed, and the lot and status of actors, except when they were serfs, was radically improved. Even Mrs. Worthington's dilemma emerged, and parents of the nobility were with increasing frequency faced with the prospect of their children entering this dubious occupation: daughters of duchesses were not always given the roles of princesses, and an actress who had recently undergone a judicial flogging might appear in the same performance cast as a general's daughter.

As in every other major national tradition of theatre, actors and playwrights in Russia were integrally linked and throve upon each other. More so than in any other country except England. The foundation of an indigenous Russian theatre (as opposed to one relying mainly upon imported talent) was primarily the work of a remarkable figure Fyódor Vólkov (1729–63). Vólkov had first attracted attention with his performances in Yaroslavl, a small provincial town. Tsarina Elizabeth duly had the entire troupe brought to the capital, now St. Petersburg, and a few years later in 1756 an Imperial Theatre was founded by royal decree. Vólkov himself became a legend. It is said that Catherine the Great, at a very tricky moment in her career, at a time when the success of her palace coup was still very much in the balance, was due to read a proclamation to her troops and found to her dismay that she had mislaid her prepared speech. The day was saved by Vólkov, who improvised so superbly, even down to the meticulous constitutional details, that Catherine drew an ovation which surprised even her.

During her reign—the latter part of the eighteenth century that is—French classicism became the inescapable model. What was good enough for Voltaire was good enough for Catherine's Court too. Playwrights were not lacking. Catherine herself wrote numerous comedies (Voltaire with typical cunning expressed his surprised admiration, pretending he had not known they were hers) and at one time she thought of following Shakespeare and writing an epic play

based on the life of Rúrik. The prolific tragedian Alexander Sumarókov (1717–77), director of Imperial Theatre and father of Russian classicism, came in for such scathing ridicule by writers of Púshkin's generation that one's instincts react towards his defence. It cannot be denied that Sumarókov committed a number of follies, including trimming *Hamlet* in such a way that the modern reader can enjoy it as straightforward farce, but the general level was no lower than that of their French models; and some consider that there is more vigour in Russian classical drama than in many of their French counterparts.

Without doubt the most important playwright of the eighteenth century was Denís Fonvízin (1744–92). Best known is his play *The Minor*, the first Russian social satire, and incidentally the only Russian play of that century still performed in the Soviet Union. The play centres around two starkly contrasted characters: the 'minor' himself, a sixteen-year-old dolt who, even had he been a prodigy, could have learnt nothing of value from the caricatures of teachers hired by fond parents for his education; and Starodúm, an admirable but somewhat puritanical plain-speaker who advocates the simple virtues of the human heart in the face of the pseudo-enlightenment beguiling the society of his day. Starodúm concedes that foreign literature uproots prejudice, but at the same time dislodges decent living and morality. The remaining figures are cartoon caricatures, and so recognizable were they to Fonvízin's contemporaries that they came close to being libellous. In Belínsky's words Fonvízin 'slaughtered the savage ignorance of the older generation as well as the crude gloss of the superficial half-education of the younger generation.' For my taste *The Minor* is marred by heavy doses of Starodúm's sanctimoniousness, and I prefer Fonvízin's other important play *The Brigadier*. Admittedly it has none of the deeper social significance of *The Minor* but it is among the funnier eighteenth century comedies of manners, not worse than anything of Marivaux for example.

Slightly later on another significant figure, the actor-playwright Plavílshchikov (1760–1812), set up a reaction against the deadening influence of French classicism. His demand was that theatre whether it dealt with princes or plebeians should be realistic and truthful. The democratic note was unmistakable, and Plavílshchchikov's crude first steps became the model for the middle-class theatre of a later dramatist Ostróvsky – 'First we have to learn about things that have taken place in our own land. Kozmá Mínin, the merchant, is a character eminently fit to be represented in a favourable light on the stage.'

Catherine established an Imperial theatrical school in the capital for the training of actors, singers and ballet-dancers. This was followed some decades later (1809) by the setting up of a State drama school in Moscow. By the time of the Napoleonic Wars the Russian theatre was thus set fair for a brilliant future.

The most striking phenomenon of the early nineteenth century was the rapid proliferation, followed by the equally rapid decline, of the serf theatre. It seems only logical that, once the aristocracy had fallen in with the fashion for theatrical pomp and luxury, they should have sought the cheapest means of developing their own ducal theatres, by making use of serf talent and labour the cost of which would approximate to nothing. At their best these serf theatres became an admirable schooling, far better than anything even the luckiest serf would get in a church school. These advantages are unfortunately eclipsed by the many abuses, when families were broken up, married couples separated. These rich landowners, to use Chátsky's words in Woe from Wit, 'bought up a serf ballet at every fair, and tore children from the arms of parents in despair'. In the worst cases serf actors were brutally flogged during entractes for the slightest slip, and were expected to perform promptly and exactly their masters' every whim, including in one celebrated case nude shows.

An outstanding figure to emerge from the serf theatre was Mikhaíl Shchépkin (1788–1863). He eventually bought, at vast cost his own freedom as well as that of his family, to become nationally famous as an actor, and great stage personality; no less than the originator of the Moscow Maly Theatre (1824) which was to become the greatest theatre in Russia and the arbiter of Russian dramatic art. Shchépkin was a brilliant 'comedian' in the widest sense of that word, and it was his collaboration with Gógol which made possible realizations like *The Government Inspector*. His technique was such that it approached true art, being no longer visible. As Hérzen said: 'Shchépkin created truth on the Russian stage; he was the first to become non-theatrical in the theatre'. It was on his foundation that later generations of actors, and eventually Stanislávsky, were to build.

While still in his mid-twenties Púshkin had written his *Borís Godunóv*, modelled after Shakespeare. It was part of his plan to reform the theatre – 'Drama was born in the city square, and was originally a form of recreation for the people.' Púshkin was incomparably more successful than any of his European contemporaries in following Shakespeare, and he is possibly the only dramatist of modern times who has managed to perform that nigh impossible graft. But high as its poetic qualities are, *Borís Godunóv* has seldom made good theatre, and will continue to be best known whether at home or abroad in Mussórgsky's operatic version. Púshkin was not to know this however, for permission to perform the play was never granted during his life-time. The Tsar (Nicholas I) thought that 'Mr. Púshkin's aim would be better achieved if, after the necessary purification, he should transform his comedy into an historical tale or novel, similar to Walter Scott.'(!)

The real Púshkin of the theatre was Alexander Griboyédov (1795–1829). The name Griboyédov is virtually unknown outside Russia. Whereas almost every Russian schoolboy knows his one outstanding comedy *Woe from Wit* (or *The Misfortune of Being Clever*) by heart; not because he has been obliged to commit it to memory, but for the very simple reason that nearly every other line of this play has become a living part of the Russian language. Blok considered it 'perhaps the greatest work in our literature' and 'a work unsurpassed, unique in the literature of the world'. 'The salt, the epigrams, the satire, this colloquial verse,' Goncharov was sure 'would never die, any more than the sharp, biting, lively Russian intelligence which is sprinkled throughout and which Griboyédov locked up, as a wizard might have locked up some sprite in his castle, where it bursts forth in peals of malicious laughter.'

And Goncharóv was vindicated: *Woe from Wit* is still very
much alive and a popular item in the repertoire. The play has
become the touchstone of actor and producer alike, rather
as *Volpone* or *As You Like It* in the English theatre. *Woe
from Wit* appeared on the eve of the Decembrist uprising of
1825, but in manuscript copies only. Packing into its high
comedy more telling criticism of his society than was ever
made by any Decembrist, the play ran smack up against the
censor. It was not even published, let alone performed, during
Griboyédov's lifetime; it saw the official light of day only in
1861 the year of the serf emancipation. Griboyédov himself
was a remarkable man. Academically brilliant, an astonishing linguist, and a fine pianist, Griboyédov was a great society
wit. Literary people he generally held in absolute contempt.
It has been suggested that he regarded even Púshkin as something of a fraud. In due course Griboyédov became a successful diplomat, negotiating a difficult treaty with Persia single-
handed. A year later he was killed in Teheran when a mob
attacked the Russian diplomatic mission and dragged his
mangled body through the streets.

If Griboyédov is strictly for Russians, or at any rate for
those with a longish familiarity with the Russian language,
Gógol is for everybody. Luckily, distinct shades of the glory
of the original survive translation. His first major comedy
The Marriage (1833), although hingeing on the long dead
custom of matchmaking, seems as fresh as the day it was
written. Podkolyósin, the reluctant wooer, like all the remaining characters in the play, is an eternally recognizable figure.
The real cornerstone of Gógol's theatrical fame is *The Government Inspector*. One's recollection of *The Government
Inspector* is always that the last time one read – or if more
fortunate, saw – the play, it was something incredibly funny.
Yet it contains no trace of farce. As we go through it scene
by scene and line by line, we are often mildly surprised that
Gógol did not try for a laugh here, or failed to follow up
something there – when all the time we are simply forgetting
that Gogol was not out to get laughs. He never aimed at anything comic in the usual sense, and it is in this respect that he
surpasses every single one of those who have attempted

comedy of situation. Khlestakóv, who lets himself be taken for a 'government inspector' is neither stupid nor clever. He is just average, or perhaps a trifle slower than average. He is not particularly quick off the mark at exploiting the situation, and seems at any moment about to mess things up. More than once his success turns on the shrewd horse-sense of his servant, and not least on the crass gullibility of the townsfolk; above all on sheer good luck. The humour that Khlestakóv dimly sees in his new predicament is mirrored back at us as the shabbiest and least funny ingredient of the entire situation. The only overplaying in the play is Khlestakóv's own. Complaining to Púshkin about the travesty that had been made of the stage performance, Gógol writes: 'Khlestakóv was made to look like a naughty boy in a French vaudeville. He has become simply an ordinary stage liar . . . Khlestakóv is not a swindler at all. He is not a professional liar; he forgets he is lying and almost kids himself into believing what he says. He lets his hair down and is in high spirits seeing that all is going well, that he is being listened to – and for that reason alone he speaks quite frankly, smoothly, unconstrainedly, and while telling his lies he reveals himself in them as he really is. . . . This, in fact, is the best and most poetic moment of his life – almost a kind of inspiration.' Shchépkin remonstrated with Gógol when later in the course of his life he wanted to raise the moral tone of his play, and to turn *The Inspector General* into an allegory of the awakened conscience of the Russian people: 'In the course of our ten-year friendship, I became so used to the Town Mayor, to Dóbchinsky and Bóbchinsky, that it would be a dishonest act to take these and all the others away from me . . . leave them as they are. I love them. . . . They are genuine persons, live men in whose midst I have grown up and have almost grown old. . . . So long as I live I will not surrender them to you.'

The experience of unexpectedly entering a room full of animated conversation is a familiar one. That is what it is like to turn up any scene at random in almost any play – almost any one of the fifty or so plays – of Alexander Ostróvsky (1823–86). Ostróvsky like Leskóv, was born into the thick of the Moscow middle classes, among odours of merchandise, counting house, and vestry. Never much of a scholar Ostróvsky left University early and went into the government service where he stayed for eight years. His first play *It's a family affair—We'll settle it ourselves* (1850) was considered in official circles a tactless and provocative exposure of the kind of bogus bankruptcy sporadic at that time in Moscow business circles. The play was banned by the censor and, was not performed for over a decade, and cost Ostróvsky his job. But by that time Ostróvsky was set on the theatre, and determined to make a success of it. His first production *Don't get on a sledge which isn't yours* in 1853 was an immediate success and inaugurated, some considered, a new era of stage realism. From then onwards Ostróvsky continued writing plays – tragedies, historical plays, but mainly comedies—and producing translations until the end of his life, leaving behind him a most astonishingly colourful panorama of slices of Russian life familiar to the ordinary member of the theatre audience. Ostróvsky was a theatre man to the core, knew all his casts personally, was an active producer, and even acted himself on occasion. Ostróvsky was convinced that the theatre was nearer to the people than any other branch of literature. All the rest was strictly for the highbrows – 'This affinity to the ordinary public does not do anything to lower dramatic art. On the contrary it enhances its power, and rules out vulgarity and any kind of degeneracy. Only those works have become immortal which were truly popular at home.'

It is unlikely that Ostróvsky will ever gain wide appeal outside Russia. For two main reasons. The dialogue is the most real, vivid and idiomatic ever to appear in the Russian language. It is not prose any more, but the actual speech of living men and women, which – as anyone knows who has tried to produce such dialogue – is a most difficult thing to attain (the dialogue of Harold Pinter might be taken as the nearest equivalent to Ostróvsky's achievement). In his later plays especially, and in *The Forest* (1871) and *Even a cat goes through lean times* (1871) above all, this dialogue attains virtuosity; and with its tension, colour and wit, its emotive halo, it enabled Ostróvsky to burst with amazing ease and fecundity into poetry, into one of the wonders of Russian folk literature *The Snow Maiden* – rivalling Púshkin in this genre, though more successful on the stage in Rímsky-Kórsakov's later operatic version than as a play. The second reason is that Ostróvsky has given expression to that elusive Russian concept *byt*, a concept quite near to 'real life' or 'being down to earth', but neither of these exactly. Add to this the local colour of Ostróvsky's Moscow Never-Never Land —'Zamoskvoréchye' – which is everywhere, yet nowhere in particular, and the English reading public is up against severe odds. Ostróvsky's milieu is as essentially Russian as Trollope's is English. Russians have always been dazzled by the illusion of reality Ostróvsky managed to spin in play after play. Alluding to one of Ostróvsky's women characters, Dostoévsky told him: 'I have seen her thousands of times. I know her well. She used to come to our house, when I was only ten years old and still living in Moscow. I remember her well.' For those who want to learn about the cards, the hucksters, the tipsters, the charmers, the men about town, the sharks and jackals, the layabouts and turnabouts of those times, not to mention an immense amount of incidental entertainment, they could not do better than read Ostróvsky, preferably in the original, and if ever they get the chance to see it on the Russian stage.

Turgénev's plays – for the most part one-act comedies – have customarily been relegated to a transitional status, foreshadowing as it is commonly supposed Chékhov's later masterpieces. They are, it is true, all very early works, written long before his first novel, and belonging to the earliest period of his literary activity. And Turgénev himself was unnecessarily modest about his own dramatic talents, rating his plays not very highly, and remarking once that 'though they were not entirely satifactory for the stage, they may afford an interest in reading'.

We know just how unfair Turgénev was being to himself, for his longest comedy *A Month in the Country* has become an established part of the theatrical repertoire, and not only in Russia. *A Month in the Country* is far more than a short story cast in dialogue, as some of the more niggardly have suggested; it is superb theatre. We have here Turgénev's typical blend of classicism and realism, a play in which the characters create their own comedy by following their own preconceived patterns of thought and action. Complications are elegantly resolved in classical fashion, but there is a residue of incongruity which points not so much to Chékhov as to Pirandello especially his *Six Characters in search of an Author*. The people, their lives and stations are such that things inevitably return to normality, even if unsatisfactorily. When Natálya's husband, sharing the general relief, tells Rakítin as he is about to leave that he is a good man, 'one of the best' Natálya replies: 'Yes, I know he is an excellent man. We are all excellent people – all of us. And yet – .'

Asked to list the world's greatest dramatists in order, most people, Russian or otherwise, would probably put Chékhov amongst their top five. And there is no denying that as far as the English stage is concerned, Chékhov has become an inalienable part of it.

Surprisingly, Chékhov did not like the theatre as such, and was invariably at odds with his actors and producers. As early as the first run of his one-act sketch *The Bear* we have the typical sour grapes: 'If in the whole of my life I somehow succeed in scribbling a dozen empty stage-pieces, I'll thank God for it. I have no love for the stage at all.' And again: 'I have succeeded in writing a silly vaudeville which, because of its silliness, is meeting with great success.' Several years later he confessed to one of his friends 'As far as my playwrighting goes, it seems to me I was not destined to be a dramatist.... While writing plays I am ill at ease, as if something were pressing against the back of my neck.' To those who doubted his sincerity Chékhov's advice was that they should try writing a play themselves. After the first production of *The Seagull*, which was a failure, Chékhov remarked that writing a play gave him 'exactly the same feeling as when you creep into an unwarmed bed on a cold night.' His distaste for the theatre extended to other dramatists – Ibsen he wrote off as a playwright – and to actors. Sarah Bernhardt he regarded as a mere conjurer, and Stanislavsky was a constant source of irritation. His realizations Chékhov considered to be travesties.

Chékhov's earliest play *Platonov* is among his posthumously published works. Chékhov was twenty probably when he wrote it. Though not by any means good theatre, the play is interesting in that it reveals the extent to which Chékhov's later outlook was already formed. 'Living life vs. clever talk' and 'Live like ordinary people, like mere mortals' are already well developed motifs. Apart from his one-act vaudevilles the next fifteen years produced only *Ivanóv* and *The Wood Demon*; and a large part of the latter was incorporated subsequently into *Uncle Ványa*. Hardly outstanding as a play, *Ivanóv* nevertheless contains some interesting life studies, in particular Ivanóv himself and the young doctor Lvov. Ivanóv characterizes himself as a strong, healthy individual, worn down to a Hamlet-like shadow of his former self: 'I was young, eager, sincere, intelligent. I loved, hated, and believed differently from other people. I worked hard enough – had hope enough – for ten men. I tilted at windmills and banged my head against brick walls. . . . And now look how cruelly life, the life I challenged, is taking its revenge. I broke under the strain. I woke up to myself at the age of thirty. I'm like an old man in his dressing-gown and slippers. Heavy-headed, dull-witted, worn-out, broken, shattered, without faith or love, with no aim in life. . . .'

One important difference between the early and the mature plays has been brought out in David Magarshack's comparison of *The Wood Demon* and *Uncle Vanya:* 'What must have struck him forcibly when he exhumed *The Wood Demon* six years after he had decided to bury it for good was that the dramatic relationships in that play were all wrong, mainly because they did not develop naturally, but were most contrived by the playwright himself.' The mature plays, *The Seagull, Uncle Vanya, The Three Sisters* and *The Cherry Orchard*, contain characters, situations and dialectic not too different from that of the early plays, but they have suddenly become three-dimensional and real. To my mind, this change is chiefly accounted for by their having become comedies in the classical sense. It is almost as if Chékhov had achieved in his later period a synthesis of his early vaudeville and serious styles, and had transposed them to a pitch of comic representation which put him on a level with Shakespeare and Molière. Chékhov was at pains to impress upon Stanislávsky that *The Cherry Orchard* in particular was meant to be a comedy, not a tragedy. All the characters in the play, with the exception of young Anya, have unmistakably ludicrous streaks in their natures which make them decidedly comic characters. When one of his correspondents complained that there were too many 'weeping characters' in his plays, Chékhov asked who they could be — 'There is only one such character — Várya, and that is because she is a cry baby by nature and her tears ought not to arouse any feelings of gloom. I often indicate "through tears" in my stage directions, but that only shows the mood of the characters, and not tears as such.'

The secret of all real comedy is that it leaves the players much leeway for interpretation, all the way from farce to deepest tragedy. It is not the width of the spectrum but the constantly shifting focus which produces the comic effect. It is only in recent times that the British public has had available to it productions of Chékhov that live up to Chékhov's specifications. Másha's famous opening line in *The Seagull* — 'I'm in mourning for my life' — is one of the numerous examples of ambivalence, combining farce and despair in the same instant. *The Seagull* begins with a play within a play, a satire on symbolistic trends in the theatre and poetry of Chékhov's day. Tréplev's 'play' in its attempt to pull out every stop in the universe, manages nevertheless to convey nothing. Trigórin by contrast is an old hand, a successful professional writer, who by his time in life has got everything into its right place, and has few illusions about himself ('I feel I must discuss ordinary people, their sufferings, their future — science, human rights, all that stuff') but when he actually encounters real life, in the form of a dead seagull which Tréplev has just shot, Trigórin far from acting according to the dictates of his own philosophy goes off instead into an emptier kind of mysticism than even the green and immature Tréplev was capable of. The seagull now represents a chunk of real life, a symbol, and a *satirization* of a symbol,

at one and the same time. It is this mirroring to and fro that
is the essence of Chékhov's and all true comedy, and is to be
found just as surely in *The Seagull* as it is, say, in *Much Ado
about Nothing.*

One October evening in 1898 in a Moscow theatre the curtain
went up on a completely darkened stage. The play was
Alexéy Tolstóy's *Tsar Fyodor Ivanovich.* Boyars stood with
their backs to the audience, and throughout the performance the actors never once turned their attention towards
the audience. Instead they talked to each other. It was as if
there existed a fourth wall, invisible but real as far as the actors
were concerned. That night theatrical history was made.

Thus came into being the Moscow Arts Theatre. Its founders
Nemiróvich-Dánchenko and Stanislávsky had met only a
short time before, and this was their first production. Their
'true to life' theatre continues to exist today in the same
theatrical institutions and its influence has spread to many
parts of the world. It is the name of Konstantín Stanislávsky
(1863–1938) that is most closely associated with this transformation in the Russian theatre, and his authority dominated
the Moscow Arts Theatre until his death. Despite a certain
egocentric crankiness and petulance Stanislávsky has been
acknowledged even by his harshest critics as an outstanding
actor. Even the demanding Chékhov, who accused Stanislávsky of changing his plays from comedy into tearjerkers,
was forced to admit: 'Your acting is excellent, only you are
not playing *my* character. I never wrote that.' Differences
apart, Chékhov and Stanislávsky shared a hatred of the
established theatre, and Stanislávsky declared himself an enemy
of that institution which had set itself so determinedly against
the truth.

The Stanislávsky Method or System, so-called, propagated
in a somewhat doctrinaire form by Lee Strasberg in America
was never intended as anything codifiable. Stanislávsky abhor-
red text-books and believed it wrong to exercise mechanic-
ally without integral reference to a specific role or play. His
System was concerned not with techniques, people going
through the motions of emulating a tree, to use the stock

example, but with the much less superficial aim of transform-
ing dramatic fiction into stage reality. The actor was required
to put himself at the service of someone else's sensibilities and
impulses, and to that end the actor had to undergo spiritual
preparation. The spirit had to be able to put on new clothes,
as it were. As for the Studio, this was never intended either
for beginners or devotees, but only for professional actors
of many years' experience – 'a laboratory for the experiments
of more or less trained actors'.

The naturalism of the Moscow Arts Theatre was all very
well for a certain type of repertoire: Ibsen or Hauptmann,
Górky or Alexéy Tolstóy; but it was much less suited to
the symbolist theatre which had risen to prominence during
the early years of the present century. Stanislávsky could see
this for himself; and it was for this reason that he collaborated
for a brief period in 1905 with an ex-pupil and former founder
colleague of the Arts Theatre – Vsévolod Meyerhóld.

Meyerhóld (1874–1940) was of 'Russian German' origin.
A born revolutionary he experimented throughout his life
with one new idea after another, and usually gave them up
just as they were gaining limited public acceptance. The early
part of his stage career is the antithesis of Stanislávsky's.
Meyerhóld's productions of Blok's *The Fairground Booth*,
Maeterlinck's *Death of Tintagiles*, and earlier (1903) of
Przybyszewski's *Snow* had confirmed Stanislávsky's view that
Meyerhóld's approach was right for symbolism and impres-
sionism as long as they remained in vogue.

The barrier of the footlights was abolished, and the proscen-
ium arch and backdrops torn down. The audience were no
longer spectators, but participants. Meyerhóld, sorely treated
by the critics, survived partly due to the active support given
him by Rémizov and Bryúsov, but mainly thanks to his
association with the greatest actress of the time, Vera
Komissarzhévskaya. Only shortly before her death did she
become disillusioned by Meyerhóld's incurable eccentricity.

Just before the Revolution Meyerhóld had reintroduced
the Commedia dell' Arte; and, like Brecht many years later,
had already felt the influence of the Japanese Kabuki and Noh
theatres, and had experimented with cinematic projection and

montage. There were few devices he had not tried by this
time. Meyerhóld's theatre was known as 'the theatre of
convention', and was seemingly diametrically the opposite
of the naturalist theatre: 'The spectator should not be allowed
to forget for a moment that an actor is *performing* before
him, and the actor should never forget that he is performing
before an audience, with a stage beneath his feet and a set
around him. . . . The more obvious the artifice, the more powerful the impression of life.' Meyerhóld wanted to drive the
'intellectual' actor away from the stage. 'The same deathly
hush prevails in the auditorium as in the reading-room of a
library, and the public is sent to sleep.' There was too much
literature on the stage in Meyerhóld's view, and if that was
what the public really wanted they could save themselves
time, effort and expense by staying at home and reading aloud
to themselves – 'To make a dramatist out of a story-teller who
writes for the stage, it would be a good idea to make him
write a few pantomimes. The pantomime is a good antidote
against excessive misuse of words.'

One of Meyerhóld's most remarkable and most lavish
productions was Lérmontov's *Masquerade*. This production
was to mark the end of an era, and was running at the time
when street fighting broke out in October 1917. Already the
enfant terrible of the critics, Meyerhóld now went on to
proclaim 'the October Revolution of the Theatre'. In the
twenties he pressed on with his gradual abolition of the box-
stage, and experimented with multi-planar constructions
which bore only the remotest resemblance to the conventional
stage, looking more like cubistic trapeze arrangements.
Scenery was virtually abolished. Reality, Meyerhóld believed
must exist not on the stage but in the minds of the audience.
The stage was no more than a convention by means of which
the spectator is led towards reality. In his production of
Ostróvsky's *The Forest* there was nothing in the stage set to
suggest a forest. Only by leaving out all scenic reference to a
forest could the audience be induced to actually see one. This
production with its rattling of tin sheets and its clatter of
boots and props has been described as what a Lewis Carroll
might have visualized while listening to a radio play.

One of Meyerhóld's boldest steps was to 'realize' many of the classics in terms of contemporary life; sometimes even to reconceive and largely rewrite them. Though his experiments were sometimes a vindication of Meyerhóld's purpose they were more often dismissed as symptoms of 'meyerholditis'. A lone tribute came from Stanislávsky not long before his death, when he told his successor: 'Take care of Meyerhóld. He is my sole heir in the theatre – here or anywhere else.' But no one did take care. Meyerhóld was arrested in December 1937, and it is believed that he was shot in a Moscow prison some time in 1940.

Let us take a passing look at two plays each of which in its own way epitomises these sharply contrasting theatres. One of the earliest productions of the Moscow Arts Theatre, Górky's *Lower Depths* gave Stanislávsky full rein. For its time the play was sensational, because it was set in and around a doss house, its characters being all social outcasts of one kind or another. In the first production (1902) Stanislávsky played the part of Sátin, and a photograph reveals a rather handsome, fiery-looking down-and-out. Naturalism in this production was carried to such excess that a real tramp was brought on to the stage. *Lower Depths* falls short of theatrical perfection, and even Stanislávsky found his own part not easy to handle. The play can be easily misinterpreted. As Helen Muchnic* has pointed out, Lúka, the 'holy' tramp, is actually the villain of the piece. He is the glib comforter, one who consoles others in order to protect himself, using a relativist humbug of an ethic: 'Whatever you believe in exists'; 'A man can live any way he likes – however his heart tells him – kind today, mean tomorrow.' His counterpoise is Sátin the daydreaming realist, of whom Górky evidently approves. Man is Sátin's affirmation: Only man exists, the rest is the work of his hands and his brain.' We have to respect man, not to pity and delude him. Obviously a play like *Lower Depths* is ideally in tune with Stanislávsky's 'theatre of truth', since everything depends for its effect on the faithful realization of the characters, their gestures, actions and setting. There is no poetry to get in the way, as in Chékhov, and nothing

* Muchnic, Helen: *From Gorky to Pasternak*, London, 1963.

that calls for any other than the box-stage set. It is a perfect example of what Meyerhóld called 'literature on the stage'.

The first ever Soviet play was *Mystery Bouffe* a joint venture of Meyerhóld and Mayakóvsky. This exercise in extravaganza which first brought this explosive couple together was followed up ten years later by productions of *The Bedbug* and shortly afterwards *The Bathhouse*. Meyerhóld was unstinting in his praise for Mayakóvsky as a man of the theatre and regarded his cooperation as indispensable: 'In his work with me, Mayakóvsky showed himself to be not only a superb dramatist but an incomparable director as well. In all my years as a director I have never permitted myself the luxury of an author's co-operation when producing his play. I have always tried to keep the author as far from the theatre as possible during the period of actual production, because any truly creative director is bound to be hampered by the playwright's interference. In Mayakóvsky's case I not only permitted him to attend, I simply couldn't begin to produce his plays without him.'

In actual fact there was nothing out of the ordinary about their production of *The Bedbug*; perhaps for the very reason that it fitted so well into Meyerhóld's frame of things. It was a popular hit despite its having been taken off a year after it was first produced. Since its revival in 1955 it has drawn enthusiastic audiences all over the Soviet Union. Topicality must be among the important reasons for its success. Prisýpkin, the hero, becomes in the second half of the play a prehistoric survival from the NEP era. He has been miraculously preserved in ice after being trapped by a fire in those bygone days. Resurrected fifty years later – the year is 1979 – Prisýpkin finds himself in an alien Brave New World in which he is quarantined as a potential source of physical and moral contamination. People come and look at him in his cage. The professor who first misclassified him as a member of the highest class of *homo sapiens* – the working class – is taken to task for his mistake. Prisýpkin in company with a fortuitously resurrected parasite *Bedbugus normalis* is reclassified as sub-human species *bourgeoisius vulgaris*. In fact Prisýpkin is none other than the most ordinary human being transposed intc the posthuman nightmare of the planned society, in which there is no place for people who don't wash, scratch themselves, use lewd language, and stick pin-ups on walls. Mayakóvsky spared neither malice nor wit in lampooning the new society which he could see springing up around him, not only in Russia but everywhere; and he foresaw very accurately the age of media control and mass brainwashing.

A third important figure on the Russian theatrical scene in the early 1920s was Evgény Vakhtángov. Stanislávsky's favourite pupil, Vakhtángov broke away from the Moscow Arts Theatre during the First World War. Not long before his death in 1923 came his superb production of *Turandot* with its romantic comedy, slap-stick and fairy-tale fantasy. The cast decked themselves out in rags, pieces of patched material, and fantastic masks. There was no scenery. Rejecting the naturalism of Stanislávsky and the stylistic fads of Meyerhóld, Vakhtángov's approach depended on 'a controlled spontaneity which broke down the barrier between performers and audience'.* The Vakhtángov Theatre in Moscow originating in the Third Studio of the Moscow Arts Theatre founded by him in 1920 has remained one of the most vital theatres in the Soviet Union.

The Russian theatre underwent one of its astonishing revivals in the late 1950s. Scores of new plays were produced, along with many plays that had been suppressed or withheld under Stalin. Some of these playwrights like Nikolái Pogódin (1900–62), Evgeny Schwartz (1904–58), and Andréi Arbúzov, whose play *The Promise* had a successful run in the London West End not long ago, had their roots in the interrupted great tradition. Others like Víktor Rózov (b. 1913), best known in the West for his film *The Cranes are Flying*, had been not unduly hampered by Socialist Realism, but came really into their own only after the thaw. Some are newcomers on the scene and not all of them are welcome to the Establishment. The contemporary Soviet theatre is wide in range, and covers everything from social satire to Alice-in-Wonderland fantasy (E. Schwartz). Some plays, for example Véra Panóva's *It's been Ages* bring out the tensions of modern living not

* Preface to *Three Soviet Plays* by Michael Glenny, London, 1966

unlike those familiar to us in the West and suggest the transformation that has taken place in Russia since the War.

Solzhenítsyn's *The Love-girl and the Innocent* actually
reached the dress rehearsal stage in Moscow when it was
banned. It has been published recently in the West. Like *One
Day in the Life of Iván Denísovich* this play is set in Campland 'that invisible country' which does not exist in geography
or history books, and the cast includes everyone from the
camp commandant to 'goners' and 'drudgers'. The play has a
central moral: to live straightforwardly and uprightly in a
labour camp is a sure passport to death. This gloomy optimism
runs right the way through Solzhenítsyn's play, starting with
the initial stage directions, which I leave as a postscript to
this survey: 'The audience will walk from a brightly lit foyer
into the darkened auditorium. In here the only light comes
from a number of tinplate hooded lanterns which are placed,
almost like crowns, on a semicircle of posts right along the
edge of the orchestra pit. The posts are quite low, so as not to
interfere with the audience's view of the stage. They are
wrapped with barbed wire. . . . The centre post carries an
indicator to mark the dividing point in the field of observation from the two nearest watch-towers. . . . Throughout the
play the towers are manned by sentries. . . .'

Appendix
SELECT BIBLIOGRAPHY

SECTION I

Historical and General Surveys of Russian Literature, Art and Ideas
The following is a selection of some of the more outstanding surveys in English:

BILLINGTON, JAMES H.   *The Icon and the Axe* (London, 1966)
  A brilliant interpretation of Russian art, literature, religious movements and thoughts from earliest times to the present.

MIRSKY, D. S.   *A History of Russian Literature*

SLONIM, MARC   *An Outline of Russian Literature* (London, 1958)
  A very concise survey, useful for ready reference.
  The Epic of Russian Literature (New York and London, 1964)
  A study from the origins to Tolstoy. A very detailed but scholarly and readable survey.
  From Chékhov to the Revolution (Russian Literature 1900–1917) (New York, 1962)
  Soviet Russian Literature: Writers and Problems 1917–1967 (New York, 1967)

MUCHNIC, H.   *An Introduction to Russian Literature* (New York, 1967)
  From Górky to Pasternák (London, 1963)
  A study of six modern Russian writers.

SECTION 2 : POETRY

In addition to the general works listed in the Appendix to Section I, the following specially relate to Russian poetry:

POGGIOLI, RENATO   'The Poets of Russia (Harvard, 1960)
  An indispensable guide to Russian poetry of the modern period.

STAKHOVSKY, L. *Craftsmen of the Word: Three Poets of Modern Russia* (Cambridge, Mass, 1949)
Includes studies of the work of Gumilyóv, Akhmátova, and Mandelstám.

Anthologies

The Penguin Book of Russian Verse (London, 1962) introduced and edited by Dimitri Obolensky. Original texts with prose translations of selected poetry from all the major and some of the minor poets, from earliest times to the present.
Modern Russian Poetry (London, 1966) edited by Vladimir Markov and Merrill Sparks. A more complete selection than the Penguin edition, with often quite good verse translations. Especially valuable for the period 1895 to 1930. Starts with the Symbolists and Decadents.
The New Russian Poetry (1953–68) edited and trans. by G. Reavey, London, 1968 (a very comprehensive survey with parallel texts).

Individual Writers

PUSHKIN: *Eugene Onegin* trans. and edited with commentary by Vladimir Nabokov (includes a facsimile of the 1837 edition (New York, 1964)
Púshkin: Selected Verse with introduction and prose translations by J. Fennell (Penguin Poets) (London, 1964).
LÉRMONTOV: *Michael Lérmontov: Biography and Translation*, by C. E. L'Ami and A. Welikotny (Manitoba, 1967). Not very good but accurate verse translations.
MANDELSTAM: The two volumes of Nadézhda Mandelstám's memoirs – *Hope Against Hope* and *Hope Abandoned* (both translated by Max Hayward) – not only contain important information on Mandelstám and his poetry, but on the times in which he lived.
MAYAKOVSKY: *Mayakóvsky* by Herbert Marshall (London, New York, 1965).
PASTERNAK: *Pasternák* edited by D. Davie and A. Livingstone (London, 1969) contains some of the more important critical essays on Pasternák, with poems quoted both in the original and in good verse translation.
Prose and Poems, edited by S. Schimanski with an intro-

duction by J. M. Cohen (London, 1959).
The Poetry of Boris Pasternák (1917–1959) translated, with a critical and biographical introduction by G. Reavey (New York, 1959)

VOZNESÉNSKY: *Antiworlds and the Fifth Ace* edited by Patricia Blake and Max Hayward, with a foreword by W. H. Auden (London, 1968). A superb bilingual edition of all but the latest of Voznesénsky, with verse translations by leading poets, including Auden and Richard Wilbur.
Selected Poems, edited and translated by Herbert Marshall (New York, 1966).

SECTION 3 : PROSE

PUSHKIN Yarmolinsky, A., *The Poems, Prose and Plays of Alexander Púshkin* (New York, 1936). More recently reprinted in the Modern Library Series: the most complete edition available.
The Captain's Daughter and Other Stories (New York, 1936) reprinted in Vintage Books
The Complete Prose Tales of Alexander Púshkin, trans. G. R. Aitken (London, 1966)

LÉRMONTOV *A Hero of our Time*, trans. by V. and D. Nabokov (New York, 1958)

GOGOL *Tales of Good and Evil*, trans. with an intro. by D. Magarshack (New York, 1957) (includes *The Portrait, The Nevsky Avenue, The Nose*, and *The Overcoat*) *
Evenings near the Village of Dikanka, trans. Gorchakov (New York, 1960)
Dead Souls, trans. with an intro. by D. Magarshack (London, 1961)
The Diary of a Madman and Other Stories, trans. by A. McAndrew (New York, 1960) (includes also *The Nose, The Carriage, The Overcoat*, and *Taras Bulba*)

TURGÉNEV Recent translations include: *Fathers and Sons*, trans. by G. Reavey (New York, 1958) R. Hare (London, 1947)

A Nobleman's Nest, trans. by R. Hare (London, 1947)
Rúdin, trans. by A. Brown (London, 1950)
On the Eve, trans. by M. Budberg (London, 1950)
Five Short Novels, trans. by F. Reeve (New York, 1960)
Selected Tales of Iván Turgénev, trans. by D. Magarshack (London, 1960)

GONCHAROV   *A Common Story*, trans. by C. Garnett (London, 1890)
Oblómov, trans. by N. Duddington (New York, 1960)

DOSTOÉVSKY   Recent translations of the major novels are available in translations by D. Magarshack (Penguin) and by A. McAndrew (Signet). Constance Garnett's translations of the *Short Stories* and *Short Novels* have been reprinted by the Dial Press (New York, 1945)
The Diary of a Writer, trans. by B. Brasol (2 vols.) (New York, 1949)

CHÉKHOV   *The Oxford Chékhov* (a three volume collection of the plays), trans. and edited by R. Hingley (London, 1967)
Lady with Lapdog and Other Stories, trans. and intro. by D. Magarshack (London, 1964)
Selected Stories, trans. and intro. by J. Coulson (London, 1963)
Chékhov: Letters on the Short Story, the Drama and Other Topics selected and edited by L. S. Friedland (New York, 1965)

LESKOV   *The Amazon and Other Stories*, trans. and intro. by D. Magarshack (London, 1949)
The Musk-Ox and Other Tales, trans. by R. Norman (London, 1944)
The Enchanted Pilgrim and Other Stories, trans. by D. Magarshack (London, 1946)
Selected Tales, trans. by D. Magarshack; intro. by V. S. Pritchett (London, 1962)

BÉLY   *St. Petersburg*, trans. and intro. by J. Cournos, Foreword by G. Reavey (London, 1960)

SOLOGUB   *The Little Demon*, trans. by R. Wilks (London, 1962)

GORKY   *Selected Short Stories*, trans. by M. Wettlin (Moscow, 1968)

Childhood, trans. by M. Wettlin (Moscow, 1968)
My Apprenticeship (ditto)
My Universities, trans. by H. Altschuler (Moscow, 1952)
The Artamonov Business, trans. by A. Brown (London, 1948)
Foma Gordeyev, trans. by M. Wettlin (London, 1956)
Through Russia, trans. by C. J. Hogarth (London, 1959)

BUNIN   *The Gentleman from San Francisco and Other Stories*, trans. by B. G. Guerney (New York and Toronto, 1964)
The Well of Days, trans. by G. Struve and H. Miles (London, 1946)
Dark Avenues, trans. by R. Hare (London, 1949)
Memoirs and Portraits, trans. by V. Trail (New York, 1951)

ZAMYATIN   *We*, trans. by B. G. Guerney (London, 1970)
A Soviet Heretic: Essays by Yevgeny Zamyátin, trans. by M. Ginsburg (London and Chicago, 1970)

PILNYAK   *The Tale of the Unextinguished Moon and Other Stories, trans.* by B. Scott (New York, 1967)
The Naked Year, trans. by A. Brown (New York, 1928)

BABEL   *Collected Stories*, trans. by W. Morison; intro. by L. Trilling (London, 1961)
Lyubka the Cossack and Other Stories, trans. by R. MacAndrew (New York, 1963)
You Must Know Everything: Stories 1915–37, trans. by M. Hayward; edited by N. Babel.

ZOSHCHENKO   *The Wonderful Dog and Other Tales*, trans. by E. Fen (London, 1942)
Scenes from the Bathhouse, trans by S. Monas (Ann Arbor, 1961)
Nervous People and Other Satires, trans. by H. McLean (New York, 1963)

ILF AND PETROV   *The Twelve Chairs*, trans. by J. H. C. Richardson; intro. by M. Friedberg (New York, 1961)
The Golden Calf, trans. by J. H. C. Richardson (London, 1962)

BULGAKOV   *The Master and Margarita*, trans. by M. Glenny (London, 1967)
The Heart of a Dog, trans. by M. Glenny (London, 1968)

Black Snow, trans. by M. Glenny (London, 1965)

PASTERNAK   *Doctor Zhivágo*, trans. by M. Hayward and M. Harari (London, 1958)

Prose and Poems, edited by S. Schimanski; intro. by J. M. Cohen (London, 1959)

The Last Summer (otherwise *The Tale*), trans. by G. Reavey (London, 1959)

An Essay in Autobiography, trans. by M. Harari; intro. by E. Crankshaw (London, 1959)

KAZAKOV   *The Smell of Bread and Other Stories*, trans. by M. Harari and A. Thomson (London, 1965)

Going to Town and Other Stories, trans. by G. Azrael (Boston, 1964)

NAGIBIN   *The Pipe: Stories*, trans. by S. Shneerson (Moscow, 1958)

AKSYONOV, VASILY   *A Ticket to the Stars*, trans. by A. McAndrew (New York, 1963)

NEKRASOV, VIKTOR   *Kira Georgievna*, trans. by N. Vickery (New York, 1962)

Both Sides of the Ocean, trans. by E. Kulukundis (New York, 1964)

KUZNETSOV   *Babi Yar*, trans. by J. Guralsky (London, 1967)

TERTZ   *The Trial Begins*, trans. by M. Hayward (London, 1960)

The Icicle and Other Stories, trans. by M. Hayward and R. Hingley (London, 1963)

SOLZHENITSYN   *One Day in the Life of Ivan Denisovich*, trans. by M. Hayward and R. Hingley; intro. by M. Hayward and L. Labedz (New York, 1963)

Cancer Ward (2 vols.), trans. by N. Bethell and D. Burg (London, 1968)

The First Circle, trans. by M. Guybon (London, 1968)

For the Good of the Cause and *Matryona's Yard*, trans. by D. Floyd and M. Hayward (New York, 1964)

General works

VARNEKE, B. V. *History of the Russian Theatre*, trans. by B.
Brasol (New York, 1951)
GORCHAKOV, N. A. *The Theatre in Soviet Russia*, trans. by E.
Lehrman (New York, 1957)
SLONIM, MARC Russian Theatre from the Empire to the Soviets
(New York, 1961)

Anthologies

SEGAL, H. B. *The Literature of Eighteenth Century Russia* (in-
cludes Fonvizin's *The Brigadier*)
Contemporary Russian Drama, Selected and trans. by F. D.
Reeve (New York, 1968) (includes plays by Rózov,
Panóva, Pogodin, and Schwartz)
Three Soviet Plays Edited by M. Glenny (London, 1966) (in-
cludes Mayakóvsky's *The Bedbug*; Babel's *Marya*, and
Schwartz's *The Dragon*)
Anthology of Russian Plays (2 vols.) Edited and trans. by F. D.
Reeve (New York, 1966) (includes a wide range of plays)

Individual Authors

GOGOL Gógol's plays are available in the Pantheon edition:
The Collected Tales and Plays of Nikolai Gógol, trans.
by C. Garnett; edited and revised by L. J. Kent (New
York, 1964)
OSTROVSKY *Easy Money and Other Plays*, trans. by D.
Magarshack (London, 1944)
CHÉKHOV *The Oxford Chékhov* (the complete plays in 3 vols.),
trans. and edited by R. Hingley (London, 1967)
GORKY *Seven Plays of Maxim Górky*, trans. by A. Bakshy
(Yale and London, 1946)
The Lower Depths in *Anthology of Russian Plays*, vol. 2
edited and trans. by F. D. Reeve (New York, 1966)
MAYAKOVSKY See above *Three Soviet Plays*.

STANISLAVSKY *My Life in Art*, trans. by J. Robbins (London, 1924)

Stanislavsky on the Art of the Stage. Translated, with an introductory essay by D. Magarshack (London, 1961)

MEYERHOLD *Meyerhold on Theatre*, trans. and edited with a critical commentary by E. Braun (London, 1969)

SOLZHENITSYN *The Love-Girl and the Innocent*, trans. by N. Bethell and D. Burg (London, 1969)

Index